Developing Management Skills for Leadership

We work with leading authors to develop the
strongest educational materials inbusiness and management,
bringing cutting-edge thinking and best learning practice to a
global market.

Under a range of well-known imprints, including
Financial Times Prentice Hall, we craft high quality print and
electronic publications which help readers to understand and
apply their content,whether studying or at work.

To find out more about the complete range of our
publishing, please visit us on the World Wide Web at:
www.pearsoneduc.com

Developing Management Skills for Leadership

Chris Parker • Brian Stone

 Prentice Hall
FINANCIAL TIMES

An imprint of **Pearson Education**

Harlow, England • London • New York • Boston • San Francisco • Toronto • Sydney • Singapore • Hong Kong
Tokyo • Seoul • Taipei • New Delhi • Cape Town • Madrid • Mexico City • Amsterdam • Munich • Paris • Milan

Pearson Education Limited

Edinburgh Gate
Harlow
Essex CM20 2JE
United Kingdom

and Associated Companies throughout the world

Visit us on the World Wide Web at:
www.pearsoneduc.com

First published 2003

ISBN 0 273 64618 4

British Library Cataloguing-in-Publication Data
A catalogue record for this book is available from the British Library

Library of Congress Cataloging-in-Publication Data
Parker, Chris.
    Developing management skills for leadership/Chris Parker, Brian Stone.
        p. cm.
    Includes bibliographical references and index.
    ISBN 0-273-64618-4
    1. Leadership. 2. Management. I. Stone, Brian, 1959- II. Title.

HD57.7 .P364 2002
658.4'092--dc21

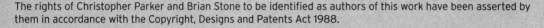

2002074808

10 9 8 7 6 5 4 3 2 1
06 05 04 03

Typeset in 9¼/12pt Stone Serif by 30
Printed and bound by Bell & Bain Limited, Glasgow.

The publisher's policy is to use paper manufactured from sustainable forests.

We are what we repeatedly do.
Excellence, then, is not an event, it is a habit.

Aristotle

Contents

Acknowledgements   ix

Introduction   1

Part one: **The foundations of leadership**   7

Chapter 1: **Managing self and self-image**   9

Self management and understanding   10
Personality   25
Image management   30
Assertiveness   37
Motivation   42
Stress and pressure management   48
Summary   65

Chapter 2: **Managing one-to-one relationships**   69

Communication and perception filters   70
Rapport and representation systems   78
Interpreting behaviour   85
Managing customers, clients and superiors   89
Interviews   97
Conflict management   107
Summary   116

Part two: **Essential leadership skills 1: creating value**   119

Chapter 3: **Developing others**   121

Learning   122
Empowerment   133
Delegation   140
Training   144
Appraisal   150
Summary   156

Chapter 4: **Leading and working in groups and teams**   160

Leadership   161
Groups and teams   176
Summary   191

Chapter 5: **Creative problem-solving**   **195**

            Managing problems   196
            Creative intelligence   210
            Summary   232

Part three: **Essential leadership skills 2: sharing value**   **235**

Chapter 6: **Selling ideas and persuasive campaigning**   **237**

            Persuasion influence and selling   238
            Persuasive presentations   247
            Persuasive report writing   256
            Persuasive campaigning   260
            Summary   266

Chapter 7: **Consultancy, negotiation and bargaining**   **271**

            Management consulting   272
            Negotiation and bargaining   281
            Summary   289

Chapter 8: **Cross-cultural management**   **291**

            Fons Trompenaars   292
            Geert Hofstede   299
            Developing cultural capability   300
            Summary   305

Part four: **Leading and learning**   **307**

Chapter 9: **Planning and managing personal development**   **309**

            Self-directed learning   310
            Dreaming and learning   312
            Summary   318

            Index   321

ACKNOWLEDGEMENTS

We are grateful to the following for permission to reproduce copyright material:

Table 1.2 from Myers, I.B. (1962) *The Myers-Briggs Type Indicator*, Palo Alto, CA: Consulting Psychologists Press; Figure 1.7 from Maslow, A.H., Frager, R. and Fadiman, J. (1970) *Motivation and Personality* (2nd edition), Glenview, IL: Addison-Wesley Longman; Figure 3.1 from Kolb, D.A. (2001) *Organizational Psychology* (7th edition), Upper Saddle River, NJ: Pearson Education US; Figure 4.1 from Tannebaum, R. and Schmidt, W.H. (1973) *How to Choose a Leadership Pattern*, Boston, MA: Harvard Business Review; Figure 4.2 from Lewin, K. (1951) *Field Theory in Social Science*, Glenview, IL: Addison-Wesley Longman; Figure 4.3 from Reddin, W. (1970) *Managerial Effectiveness*, New York: McGraw-Hill; Table 4.9 from Belbin, M. (1981) *Management Teams: Why They Succeed or Fail*, Oxford: Butterworth Heinemann, www.belbin.com; Figure 6.1 from Argyle, M. (1994) *The Psychology of Interpersonal Behaviour* (5th revised edition), London: Penguin Books. Reproduced by permission of Penguin Books Ltd.; Figure 7.1 from Maslow, A.H., Frager, R. and Fadiman, J. (1970) *Motivation and Personality* (2nd edition), Glenview, IL: Addison-Wesley Longman.

Text extract, p.19 from Senge, P. (1994) *The Fifth Discipline*, London: Century Business. Used by permission of The Random House Group Limited; Text extract, p.22 from Goleman, D. (1995) *Emotional Intelligence*, London: Bloomsbury; Text extract, p.27 from Guilford, J. (1959) Personality, New York: McGraw-Hill; Text extract, p.48 from Robbins, A. (1991) *Awaken the Giant Within*, Simon & Schuster Adult Publishing Group. Reprinted with the permission of Simon & Schuster. Copyright © 1991 by Anthony Robbins; Text extract, p.56 from Sondhi, R. (1999) *Total Strategy*, London: Airworthy Publications International; Text extract, p.79 from O'Connor, J. and Seymour, J. (1993) *Introducing NLP*, London: HarperCollins. © 1993 by Joseph O'Connor and John Seymour; Text extract, p.85 from Guirdham, M. (1995) *Interpersonal Skills at Work* (2nd edition), Harlow: Pearson Education; Text extract, p.116 from Oliver, M. (1994) *Mockingbirds*, The Atlantic Monthly, vol. 273; Text extract, p.127 from Honey, P. and Mumford, A. (2001) *The Learning Styles Questionnaire*, Maidenhead: Peter Honey Publications; Text extract, p.134 from Block, P. (1991) *The Empowered Manager: Positive Political Skills at Work*. © 1991 by Peter Block. This material is used by permission of Jossey-Bass, Inc., a subsidiary of John Wiley & Sons, Inc.; Text extract, p.137 from Knight, S. (1999) *NLP Solutions*, London: Nicholas Brealey Publishing; Text extract, p.138 from Golembiewski, R.T. and McConkie, M. (1975) 'The Centrality of Trust in Group Processes' in Cooper, C. (ed.) *Theories of Group Processes*, New York: Wiley. © 1975 John Wiley & Sons Limited. Reproduced with permission; Text extract, p.143 from Handy, C. (1999) *Understanding Organizations* (5th edition), London: Penguin Books. Copyright © 1999 by Charles Handy. Reproduced by permission of Penguin Books Ltd; Text extract, p.149 from Conway, C. (1998) *Strategies for Mentoring*, Chichester: John Wiley & Sons Limited. Reproduced with permission; Text extract, p.161 from Bennis, W. (1998) *On Becoming a Leader*, London: Random House Business Books. Used by permission of The Random House Group Limited; Text extract, p.170 from Brown, A. (2000) *The Six Dimensions of Leadership*, London: Random Hose Business Books. Used by permission of The Random House Group Limited; Text extracts, pp.176 and 191 from Jordan, M. (1994) *I can't accept not trying*, New York: HarperCollins. Reproduced by permission of HarperCollins Publishers Inc.; Text extract, p.238 from Wickham, P. (1999) *Management Consulting*, Harlow: Pearson Education; Text extract, p.276 from Schein, E.H. (1997) *Organizational Culture and Leadership*. © 1997 by Edgar Schein. This material is used by permission of Jossey-Bass, Inc., a subsidiary of John Wiley & Sons, Inc.; Text extract, p.282 from Kennedy, G. (1997) *Everything is Negotiable!*, London: Random House Business Books. Used by permission of The Random House Group Limited; Text extract, p.311 from Piskurich, G.M. (1993) *Self-Directed Learning – A Practical Guide to Design, Development and Implementation*. Copyright © George Piskurich. This material is used by permission of Jossey-Bass, Inc., a subsidiary of John Wiley & Sons, Inc.; Text extract, p.312 from Watkins, K.E. and Marsick, V.J. (1993) *Sculpting the Learning Organization*. Copyright © Karen Watkins and Victoria Marsick. This material is used by permission of Jossey-Bass, Inc., a subsidiary of John Wiley & Sons, Inc.

In some instances we have been unable to trace the owners of copyright material, and we would appreciate any information that would enable us to do so.

☐ Author's acknowledgements

Books are not written without the personal and professional encouragement and support of many people. As authors, we wish to thank the many students we have taught and from whom we have learnt, our families for their understanding and patience, and the team at Pearson Education, particularly Jacqueline Senior, Janey Webb and David Cox, for their unswerving enthusiasm and support.

The beginning is the most important part of the work.

(Plato)

Nature and purpose

This is a skills book. Its purpose is three-fold:

- ☐ To raise awareness by identifying key personal and interpersonal management skills, and highlighting the relationships that exist between them
- ☐ To increase knowledge by providing an overview and discussion of relevant management theory and research
- ☐ To develop capability by offering a variety of practical activities.

Audience

These three elements ensure that the book is of value to:

- ☐ Undergraduates of business and management studying a module on skills
- ☐ Post-graduates of business and management studying a skills, management development or leadership module
- ☐ Prospective or current managers wishing to develop their awareness, knowledge and capability.

Rationale

The authors believe that personal and interpersonal management skills cross professional boundaries; that the insights and abilities needed to manage oneself and then others successfully are essentially the same whether the manager is working in a leisure centre, a school or a blue-chip organisation. We also believe that the best managers are leaders. *This, then, is a book for those wishing to develop their ability to manage and lead in any environment.*

We refer primarily to 'managers', not 'managers who are leaders', throughout the book, purely for the sake of brevity. The personal and interpersonal skills that follow are intended to enable managers to lead to the best of their ability, not simply to manage.)

Structure

While each chapter can act as a stand-alone area of study, no management skill exists in isolation. Skills overlap, interact and support - a fact highlighted by the 'content maps' at the beginning of each chapter. These serve two functions:

1. They act as content guides, enabling you, the reader, to find specific topics with ease.

2. They stress the systemic nature of skill development.

Some skills, however, do provide a foundation for others. The chapter progression reflects this.

Part One

☐ Chapter 1: Managing self and self-image

☐ Chapter 2: Managing one-to-one relationships

This section develops the core skills, knowledge and attitudes that underpin all subsequent topics. For this reason, we suggest you study these chapters fully before selecting topics from subsequent chapters. (The authors appreciate that some readers might question our chapter sequencing and/or the inclusion of particular skills within certain chapters. While this is an interesting topic for debate, it is primarily a reflection of the difficulties of presenting a complex system through the essentially linear structure of a book and should not distract from the practical nature and purpose of the text.)

Part Two

☐ Chapter 3: Developing others

☐ Chapter 4: Leading and working in groups and teams

☐ Chapter 5: Creative problem-solving

This section explores the differences between managers and leaders, explains why the best managers are also leaders, and develops essential management and leadership knowledge, roles and skills.

Part Three

- ☐ Chapter 6: Selling ideas and persuasive campaigning
- ☐ Chapter 7: Consultancy, negotiation and bargaining
- ☐ Chapter 8: Cross-cultural management

This section builds on what has gone before, further testing and developing existing skills in addition to providing new insights and capabilities. It not only provides new learning, but draws together many of the previous skills and attitudes.

Part Four

- ☐ Chapter 9: Planning and managing personal development

This reflects the systemic, holistic nature of the book by returning to the key learning points made in Chapter 1 and providing additional self-evalution and personal and professional development strategies.

Developing personal and interpersonal management skills

The development of skill is not a purely intellectual exercise. Neither is information the same as knowledge. One way to distinguish between the two is to regard the material contained within this book as information that will become *your* knowledge once you have interpreted and absorbed it. Knowledge, then, is the result of a mental conversion process. One thing it is not is power. Knowledge is a precursor to power.

Power is the ability to take appropriate action. The greater our knowledge, the more resources at our disposal, the greater our potential to take action. How the appropriateness of an action is determined and measured is an issue we will explore later in the book.

The generic definition of power (that is, the rate at which a body or system does work) is applicable here since the primary purpose of a skills-based book is to improve the rate and quality of performance. However, Andrew Brown's definition of power (that is, 'the capacity to listen to others, to resolve conflicts, to persuade ... to stifle discontent when it is destructive, to prevent potentially damaging issues from being discussed, and to silence unhelpful critics' (Brown, 2000: 100)) is far more insightful and indicates the range of skills needed. His conclusion, that 'power to the leader is like energy to the physicist' (Brown, 2000: 101), emphasises its importance further.

There are, however, different types of power. Coercive power is that applied by an authoritarian leader and centres around rules, results and control. Expert power is that displayed by a technical wizard. Our focus is on generative power: the enabling skills that allow creative problem-solving and the management of change; the skills that act as a vehicle for personal and professional growth and achievement.

While the warning in Lord Acton's dictum that 'power tends to corrupt and absolute power corrupts absolutely' should be borne in mind, it is not an argument against the acquisition of power. Rather it is a reminder of the need for power to be developed in tandem with personal and interpersonal skills that are based on a positive set of beliefs and values, a clear and empowering sense of identity, an ability to create and maintain meaningful relationships, and an acute awareness of the responsibilities that accompany the different roles we play.

Unlike Napoleon, who confessed, 'Power is my mistress. ... I have worked too hard at her conquest to allow anyone to take her away from me or even covet her', modern managers have to be willing to share, to create empowering situations for those around them. The rapid rate of change that is synonymous with our Communication and Information Age demands that people become more adept at learning, at acquiring knowledge and developing skills, than at any other time in our history, and managers who are generative learners and leaders can do much to encourage and enable this process.

Interestingly, the word 'generative' shares the same root as 'generous', 'genial' and 'genius'. Managers who are generative learners and leaders can therefore be described as:

highly skilled and knowledgeable individuals who, through their example, the environments and systems they create, and their willingness to share their expertise, encourage and enable the personal and professional development of others while in pursuit of a meaningful shared vision.

This book does not purport to provide all the answers (indeed, in part, it encourages questioning and further study), but it does provide a focus and a stimulus. It is a practical and accessible text, concerned with the realities of current management and leadership issues. If does, importantly, demonstrate the relationships that exist between a variety of skills, attitudes and applications across a range of topics and in a variety of arenas.

A journey shared

The relationship between writers and readers is, at once, distant and close. At its best, both parties experience a sense of excitement, enthusiasm and urgency; time is measured in pages and chapters rather than minutes and hours and, when the final page is turned, there is an awareness that a journey has been shared. Readers have certain expectations and make silent demands of their writers. In return, the writers of this particular work have only one request: If you own this book, don't simply read it. *Use it.*

Back to the present!

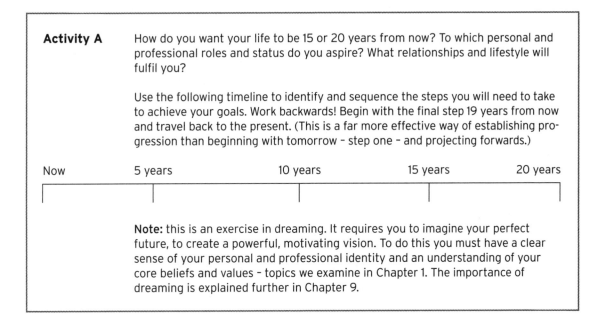

| Activity A | How do you want your life to be 15 or 20 years from now? To which personal and professional roles and status do you aspire? What relationships and lifestyle will fulfil you? |

Use the following timeline to identify and sequence the steps you will need to take to achieve your goals. Work backwards! Begin with the final step 19 years from now and travel back to the present. (This is a far more effective way of establishing progression than beginning with tomorrow - step one - and projecting forwards.)

Now   5 years   10 years   15 years   20 years

Note: this is an exercise in dreaming. It requires you to imagine your perfect future, to create a powerful, motivating vision. To do this you must have a clear sense of your personal and professional identity and an understanding of your core beliefs and values - topics we examine in Chapter 1. The importance of dreaming is explained further in Chapter 9.

Reference

Brown, A. 2000. *The 6 Dimensions of Leadership*. London: Random House.

01 The foundations of leadership

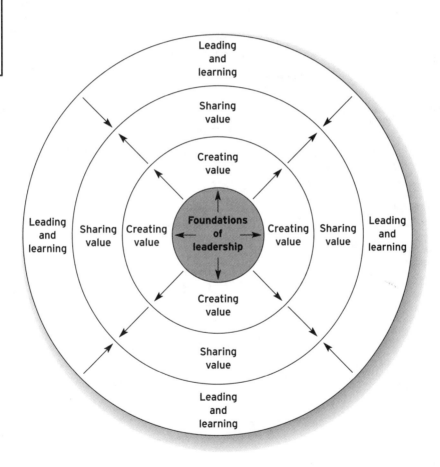

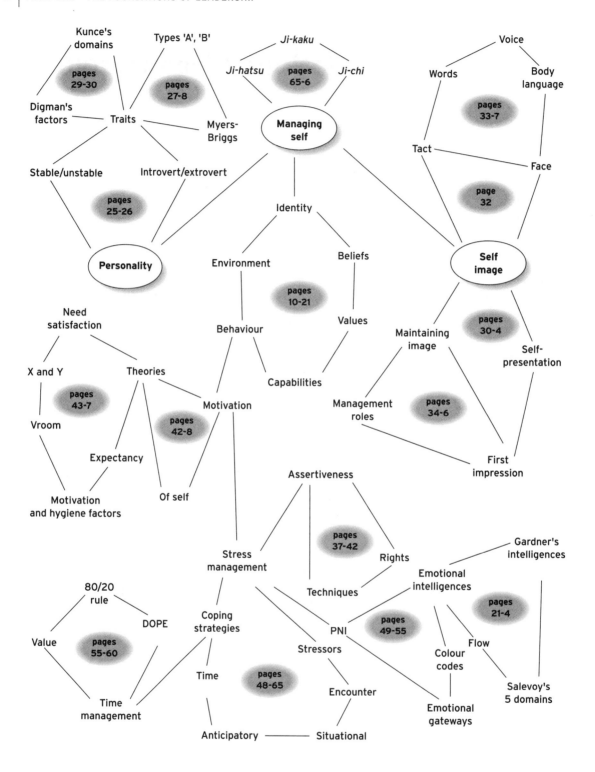

01 Managing self and self-image

Self understanding is a prerequisite for leading and managing others effectively, responsibly and honourably.

(Roy Williams, Chairperson of the Association for Management Education and Development)

This chapter will develop your:

Awareness of:	Knowledge of:	Capability to:
The concept of identity.	The relationship between beliefs, values, capabilities and environments.	Manage personal beliefs. Create personal alignment.
The concepts of emotional intelligence and 'flow'.	Seven key intelligences.	Identify and apply positive emotional states.
The concept of personality.	Personality traits.	Evaluate your own personality in the light of management role requirements.
The concepts of self-presentation and self-image.	The key elements of face-to-face communication. Assertive behaviours and strategies. Motivational theories.	Create and maintain an appropriate personal image. Be assertive. Motivate yourself. Motivate others.
The concept of stress.	The biology of stress. Primary stressors.	Apply appropriate stress management techniques, including time management.
The concept of Balanced Learning Performance.	The difference between balanced and peak performance.	Maintain high-level, balanced performance.

☐ Self management and understanding

The pioneering work done by Richard Bandler and John Grinder in the 1970s, leading to the formal creation of Neuro-Linguistic Programming (NLP), provides essential models and training methods for developing our understanding of human communication and provides a useful starting point for answering the question 'Who am I?'

The five-step model shown in Figure 1.1 identifies the relationship between a person's thoughts, beliefs and behaviour and the environments in which he/she operates.

Figure 1.1
Who am I?

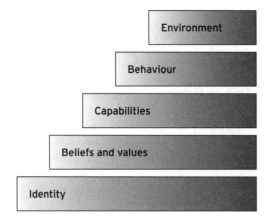

Personal identity

The first step focuses on an individual's personal sense of identity. Who you think you are influences the way you view the world, your relationships, how you wish to be regarded, how you think you are regarded, and the challenges you accept or reject. How is individual identity determined?

Imagine a social meeting between two strangers. Listen to their conversation. Notice how quickly one asks the other: 'What do you do for a living?' The reply comes back: 'I'm a Marketing Manager', or 'I'm a Headteacher', or 'I'm a Doctor'. It is easy for us to imagine this exchange because it is repeated whenever two strangers meet. Common practice is for people to identify themselves in accordance with their professional title. However, if we want to explore and, perhaps, share our personal identity more fully, we may be better advised to consider the roles we play within our job.

The writers of this book are both lecturers (among other things). But what does it mean to be a lecturer? On one level it means being a perpetual student, committed to one's own personal learning and growth. However, when a lecturer is in front of a group of students, he/she has three other responsibilities. These are to:

☐ Educate
☐ Entertain
☐ Inspire.

Essentially a lecturer's purpose is more than simply passing on information. Lecturers, like all other teachers, encourage and enable personal and social change. For many teachers and trainers, their work is more a sacred trust than a day job. While there are many ways to educate and inspire, the concept of entertainment is central to the practice. Why? Because people learn best when they are having fun.

So, by considering the roles played and the responsibilities accepted, by moving beyond the traditional labels of job titles, we can reach a deeper understanding of our personal identity.

'Hello, Chris. I'm pleased to meet you. What do you do for a living?'
'Actually, I'm a change management consultant, a learner, entertainer and story teller.'
'Oh. I'd heard that you were a lecturer. I must have been mistaken...'

Activity 1.1   Consider your current or a previous job (in this context, you can consider 'student' as a job). List the traditional titles you are given.

Now spend some time reviewing all the things you are required to do during a working day and replace the titles with more positive - and revealing - role labels.

Imagine how an advert for your job would read if it focused on these roles and responsibilities, rather than just the qualifications, experiences and key skills required.

And then, of course, there is one's personal self, which can also be lost behind traditional titles. What does it really mean to be a parent, partner, son, daughter or friend? What are the roles we play and the responsibilities we assume under these headings?

A powerful sense of personal identity can help individuals achieve their goals and shape their future. Steven Spielberg always saw himself as a film director. He knew who he was before he had acquired the title. It was that clarity that enabled him to turn his personal vision into reality. Imagine a sporting competition – a tennis final on the Centre Court at Wimbledon, perhaps – between an established champion who has won there many times and a newcomer who had not expected to get past the early rounds. Consider how their sense of identity will influence their performance. How easy to imagine the champion relaxing and playing at her very best because she *knows who she is*, while the newcomer struggles to see herself as this year's winner.

Another useful way to consider personal identity is through the use of metaphor. A favourite of many creative consultants, metaphors encourage people to reveal exactly how they perceive themselves.

Activity 1.2   Select one of your role labels. Convert it into a metaphor by comparing your per-formance and style in that role to an animal. For example, a person says: 'As a learner I am like a bear in a trailer park – eating everything I can lay my paws on.'

What insight does that give you into the individual concerned? What do you learn from your own metaphor?

As this chapter is also concerned with managing self-image, you may want to ask a number of appropriate people to create their metaphor for you in the role under question.

If, for example, the common response to the person quoted above is 'As a learner you are like a mouse, running out from the floorboards to nervously nibble some cheese', that person may need to consider how accurate his/her self-percep-tion is, or how well he/she is managing his/her self-image.

Personal identity, then, is the foundation for self-knowledge and for creating rapport between the different elements of our personal and professional lives. Most directly, personal identity influences the beliefs you hold and the values you strive for.

Beliefs

What is a belief? Expressed most simply, a belief is a feeling of certainty. It is stronger than a mere opinion but less powerful than a personal conviction. Beliefs grow out of ideas and are influenced by such powerful forces as:

☐ Religion
☐ Education
☐ Organisational and/or national culture
☐ Personal experiences.

Beliefs affect individual and group behaviour in a positive or negative manner. Positive beliefs are those which:

☐ Make people feel good about themselves
☐ Encourage people to take risks
☐ Enhance performance.

Negative beliefs have the opposite effects. They:

☐ Make people feel bad about themselves, or a part of themselves
☐ Limit risk-taking
☐ Impair performance.

Those beliefs held to be true by the majority of a society establish the bound-aries within which most people operate. They create a sense of what psychologists call 'social proof' – a widely accepted agreement of what is right or wrong, possible or impossible. For example, in the world of athletics, breaking the four-minute-mile barrier was considered to be impossible for many years. Many runners tried and failed, and with each failure the social proof was strengthened. It seemed there really was a limit as to how fast a human being could run. As with all examples of social proof, this belief was so widely accepted that it was regarded as a fact by many, but not all. In 1954, the Englishman Roger Bannister broke the four-minute-mile barrier. The world was reminded once again that exceptional people, capable of ignoring the negative beliefs of others, redefine the realms of the possible. With the barrier and (more importantly) the belief broken, athletes now approached the task in a different frame of mind, unfettered by the burden of social proof.

The result? Within 12 months of Bannister's achievement, 37 athletes had also run a sub-four-minute mile. In 1956, several hundred runners followed suit. Nothing had changed in terms of athletic coaching or human capability. The difference lay simply in the beliefs people held.

That is why this topic features in a management book. Beliefs influence behaviour and performance, and people *hold* beliefs. That means we can learn to let go of any beliefs that harm us or limit our ability to perform effectively. We can manage our personal, functional or corporate belief systems as deliberately as we manage our wardrobe. And that analogy is not inappropriate. How many people hold on to pieces of out-dated, worn out, possibly ill-fitting clothing because they have become so comfortable they cannot bear to throw them away? People do the same with negative beliefs.

At its most extreme, adherence to a predominantly negative set of beliefs creates a state of learned helplessness: a permanent, pervasive sense of inadequacy and lack of control. At the other end of the scale, a positive belief system encourages learned optimism: self-confidence, the ability to learn from all experiences, to see opportunities where others might see only threats. As creative, adaptive beings we have a choice where we position ourselves on the scale between learned optimism and learned helplessness. Managing our personal belief system is at the very heart of this process.

Children understand that beliefs need not be permanent. Indeed, as parents we teach them that. Can you remember as a child being encouraged to believe in Father Christmas only to discover that the provider of presents was actually your mother or father? By definition, a belief is not something we can prove. Its value is associated directly with the way it influences our thoughts and behaviour. Why would anyone choose to hold on to negative beliefs? Perhaps it is because, in some perverse way, we have become comfortable with them. Perhaps it is because we have held them for so long we now regard them as facts and have forgotten what we teach our children. Or perhaps it is because we simply do not know how to change?

The three-step process in belief management is as follows:

1. Understand how beliefs work.
2. Perform a personal belief audit.
3. Select and apply appropriate techniques to strengthen positive beliefs and remove negative beliefs.

How beliefs work

Beliefs operate in cycles (see Figure 1.2) and are continually strengthened or weakened by an individual's thoughts and actions. Negative beliefs create negative cycles, which invariably reinforce a feeling of failure or under-achievement. Positive beliefs create positive cycles, which have the opposite effects. The key point here is that beliefs should be regarded as living, growing organisms, at once fuelling and feeding off mindsets and behaviours. Beliefs do not naturally stagnate. People's internal response to a particular stimulus and their subsequent action either challenges or reinforces their belief system.

Figure 1.2
A negative belief cycle

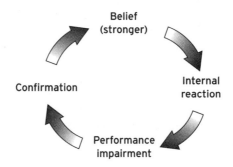

Belief (stronger)

Internal reaction

Performance impairment

Confirmation

Consider a young manager, let's call him James, who doubts his ability to deliver an effective, stimulating presentation. When required to do so, perhaps with the aim of winning a new customer, James feels an immediate sense of doubt and fear, feelings which grow as the day of the presentation nears. No matter how much time James spends in preparation and practice, he can do nothing to increase his confidence. He is aware only of his perceived lack of ability. Sure enough, on the day of the presentation, James stutters and stumbles, unable to present a positive image or to create rapport with his audience. The opportunity to develop a new client is lost. This confirms what James already believed – that he lacked the necessary skills – and his negative belief is strengthened.

However, James may not be as bad at delivering presentations as he thinks. Once a belief has been accepted, it encourages us to interpret events in ways that support and, therefore, strengthen it. James might have made a better start to his presentation than he realised, he might have appeared more confident and relaxed than he thought, but such was the power of his negative belief that he only recognised, and was affected by, those indications that he was failing.

Beliefs influence not only what we think, but how we see and interpret events. Consider how difficult it would be to convince a person who does not believe in ghosts that they do exist! If a ghost appeared in front of that person, would it change his/her belief or would he/she find a different explanation for what he/she had witnessed? It is easy to imagine that (like us) the person would create an explanation to support his/her existing beliefs.

Beliefs help us to make sense of our world, but negative and limiting beliefs blind us to opportunities, confine our imaginations and prevent us from creating valuable new realities. Bill Gates held such positive beliefs that he was able to think the unthinkable – 'a computer in every house' – at a time when most people knew it to be an impossibility. His belief system was so strong that he was then able to turn the unthinkable into a reality that transformed the world.

Techniques

Anthony Robbins, a leading NLP practitioner, discusses three techniques for letting go of negative beliefs. These are:

☐ Associate great pain with a belief
☐ Create doubt about the validity of the belief
☐ Reframe the way you regard and interpret events and associated beliefs.

Associate pain

Take time to consider all the ways a particular belief has hurt, or limited, you in the past. How has it made you feel inadequate or insecure? What opportunities have you missed because of it? Now consider the extent to which your negative belief, and the ways it makes you behave, has caused pain to those around you – your family or work colleagues perhaps. Why would you want to hold on to such a harmful belief? According to Robbins: 'If we associate enough pain to anything, we'll change. The only reason we have a belief about something is that we've linked massive pain to not believing it or massive pleasure to keeping it alive' (Robbins, 1992: 85).

Activity 1.3 **A personal belief audit**

The purpose of this exercise is to determine the positive and negative beliefs you currently hold and their relative power.

1. Brainstorm your personal beliefs. List what you believe to be your physical, emotional, social and intellectual strengths and weaknesses, the aspects of yourself you like and those you don't, the ways you believe you are perceived by others, etc. Don't stop to evaluate, simply write them down.
2. When the list is as complete as you can make it, divide the beliefs into two columns: positive and negative. Count the number in each. Are the columns evenly balanced, or do you have more beliefs in one than the other? What does that tell you?
3. Rearrange the beliefs in each column according to their relative strength. Place the weakest belief - the one that is the least positive and least negative - at the bottom and work your way up so that, in both columns, the most powerful belief is at the top.
4. Now make a commitment to let go of the least negative belief you hold. Why begin with this one? Because it is important to succeed, to establish a winning streak, and the weakest belief will be the easiest to lose.
5. Select from the following techniques the ones that work best for you, and restructure your belief system.

Create doubt

Select your weakest negative belief and question its validity. Remember a time when you changed your opinion, or perhaps even a belief, and notice how often, as a result of an experience, you began to doubt that which you thought was true.

The key to creating doubt is to question. Try working from the principle that none of your negative beliefs is true 'beyond a shadow of a doubt'. Negative beliefs influence us only because we give them the power to do so. Much as we might have wanted Father Christmas to exist, the good news is that we can lose our negative beliefs as easily as we lost our belief in him. If you want to let go of a negative belief, question it continually until you begin to doubt. Then, as you question it even more rigorously, associate massive pain with it.

Reframing

A third technique is known as reframing. This involves changing the way you think about, or regard, a particular belief or experience; changing your frame of reference from negative to positive, for example. If you have ever purchased an unframed painting, you will appreciate the impact different types of frame can have on your picture. Even a beautiful painting by a great artist is dependent on the right frame if it is to be seen at its best. The same principle holds true for the events we experience and the beliefs we develop as a consequence.

Shakespeare wrote: 'There is nothing either good or bad, but thinking makes it so.' But the ability to reframe – itself a powerful tool in the process of belief management – cannot turn a painful or unpleasant experience into a totally enjoyable one. Reframing enables us to see possible gains in what, at first glance, might seem a no-win situation. It allows us to represent and inter-pret experiences in ways that support our outcomes. Reframing reminds us that experience is not what happens to a person, but rather how that person uses what happens.

There are two main types of reframe:

1. Context reframing.
2. Content reframing.

1. Context reframing

Context reframing is based on the principle that most behaviours are useful somewhere, in a certain context. Standing to attention and singing the national anthem while in the middle of an examination will probably result in your exclusion from the room. However, if you do the same at Twickenham, moments before England play the All Blacks at rugby, you will be in the majority, creating a sense of belonging and anticipation. Likewise, doing a great impersonation of Whitney Houston might not be a good idea in the middle of a job interview, but it would probably impress a lot of people in a karaoke bar!

The key to context reframing, then, is to identify the situations in which particular behaviours are most appropriate and to prepare for those.

2. Content reframing

Content reframing focuses on the meaning given to a situation or experience. It is based on the understanding that we have a choice about how we interpret our experiences and the value we place on them. Content reframing is the ability to apply the most suitable meaning to an event, to focus on the content in such a way that it provides some positive purpose. Politicians are excellent content reframers. If you provide the same data to members of three different political parties, you will hear three different interpretations and be asked to choose between three different meanings.

Values

Oscar Wilde defined a cynic as a person who 'knows the price of everything and the value of nothing'. What exactly are values?

Like beliefs, values determine not only why we do something but, to a great extent, the manner in which we do it. Values are those behaviours, practices or principles that are important to us. They are supported by our beliefs and, like them, they are developed through our experiences and our choice of role models. Values are directly related to our sense of personal identity. They are a source of motivation and direction and yet, as with beliefs, their influence is often at a subconscious level. Individuals committed to managing their values in much the same way as they manage every other aspect of their life need to evaluate and express their values in a conscious, deliberate manner. Values are best expressed in a positive way, and can be divided into two types. These are:

☐ Means values
☐ End values.

People's end values reflect the ultimate reason(s) why they behave in a certain manner. Means values precede and feed end values. Means values provide the motivation to achieve desired goals. Both types of values are expressed in the following statement:

> *It is important for me to develop my academic ability (means value) so that I achieve a first class degree (means value), which will enable me to get the job of my dreams (end value).*

In *The Nature of Human Values* (1973), Rokeach argues that people share many end values, differing only in the extent to which they prioritise them. Rokeach called end values 'terminal' and means values 'instrumental'.

Instrumental values relate to morality and/or competence. Failure to behave in ways that reflect one's instrumental values leads to feelings of guilt or shame. Terminal values relate to desired outcomes or goals, and can be either personal (for example, happiness) or social (for example, equality).

Table 1.1 lists what Rokeach identified as 'the most important terminal values in American society'. It is important to bear in mind that the priority given to values is driven to some extent by the influence of national culture. The reasons for such cultural differences will be explored more fully in Chapter 8.

Table 1.1
The Rokeach
Value System

Terminal values

A comfortable/prosperous life	Inner harmony
An exciting life	Mature love
A sense of accomplishment	National security
A world at peace	Pleasure
A world of beauty	Salvation (Eternal life)
Equality	Self-respect
Family security	Social recognition
Freedom	True friendship
Happiness	Wisdom

Source: Rokeach (1973)

Activity 1.4   Prioritise the values listed in Table 1.1. Do you have any terminal values that are not included? If so, add them to the lists in the appropriate place(s). Identify the core instrumental values you hold.

Values can change as changes occur in a person's life. For example, individuals who have never valued exercise might change their value if told by their doctor that they need to begin a gentle exercise programme. Analysis of our current values enables us to evaluate and, if necessary, re-establish our priorities. In a rapidly changing, often complex and dynamic environment, achieving and maintaining a sense of balance between personal and professional roles and responsibilities can be a difficult task. A useful starting point is to ensure that our behaviours always reflect our values.

Capabilities

It is important to distinguish between resources and capabilities. Knowledge is a resource. Capability is the manner in which the knowledge is used. However, capability is more than just a skill. Presented with the same situation, people with identical knowledge and skills will apply them differently.

These differences are influenced by the previous two steps – identity and beliefs/values – which in turn influence the distinctions people make when preparing for, or engaged in, a situation. Personal distinctions, or areas of focus, determine how knowledge and skills are applied. For example, a group of people in a meeting will respond differently to the same stimulus because of the different distinctions they make. One person may need to speak, another wants to listen further, while a third threatens to withdraw.

Remember James, the nervous presenter? Imagine the distinctions he makes as he struggles to provide that winning presentation, hampered by his negative beliefs and a personal identity that is not consistent with his role. In this situation, is James working to the best of his capabilities? Certainly not. Will the distinctions he makes reinforce his sense of incompetence? Almost certainly. They will also influence the goals he sets himself prior to, and during, his presentation.

A strong identity, consistent with the role and task at hand, supported by positive, empowering beliefs, will lead to the development of clear, meaningful goals and equally clear distinctions. With James's internal support structure so weak, it is easy to imagine him setting limited goals, and changing them as he perceives the presentation to be floundering. His behaviour will deteriorate as his primary goal becomes simply to complete the presentation and get the heck out of there! His area of focus will no longer be to win a new client, but simply to escape.

The distinctions we make also influence the learning we take from different experiences. This, in turn, affects our capabilities. In our rapidly changing world, the ability to learn quickly, to be flexible, to be comfortable with newness, is a core skill. It might even be the most important. Peter Senge explains the meaning and purpose of generative learning, and shows how it is far removed from the mere acquisition of knowledge, when he says:

> *Real learning gets to the heart of being human. Through learning we re-create ourselves. Through learning we become able to do something we were never able to do. Through learning we re-perceive the world and our relationship to it. Through learning we extend our capacity to create.*
>
> (Senge, 1993:14)

Learning, then, demands a willingness on the student's part quite literally to change his/her mind, to let go of previously held assumptions and beliefs, and to develop new perceptions based on the results of his/her study. It is through this process, Senge argues, that capabilities are developed.

Much traditional learning has focused on the acquisition of knowledge and, at best, skills relevant only to a specific context. As no two situations are ever exactly the same, this approach to learning actually limits an individual's chances of success. To repeat behaviour because it appeared to provide the best solution in the past is no guarantee of success in the present. Contexts change because people and environments change. As they continue to do so with increasing rapidity, the need for the flexible, creative skills that can best be developed through generative learning grows ever greater.

Behaviour

While the things we do and say are influenced by the subconscious sub-text of our beliefs and values, they are also learned from those people we regard as role models. If we are lucky, we are born into a family with good role models and, as we grow, we surround ourselves with family members, friends and colleagues who are positive and perhaps inspiring influences.

Managers – particularly those who are leaders – are also role models. The ways in which they solve problems, relate to others, exercise power and respond to pressure, for example, will be copied to varying degrees by those around them. This is a weighty responsibility. It implies that managers concerned with creating behavioural change in others have, among other skills, to be able to demonstrate their own capacity to change.

Habitual behaviour is a fact of life and it is essential that some habits, like stopping your car at a red light, are maintained. However, in dynamic, rapidly changing environments an unwillingness or inability to change behaviour, to let go of limiting, out-of-date habits in favour of new systems, practices or skills, results in sterility and performance impairment at best, and decay leading to eventual demise at worst. Managers who are role models may begin an evaluation of their own behaviour by exploring the value and power of their personal habits.

Activity 1.5   Review your behaviour yesterday. Imagine you had been filmed throughout the day. Close your eyes and watch the film.

Make a list of all the habitual behaviours you observe. Divide them into positive, essential behaviours and those that serve no useful purpose but have become part of the way you behave. How much of your day was simply a matter of habit?

The ability routinely to engage in creative behaviours grows out of the ability to manage our habits, to ensure that they are our servants and never our master. As with all skills, this requires regular and deliberate practice.

Activity 1.6   Break a habit! Do one new thing every day.

Environment

Environments have a powerful effect on an individual's emotional state and behaviour. The most appropriate environments are those which encourage and enhance performance while providing sufficient opportunities for meaningful feedback. It is also true, though, that individuals who recognise beliefs and values as powerful drivers of behaviour, and who manage them accordingly, can achieve amazing results and gain significant insights and learning even in the most negative of environments.

Environments can be created or chosen and, while it is possible to overcome the negative influences of uninspiring or even threatening environments, it makes sense to create or to choose those environments that inspire commitment, enthusiasm and effort, and in which high-level performance is the norm.

This can also present challenges. Consider the issues facing the manager who determines to create an environment that will keep his/her team's spirits high and encourage creativity and the sharing, evaluation and implementation of new ideas. Perhaps this manager begins by asking each member of the team to describe his/her vision of a creative environment. Can you imagine the different responses he/she would receive? From the individual who needs a calming, peaceful setting to the one who needs rock music blasting out all the time? From the person who feels that an open-plan design will encourage the sharing of ideas to the person who requires solitude?

This is not to suggest that this is an impossible task. Far from it. However, few environments have a universal impact or appeal. Creating organisational environments that positively affect everyone involved means taking into account individual differences and requirements. It is a far easier task choosing or creating environments only for oneself.

Activity 1.7   Imagine, then create, your own personal learning environment. Design the perfect environment in which to study. Pay attention to every detail, from the practical to the atmospheric. Consider availability of equipment and books, lighting, colour schemes, noise levels etc.

When the ideal is complete, remind yourself of the realities of your situation.

Within which boundaries do you have to work? Review your perfect environment with these in mind. Make whatever changes, or compromises, you have to.

Now turn your design into a reality.

The five steps we have used as a starting point for answering the question 'Who am I?' impact one upon another. Behaviour is driven by beliefs and environments reflect values. This systemic perception is best represented in the form of a simple interacting loop (see Figure 1.3).

Figure 1.3
Who I am

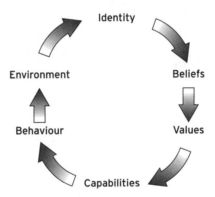

Managing emotions
===

The pioneering work of Daniel Goleman, sometimes referred to as the 'father of emotional intelligence', has done much to focus attention on the proposition that a successful, balanced life requires a high level of emotional intelligence in combination with an average level of traditionally measured intelligence. Goleman reports how Howard Gardner, a psychologist at the Harvard School of Education, proposed a shift away from the commonly-held view of one crucial intelligence to an acceptance of a wide spectrum of intelligences within which were seven key varieties. Gardner included the two basic academic types, verbal and mathematical, but added the following:

☐ Spatial
☐ Kinesthetic
☐ Musical
☐ Interpersonal
☐ Intrapsychic.

Intrapsychic intelligence, according to Gardner, includes the ability to 'access one's own feelings ... to discriminate among them and draw upon them to guide behaviour' (Gardner, 1999). Gardner continues to explore the possibility of additional intelligences that meet the criteria he sets and, in his work *Intelligence Reframed*, he evaluates the notion of Existential and Moral Intelligences.

Peter Salovey, a Yale psychologist, offered a basic definition of emotional intelligence that subsumed Gardner's intelligences into five domains. While two of these, 'recognising emotions in others' and 'handling relationships,' will be discussed in Chapter 2, Salovey's first three domains are at the heart of managing self and self-image. These are:

1. Knowing one's emotions.
2. Managing emotions.
3. Motivating oneself.

1. Knowing one's emotions

This is dependent upon a high level of self-awareness. Goleman describes the ability to recognise a feeling as it occurs as 'the key to emotional intelligence. ... An inability to notice our true feelings leaves us at their mercy. People with greater certainty about their feelings are better pilots of their lives...' (Goleman, 1996: 43). Self-awareness in this regard is primarily objective in nature. It means, says John Mayer, a psychologist from the University of New Hampshire, being 'aware of both our mood and our thoughts about that mood' (Mayer and Stevens, 1993). To achieve this sense of detachment, what Freud called 'an evenly hovering attention', is perhaps easier said than done. When individuals recognise a particular mood, the temptation to assign an immediate value or goal to it is often difficult to resist. Thoughts such as 'I must stop feeling like this, it isn't doing me any good' or 'I need to cheer myself up' are typical examples. Mayer identified three distinct styles that people demonstrate when dealing with their emotions.

Self-aware
Are those who recognise specific moods with speed and clarity, and are able to change them if necessary. Such people tend to have a positive outlook on life.

Engulfed
Are those who often feel dominated by their emotions. Such people feel unable to resist or escape their emotions. They cannot access the 'observing ego' at the heart of self-awareness, and have minimal control over their emotional self.

Accepting

Are those who often recognise their moods, but do little, or nothing, to change them. Some people may experience primarily positive moods and so feel little need for such management. There are, however, also those who accept negative moods and associated distress. Such people often display a sense of resignation.

2. Managing emotions

Ensuring that emotions are controlled and/or displayed appropriately enables people to manage negative states such as fear, anxiety or anger more effectively, and to recover more quickly from potentially distressing situations. Although Mayer acknowledged the difference between awareness of feelings and acting to change them, he did conclude that the two tend to be interrelated. Once we become aware of the fact that we are in a negative, unproductive or potentially harmful mood, we do want to get out of it. Our capability to employ appropriate strategies depends upon our self-awareness and subsequent level of emotional intelligence.

Awareness of the emotion we are feeling can lead to a far more complete resolution than focusing only on the behaviour spawned by that emotion. For example, should you become angry with a fellow driver you might be able to stop shouting and pressing the horn after only a few seconds. Yet, even if you do control your temper, you will still feel the emotion for sometime afterwards. Behavioural management, physical self-control, does not guarantee, or necessarily reflect, emotional change. Self-awareness, on the other hand, focuses directly on the emotional root. The recognition that 'I am feeling angry now' brings with it not only the option to remain physically calm but, more importantly, the opportunity to let go of the emotion if it is deemed inappropriate or potentially harmful.

3. Motivating oneself

Goleman reports that: 'Studies of Olympic athletes, world-class musicians, and chess grand masters find their unifying trait is the ability to motivate themselves to pursue relentless training routines' (Goleman, 1996: 79). Emotional self-control, including the capacity to disregard impulsive urges and delay rewards until the goal is achieved, is a prerequisite for accomplishment. The channelling of appropriate emotions, an essential part of self-motivation, is the path along which a state of seemingly effortless peak performance, or 'flow', can be attained.

People who are confronted by challenges that test their capabilities are most likely to experience flow. Tasks that are perceived as too easy become boring, while tasks that are viewed as beyond 'our measure' create anxiety. People who can summon the state of flow tend to be hopeful, optimistic individuals, driven by a passion for their chosen activity. They are not motivated by thoughts of material reward. They *have* to do what they do.

Knowing, and then creating, the optimum emotional state for a given activity is an additional measure of emotional intelligence. For writers and others in creative employment, a mildly elated state – hypomania – best encourages imaginative responses and associations. The key here is 'mildly elated'. A manic state does not increase creativity, but rather anxiety and severe mood swings that block the creative process.

Psychologists have long explored the relationship between anxiety and all types of performance, representing it as an upside-down U (Figure 1.4). Too little anxiety, as depicted by the first side of the U, leads to apathy and insufficient motivation. Too much anxiety, the other side of the U, can lead to performance impairment. The ideal relationship, enough nervous tension to stimulate high levels of motivation and a subsequent state of flow, is shown at the peak of the U.

Figure 1.4
Anxiety and performance

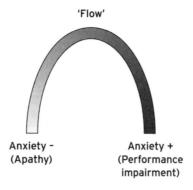

'Flow'

Anxiety –
(Apathy)

Anxiety +
(Performance impairment)

The root meaning of the word 'emotion' is 'to move'. Emotions create impulses to act. Sometimes those impulses need to be ignored, sometimes embraced. People with a high level of emotional intelligence distinguish between the two, and move in directions and ways that support and increase their sense of identity, their beliefs, values and capabilities.

Activity 1.8   What emotional states enable you to perform at your best? What behaviours, thoughts, environments encourage those emotions? How can you create and/or use those to help you access the desired state?

Practise observing your moods. Identify them to yourself. Ask yourself the following questions:

'Am I enjoying this mood?'
'Is it improving the quality of what I'm doing?'
'What effect is it having on those around me?'
'If I need to let go of this mood, what shall I replace it with? What thoughts, behaviours and/or environments help me to access the preferred emotional state?'

Self management and understanding: key points!

☐ The NLP approach to self management and understanding is based on recognising the relationships that exist between:
  ☐ Identity
  ☐ Beliefs and values
  ☐ Capabilities
  ☐ Behaviour
  ☐ Environment.
☐ Managers who achieve this have established alignment, a sense of rapport with themselves.
☐ Such people demonstrate:
  ☐ A level of balance and purpose in both their professional and personal lives
  ☐ A clear understanding of who they are, what they aim to accomplish and how they will do so.
☐ Their focus is on such questions as:
  ☐ 'Am I behaving in a way that is true to who I am?'
  ☐ 'Am I influencing my environment in the ways I find most acceptable?'
  ☐ 'Am I achieving my potential?'
☐ An understanding of emotional intelligence and its value in managing self and self-image leads to a shift away from traditional definitions and measures of intelligence.
☐ Managing self and self-image is dependent upon:
  ☐ Knowing one's emotions
  ☐ Managing emotions
  ☐ Motivating oneself.

☐ Personality

I yam what I yam, and that's all that I yam.

Popeye

People have differing personalities, which affect the way they interact and work. Categorising these personalities has long been a popular human pastime. Eysenck suggested there are two main categories. These are:

Introvert -- Extrovert

(Seeking within yourself to find your true self) (Seeing yourself reflected in others)

Stable --- Unstable

(Moods changing only slowly or rarely)   (Moods change frequently)

Activity 1.9   Having considered the definitions of Eysenck's categories of personality, write a statement about whether you feel yourself to be extrovert or introvert, stable or unstable. Now try the following test to see where you locate yourself on this type of personality analysis. Ignore column 2 in the first instance.

	Column 1 Yes/No	Column 2 Yes/No
1. Do you sometimes feel happy, sometimes unhappy, with no real reason?		
2. Do you frequently lose concentration on the subject in a conversation?		
3. Are you often moody and difficult?		
4. Do you sometimes burst with energy, but are sometimes lethargic and dull?		
5. Do you have difficulty concentrating, and does your mind often wander?		
6. Do you have ups and downs of mood, with or without reason?		
7. Do you prefer to do things actively rather than to plan for them?		
8. Do you usually take the initiative in starting conversations and making friends?		
9. Are you stimulated and happy when you have to act quickly?		
10. Would you describe yourself as a lively person?		
11. Are you usually confident and sure in your actions?		
12. Would you be very unhappy if you could not often meet lots of new people?		

To assess your responses, give yourself a point on the following extrovert–introvert axis for every 'yes' in the first six questions, and a point on the stable–unstable axis for every 'yes' in the last six questions.

```
                        Stable
                          6
                          5
                          4
        Extrovert  6  5  4  3  2  1  0   Introvert
                          2
                          1
                          0
                       Unstable
```

As a supplementary activity, ask a close friend and/or a work colleague to answer the questions about you, using column 2. Mark his/her responses on the diagram and contrast these with what you have said about yourself.

Personality traits

Personality traits are habitual responses to specific stimuli or situations. Guilford defined personality as 'the interactive aggregate of personal characteristics that influence the individual's response to the environment' (Guilford, 1959). More commonly, the term is used to summarise a collection of traits. Individuals are described as 'honest', 'good-natured', 'introverted' or 'aggressive'. Such summary judgements are, by definition, based on past experience. The fact that they are often used to predict likely future responses is no indicator of their accuracy.

Some traits are difficult to identify because they are not directly linked with specific behaviours. 'Sensitivity', for example, can be difficult to observe. Another difficulty lies in determining the reliability of the individual defining the traits. Many people find it difficult to identify their own traits with a great degree of accuracy, and most observers have only a limited time frame in which to make assessments. (Your responses to the previous activity probably reflect this.) Nevertheless, the fact that the qualities and behaviours connected to traits are repetitive, has encouraged psychologists to devise various personality trait measures.

Type A and Type B

For several decades now, scientists have accepted the link between certain personality traits and various physical and psychological problems, particularly anxiety, heart disease and unsuccessful relationships. Friedman and Rosenman (1959), cardiologists working in the 1950s, defined this personality as Type A.

Type A
Type A individuals demonstrate such traits as impatience, extreme competitiveness, restlessness, explosive speech patterns and physical tension. They are often driven by a strong urge to be acknowledged as an expert on a given subject and, failing this, may refuse to become involved. Type A individuals often appear to be in a hurry, can experience feelings of guilt when relaxing and are always trying to do several things at once.

Type B
Type B personalities demonstrate opposite traits, appearing to be more relaxed, less hurried and competitive, less driven by measurable results, more aware of the bigger picture and the effects of their actions on the broader environment.

An eight-year survey of 3,400 men aged between 39 and 49 found that Type A personalities were approximately 6.5 times more likely to suffer heart disease, but were more capable of recovering from heart attacks than their Type B counterparts. However, the most debilitating Type A factors have yet to be agreed. Rosenman argued that anger, competitiveness and impatience were the most potentially harmful traits, while Kobasa (1979) suggested it was the feelings of urgency that ensured a constant flow of adrenalin and cortisol into the system, and Greenberg (1987) opted for hostility. The issue and effects of constant adrenalin release is a relevant and important topic, and will be returned to later in this chapter when we consider managing pressure and stress.

Myers-Briggs Type Indicator

Myers and Briggs's (1962) work on personality, and the measures they use, reflect the theory that traits evolve as a result of experience. People prefer the ways of doing things that have been most productive in the past. Behaviours that have been rewarded and/or have resulted in the desired outcome are repeated in preference to experimenting with new alternatives. These new methods of behaviour are less likely to be as successful because, by definition, they are less practised. This awareness also limits the likelihood of change.

The four traits that Myers and Briggs concentrate on (see Box 1.1) are closely related to work activities and have been used by many organisations in the assessment of people and management training. This does not mean, however, that the Myers–Briggs Indicator is exempt from the criticisms that can be levelled against all trait theories.

Box 1.1 | ## Myers-Briggs's personality traits

Generating Information

Sensing -- Intuition

(Using data from the environment)   (Using insight, memory, imagination)

Decision-making

Thinking -- Feeling

(Using logic, analysis)   (Using personal values, experience)

Prioritising

Perceptively -- Judgementally

(Prefer to understand the situation fully)   (Prefer to resolve issues)

Managing Relationships

Extroversion -- Introversion

(Prefer company and interaction)   (Prefer to work alone)

Activity 1.10   Decide where you would place yourself on each of the four Myers-Briggs lines. Ask members of your family, your closest friends and some work colleagues to evaluate you in the same way. How significant are the differences? How do you explain them?

Kunce's Personal Styles Inventory

Based on studies that indicate there are several different 'domains' of behaviour, Kunce's Personal Styles Inventory (PSI) (Kunce et al., 1991) enables the assessment of characteristics in three specific domains:

☐ Emotional
☐ Activity
☐ Cognitive.

The range within each domain is as follows.

Emotional
Enthusiastic ------------- Reserved
Sympathetic ------------- Restive
Patient ------------- Confronting
Modest ------------- Expansive

Activity
Affiliating ------------- Autonomous
Amicable ------------- Restless
Regulating ------------- Venturing
Introspecting ------------- Excitement-seeking

Cognitive
Ideological ------------- Empirical
Conventional ------------- Individualistic
Convergent ------------- Divergent
Realistic ------------- Abstract

With eight elements in each domain, individuals' scores on the 24 scales are recorded in two ways. First, respondents select the most accurate descriptors. This set of results makes up the respondents' PSI. Secondly, respondents determine the degree to which a definition of each element describes them. This set of results reveals their self-rating.

Apart from identifying the most, and least, characteristic personality clusters, Kunce also claims that significant differences between the PSI and self-rating scores can indicate sources of potential negative stress. This is because the PSI scores reflect the most enduring personality traits, whereas the self-ratings reveal how a person is currently behaving.

Digman's Five Factor Model

This reflects the growing body of research that suggests there is a larger set of personality dimensions than previously identified. The dimensions assessed are:

1. Extroversion – meaning fun-loving, sociable, affectionate and friendly.
2. Openness to experience – meaning imaginative, daring, having a broad range of interests.
3. Agreeableness – meaning cooperative, sympathetic, trusting and polite.
4. Conscientiousness – meaning hardworking, energetic, ambitious and persevering.
5. Neuroticism – meaning the opposite of emotional stability: self-conscious, insecure, worrying.

Personality: key points!

☐ Personality affects the ways individuals interact and work.

☐ Personality traits are habitual responses to specific stimuli or situations.

☐ Two main personality categories are:

    ☐ Introvert ------------ Extrovert

    ☐ Stable ------------ Unstable.

☐ Some traits are difficult to identify because they are not directly linked to specific behaviours.

☐ Trait theories and models include:

    ☐ Type A and Type B

    ☐ The Myers-Briggs Indicator

    ☐ Kunce's PSI

    ☐ Digman's Five Factor Model.

☐ Trait-based approaches to understanding and evaluating personality have proved useful in the workplace. However, they still fail to explain how an individual's personality develops or why it is what it is.

☐ The task of identifying and assessing one's traits presupposes a level of objectivity that can be difficult to achieve.

☐ Image management

There are two different aspects of personality. These are the person we perceive ourselves to be and the person others perceive us to be. Which perception is right? Both are. We play different roles in different aspects of our lives and, for most of us at least, there are elements of our persona that are best (perhaps only) seen by others. Understanding this duality lies at the heart of managing self-image.

While it is not essential for managers to undertake a study of psychology, philosophy and Zen in order to reach a deeper understanding of their true selves, it is the case that many successful managers create a synergy between these two different aspects of personality. How they see themselves has much in common with how their colleagues see them.

The Johari window (Figure 1.5) is a useful tool for reminding us of the relationship that exists between the different elements of personality and personal versus public perception.

Figure 1.5
The Johari window

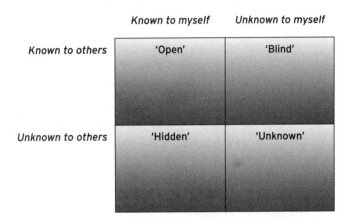

	Known to myself	Unknown to myself
Known to others	'Open'	'Blind'
Unknown to others	'Hidden'	'Unknown'

Activity 1.11 Draw the Johari window. Put three things in the 'Open' box and three in the 'Hidden' box. Consider why you have made these things 'Open' and 'Hidden'.

What aspects of your personality do you feel (would) need to be 'Open' in your role as a manager/leader, and what aspects (would) need to be 'Hidden'? Justify your response.

Self-presentation

Erving Goffman (1959), the American sociologist at the forefront of the study of managing self-image and understanding the impressions we make on others, coined the phrase 'self-presentation', linking human behaviour in a variety of personal and professional settings to theatrical performances. The key difference is that, in real life, the aim is not solely to entertain or educate but rather to behave in a manner that reflects our perception of what is real and important. For example, a top sports coach will interact with her athletes in ways that support her definition of the situation–namely, that she is responsible for their progress. Thus, she will plan training programmes, dietary regimes, rest periods and, possibly, even the competitions to be entered. While this will be done in consultation with her athletes, the coach's behaviour will determine the nature of her relationships with them and constantly reinforce the situation as she defines it.

This type of self-presentation is dependent on two things. First, the success of the coach in improving athletic performance. Secondly, the willingness of the athletes to accept the coach's definition of the situation and the manner in which she performs her role. The relevance of the former is self-explanatory. The latter reflects the close relationship that exists between self-presentation and establishing and maintaining one's required status or 'face'.

'Face', or public image, cannot survive without the acceptance of those with whom we come into contact. Loss of face, resulting from the behaviour of others and/or inappropriate personal actions or words, is not only humiliating for the individual but can also be a source of embarrassment for all concerned. For this reason, most people feel an obligation to defend others' 'faces' along with their own. The behaviour that accomplishes this is known as 'tact'. For the most part, we accept the image presented by those we meet and respond to them accordingly. Without such tact, self-image would be almost impossible to maintain. There are occasions, however, when tact is missing, when people inadvertently or deliberately challenge or disregard another's image. Such power-plays can be successful as a form of self-promotion, or as a method of reprimanding an individual who has crossed a formal (or informal) line.

However, as a general rule, causing loss of face usually provokes a negative reaction at least and retribution at worst. Also, such behaviour is likely to unsettle any observers who may then involve themselves. After all, if you are willing publicly to humiliate one person, you are probably capable of doing it to another – including them! Given this, the wise manager will rarely use this tactic. The social structure of groups, teams and organisations depends to varying degrees on tact and 'face-saving'. Deliberate tactless responses are perhaps best saved as a last line of self-defence when all else has failed.

First Impressions

As mentioned earlier, the beliefs we hold create mindsets through which we make sense of our world and the people in it. The first impressions we give, and those we receive from others, go a long way to determining future expectations and the nature of relationships.

Why are we so quick to make judgements about others? One reason is because it is easy. It takes far more effort, skill and sensitivity to gain a meaningful understanding of another human being in a relatively short space of time than it does to make a snap decision. Secondly, much of our education system encourages us to find the right answers as quickly as possible. The successful student is the one who answers the question the fastest. How many teachers did you have who encouraged you to spend time identifying the most relevant questions, rather than rushing to the most obvious answers? Finally, and connected with the other two, we tend to be influenced by first impressions because of the way mindsets work.

Throughout every day of our lives, our brains are literally bombarded with millions of stimuli. To manage and make sense of these, we subconsciously select the stimuli to focus on. This process is driven by our existing beliefs and assumptions.

Activity 1.12 The next time you are on a busy street, take a moment to observe a passing stranger. Try not to make any judgement about him/her. Then think of a colleague or a friend. Can you remember your first impression of them? How much has it changed? When was the last time they did anything that surprised you? How easy would it be for you to change your current impression of them? When was the last time you tried?

Introductions

For the reasons mentioned earlier, self-presentation skills are especially important when introducing yourself. Whether meeting new colleagues or potential clients, whether beginning a presentation or meeting representatives from other organisations with interests of their own, the first few minutes are vital in determining whose definition of the situation will be accepted. Some key points to bear in mind are as follows:

1. In face-to-face communication every message we give is a combination of the words we use, the tone, pace and clarity of our voice, and our body language. Creating a good impression is based on getting the mix between these three elements right.
2. Your manner in the first meeting will be viewed as indicative of your general manner and behaviour. Although some people may resist the temptation to jump to conclusions and take into account the nature of the situation, it is best to work on the principle that first impressions really do count. Unless you are commenting on an issue regarded as vitally important by your listeners, your behaviour will have more impact than what you say. Therefore, you need to ensure that your style reflects the manner you intend to show in future meetings.

Activity 1.13 How do you rate the importance of each of the three elements of face-to-face communication?
What percentage of the message is determined by:

☐ the words
☐ vocal tone, pace and clarity
☐ body language?

(You will find the answer at the end of this section, see page 42.)

3. A low-key approach reduces the risk of saying or doing the wrong thing based on lack of knowledge. This is a particularly useful tactic when meeting superiors for the first time. Again, ensure that your body language does not imply an unintended air of authority.
4. When first meeting colleagues, or at a social gathering, a quick way to create a non-threatening, likeable impression and gain rapport is to emphasise the things you have in common with those around you.

5. However, if the situation requires you to demonstrate authority, do so from the very beginning.

6. If at all possible, spend more time listening and less time talking. Have at least some of the questions you want to ask prepared before the first meeting. Show an interest in the answers you get, but avoid passing judgements that might inadvertently draw you into a long-standing argument or debate. If asked for your opinion and you sense a potential pitfall, it is quite reasonable to refuse to commit yourself on the grounds that you have not had time to study the situation as fully as you need.

Being a good listener is not only an important aspect of self-presentation, it is also a core communication skill. NLP practitioners teach and practise a comprehensive approach to listening, referred to as 'whole-body listening'. This skill, along with techniques to develop it, is covered in Chapter 2.

Although it is important to make the correct impression when first meeting others, it is at least equally important to be able to maintain the image you present over a longer period of time. First impressions are significant, but if the subsequent image you offer contradicts that first impression, colleagues will begin to doubt your honesty, reliability and integrity. Creating the most appropriate image in the first meeting is only the first step in an ongoing managerial process. The responsibility for defining the situation requires that managers are skilled at self-presentation and comfortable with the personal image(s) they choose to present. The adage 'It isn't what you do, it's the way that you do it' is appropriate here. Establishing the correct relationship between substance and style is essential for maintaining an impression.

Maintaining personal image

Once you have successfully defined the situation and the nature of the relationships you are going to share within it, the issue becomes one of preservation. To preserve those relationships as intended, managers need to determine how much information and time they will share with the individuals concerned. Managers also need to decide upon the style of interaction. The following questions reflect some of the issues they need to address:

☐ 'Will I treat everyone the same, or will I obviously take certain individuals more into my confidence?'
☐ 'To what extent do I need to demonstrate my independence from the team I manage?'
☐ 'How will I demonstrate that independence?'

According to Goffman, managers should resist the temptation to behave like those they manage. If they do not remain a step removed, he argues, there is the risk that lines will become blurred and the clarity of the situation lost (Goffman, 1972).

Activity 1.14   'Managers are not in the team, they are *of* the team; they must maintain a sense of distant dignity.'

Do you agree with this statement?

Consider two managers you have worked with or observed. Review the degree to which they have/have not applied this principle. How successful were they as managers?

To what extent is a manager a symbol of the organisation? Consider different organisations and levels of seniority as you answer this question. How does the concept of the 'manager as a symbol' impact on the whole issue of self-presentation?

As a manager how would/do you define and maintain the situation and your personal image?

The ability to maintain a personal image for extended periods also requires a degree of honesty. It would be unrealistic and, eventually, counterproductive to expect managers to behave constantly in a way that is at odds with their essential nature. Goffman's observation about the relationship between human behaviour and theatrical performance is at once useful and challenging in this regard. It implies that managers, like actors, play roles. And, more significantly, that managers, like actors, should have the ability to play a variety of roles with equal conviction. This does not equate to dishonesty. Actors will explore and apply aspects as their real selves to a role they are playing. And successful actors are so good at creating and defining situations that audiences never question or challenge them.

Managers, then, should be able to play more than one role and be able to change their personal image to suit the requirements of a new environment with the same honesty and thoughtfulness as a great actor. The key here is to be prepared to make significant changes only when we change environments. As mentioned earlier, role-playing does not equate with dishonesty, but inconsistency in self-presentation is often regarded as such by colleagues.

Activity 1.15   Prioritise the following list of management roles:

☐ Teacher
☐ Creator and steward of a vision
☐ Rule maker
☐ Enforcer
☐ Conflict manager
☐ Figurehead
☐ Designer
☐ Motivator
☐ Delegator
☐ Team builder.

Would you remove any of these roles from the list? Why?

Are there any other roles you would add to this list? Where would you place them?

Which roles can you play most easily? Why?

How could you learn to play the others?

The research carried out by E.E. Jones (1964) shows that people's capacity to choose a specific style of self-presentation can also be severely limited by the role they feel required to play. There may, for example, be a perceived need to demonstrate to a superior how strict and authoritative you can be. If this need is great enough, other options will be rejected and the image you create, and the manner in which you are perceived by your subordinates, will be set. There are, according to Goffman, other factors which can negatively influence self-presentation. These are:

☐ *External preoccupation.* This refers to those times when one's mind wanders, attention is diverted, and others notice the distraction and resultant changes in image.

☐ *Self-consciousness.* Feelings of uncontrollable nervousness or awkwardness are visible and, again, the public image is lost as the more private face appears.

☐ *Over-consciousness of the other person.* This occurs when the manager becomes too interested in or concerned by a particular individual. Examples would include being unnerved by or sexually attracted to a colleague.

☐ *Over-consciousness of the interaction process.* Often a result of the previous two factors, this refers to those times when individuals become too concerned with how they will be perceived or how others will respond.

Any combination of the above factors is likely to result in unwanted revelations and inconsistency in the desired image. Emotions and thoughts influence physicality. Often, no matter what we say, our body language reveals the real truth.

Image management: key points!

☐ Personal image, like organisational culture, is inevitable.

☐ Personal image can be:
  ☐ Deliberately created and managed
  ☐ Left to chance.

☐ Self-presentation has much in common with theatrical performance.

☐ Managers should:
  ☐ Have the ability to play the roles that most suit the needs and expectations of the people around them
  ☐ Be able to create appropriate first impressions
  ☐ Recognise that these are only the first stage of the managerial process.

☐ Consistency is essential if trust is to created.

☐ Personal image is dependent on:
  ☐ Other people's tact; loss of face can be hurtful to the individual and threatening to the group
  ☐ An honest commitment to, and an understanding of, the role that has to be played.

☐ Self-presentation is demonstrated not least through the ways in which the manager is assertive, motivates others and manages pressure.

Response to Activity 1.13

According to the work of Professor Albert Mehrabian, the answer to Activity 1.13 is: Body language, 58 per cent; tone, pace and clarity of voice, 35 per cent; words used, 7 per cent. More recently, tests in business environments have suggested that the importance of words can be as great as 40 per cent.

☐ Assertiveness

There is a significant difference between assertive and aggressive behaviour. The *Collins Dictionary* defines 'aggression' as 'violent, hostile and unprovoked', while 'to assert' means to 'insist upon one's rights'. Assertive behaviour, then, is confident and direct, based on an awareness of one's own rights and the rights of others. It can be seen as the middle path, the balanced approach between being too submissive and too aggressive. Basic rights we can expect and declare include:

☐ The right to ask for what we want and don't want
☐ The right to be listened to and respected
☐ The right not to know something and not to understand
☐ The right to make mistakes
☐ The right to change our minds
☐ The right to judge our own behaviour and take responsibility for the results.

As with so many aspects of management skills, these rights do not exist in isolation. The right to make a mistake, and to see this as part of a learning, creative process, underpins both assertiveness and creativity. The right to be listened to and respected is also at the heart of communication. The right to judge our behaviour and accept responsibility for the consequences is a key element of personal development. *Understanding the relationships that exist between personal and interpersonal skills is a core requirement for the modern manager.*

Assertive behaviour is relatively easy to apply in situations that are not threatening or stressful. It is of most value, however, in precisely those situations. To become really angry for the most part reflects a loss of control. To submit to demands we would rather withstand is a weakness of a different kind. While most of us would prefer to live without conflict, there are times when it is unavoidable. The willingness to avoid conflict at all costs is no guarantee of outcomes with which we are comfortable or happy. To go along with another's wishes when we would rather not may keep the peace in the short term but demonstrates a lack of mental fortitude rather than the application of high moral values.

It can be difficult, however, knowing when to be assertive. In part, this knowledge comes from recognising when our boundaries are being crossed and from understanding the motives of others. A useful approach is to consider assertiveness as the middle path in what can be termed the '3 As'. These are:

1. *Avoidance.* If a problem or possible conflict is brewing, an early response may nip the problem in the bud or enable us to avoid it should it happen.
2. *Assertiveness.* Unable to minimise or avoid the issue, we have to be able to assert our rights.
3. *Aggression.* The least preferable option, it is rarely the most appropriate response.

The need for assertive behaviour in the workplace is often different from that outside. People in organisations do need to have their rights recognised and respected, but managers must be assertive to ensure that behaviours and achievements are to the standard required and that deadlines are met. Assertiveness can be demonstrated in two ways:

☐ Through what we say
☐ Through our body language.

Activity 1.16   To asssess your own level of assertiveness, decide where you would place yourself on the following scales.
When I need to be assertive I:

Take responsibility for what I say

Always -- Never

State limitations and alternatives

Always -- Never

Repeat key assertions when necessary

Always -- Never

Don't allow myself to be distracted

Always -- Never

Ask for more information if needed

Always -- Never

Share my feelings

Always -- Never

Acknowledge the other person's feelings

Always -- Never

Give reasons, not excuses

Always -- Never

Avoid using threatening language

Always -- Never

Am willing to compromise

Always -- Never

Box 1.2

Verbal Assertiveness – 15 Tips

1. Take responsibility for everything you say.
2. State your specific limitations and alternatives.
3. Repeat what the other person requests before you reply.
4. Repeat your key assertions if necessary.
5. Don't allow yourself to be distracted from the issues you want to discuss.
6. Be willing to ask for more information.
7. Share your feelings and how you are going to respond.
8. Acknowledge how the other person is feeling.
9. Don't apologise for the way you feel or for what you are going to do, unless there is a very good reason.
10. Give reasons not excuses.
11. Maintain a firm, even tone of voice.
12. Avoid the language of blame.
13. Never threaten.
14. Use questions to draw attention to issues.
15. Be willing to compromise.

Body language

Remember, in face-to-face communication the majority of our message is determined by body language and the tone, clarity and pace of our voice. Clearly, then, being assertive is about far more than what we say. A calm, confident and deliberate manner provides the foundation for assertive language. It can also help overcome the problems people face when being assertive, the most common of which are:

☐ How to say 'No'
☐ How to avoid interruptions
☐ How to elicit a response
☐ How to give and accept compliments.

How to say 'No'

Solutions include:

☐ Using repetition
☐ Saying 'No' on its own
☐ Using specific body language to emphasise the point.

Repetition can be a powerful and persuasive tool. The 'rule of three', which requires the use of three examples or repetitions, is favoured by public speakers and politicians because it fixes the message clearly in the listener's mind. An example of the 'rule of three' in operation would be Tony Blair's promise to the electorate that his priority would be 'Education! Education! Education!'

Many people find it difficult to say 'No' on its own. Therefore, very few people do. For that reason, it can have great impact if delivered in a calm and confident manner.

Decide whether to use open or closed postures to support an assertive refusal. Both can be successful, depending on how they are applied and, particularly, the personal image you have already created. A relaxed, open stance supported by open-handed gestures can give the impression of absolute confidence or can suggest that you are easily swayed. While sitting down, crossing both arms and legs could imply absolute refusal or defensive retreat.

How to avoid interruptions

Solutions include:

- ☐ Speaking at a constant speed
- ☐ Avoiding unnecessary pauses
- ☐ Avoiding eye contact.

Under pressure, with the release of adrenalin and cortisol into the system, breathing quickens and the capacity to construct cohesive arguments can diminish. For these reasons, the pace of a person's speech can either speed up or slow down. Under extreme duress language often becomes monosyllabic and repetitive. Maintaining a constant speed disguises any feelings of nervousness, suggesting confidence in both your knowledge of the topic and your capacity to manage the situation. Unnecessary pauses indicate the opposite and encourage interruption.

While maintaining eye contact is a sign of confidence or interest, it also invites a response. So, if it is essential that your audience remains silent while you speak, avoid overlong direct eye contact with any individual.

How to elicit a response

Solutions include:

- ☐ Gaining eye contact
- ☐ Using silence.

When you have finished talking to a group, establish eye contact with the person you most want to respond first. You may select him/her because he/she is likely to agree with your viewpoint, or because you know what he/she is going to say, or simply because of his/her status. Whatever the reason, this tactic can help you maintain a degree of control of the situation.

To create and hold a silence implies great confidence. Experienced speakers will often take a second or two before beginning their address, during which time they may cast their eyes over the audience, perhaps smiling as they do so. The message is: I am relaxed, confident, in control and comfortable with your attention. Silence can also be used to show interest in someone else's comment. People who think for a few seconds before replying are paying obvious respect to the value of what they have just heard. (This is, of course, dependent on their body language being congruent with their thoughtful expression.) Finally, when needing to elicit a response, silence can be used to pressure the other person into speaking. Silences occur infrequently in many conversations. When they do, they are often the result of boredom or a lack of things to say! Knowing this, we can be fairly certain that if we create a silence, someone will feel obliged to speak – probably sooner rather than later.

How to give and accept compliments

When giving compliments:

- ☐ Be clear and precise
- ☐ Refer to appropriate examples
- ☐ Offer the compliment as soon after the event as possible
- ☐ Use your knowledge of the person to determine whether to compliment publicly or privately.

Acknowledgement of good work or a good attitude or effort can motivate and inspire. The most meaningful compliments:

- ☐ Are specific
- ☐ Include examples of the behaviours or results that are being praised
- ☐ Are offered promptly.

Not everyone enjoys public recognition and, as a compliment given at the wrong time and place can have a demotivating effect, astute managers base the style and setting of the compliment on their understanding of the person concerned.

For many people, receiving a compliment can be more awkward than giving one. Techniques for receiving compliments centre upon being able to accept praise at full value. Resist the temptation to downplay the quality of your work or its value in the eyes of others. A simple 'Thank you' is a more than suitable response, but if you are able, you can also agree with what has been said about you. A third alternative is to offer your thanks and then return the compliment.

Activity 1.17 Identify situations you encounter that call for assertive behaviour. List any common problems you face when being assertive. Determine a plan of action to overcome them. Deal with your problems one at a time, beginning with the easiest to resolve and leaving the toughest problem until last.

Assertiveness: key points!

☐ Assertiveness is founded on an awareness of human rights – ours and those of the people around us.

☐ It is the manner in which we insist on getting what is right for us, without abusing others.

☐ In the workplace, a manager's assertiveness is usually intended to ensure that standards and deadlines are met.

☐ Assertiveness enables people to:
 ☐ Say 'No'
 ☐ Avoid interruptions
 ☐ Elicit responses
 ☐ Give and accept compliments.

☐ Assertive individuals:
 ☐ Take responsibility for everything they say
 ☐ Are willing to ask for more information when necessary
 ☐ Share their feelings
 ☐ Avoid the language of blame
 ☐ Never threaten
 ☐ Are willing to compromise
 ☐ Create synergy between their verbal and body language.

☐ Most people are capable of being assertive in non-threatening or stressful situations. The aim is to use those same techniques under pressure.

☐ Motivation

There are two aspects of motivation that need to be studied, understood and applied. These are:

☐ Motivating oneself
☐ Motivating others.

Managers need to do both. Ensuring the acquisition of knowledge and the development of key skills in oneself and others does not alone guarantee success. To use an analogy, motivation is the engine that drives behaviour. Paul Anderson, the legendary weight lifter and strongman, famously talked about the champion's willingness to 'go that extra mile' in pursuit of excellence. Anderson might have had outstanding genetics, he might have been naturally stronger than the average person, but his extraordinary feats were ultimately a testimony to his ability to motivate himself to a degree that few could equal. He was always prepared to 'go that extra mile' and, as is always the case with well-motivated people, his sense of drive and purpose was crucial in creating an ongoing virtuous motivation circle (see Figure 1.6).

Figure 1.6
A motivation cycle

Motivational theories and models

A number of often overlapping theories and models have been presented with the aim of helping us understand how to establish such a virtuous circle and avoid its negative counterpart. We will consider the following:

- ☐ The expectancy theory
- ☐ Vroom's two-factor theory
- ☐ McGregor's Theory X and Theory Y assumptions
- ☐ Maslow's hierarchy of needs
- ☐ Herzberg's motivators and hygiene factors.

The expectancy theory

The expectancy theory identifies the elements that must be in place if a high level of motivation is to be achieved. These are:

Effort ------------------------ Performance ------------------------ Outcomes

The perceived quality of the outcome(s) determines the degree of effort exerted in the future. It is important to remember, however, that it is usually a third party who determines the value of the outcome. It is the third party's response – reward, punishment, indifference – that is the key motivating factor. Increased effort on the part of the 'performer' is a reflection of the level of motivation created.

While some individuals are capable of pursuing their goals and improving their performance without the stimulus of feedback, most of us are motivated by and are, to a greater or lesser extent, dependent upon the responses of others. It should also be noted that the connection between the three elements of effort, performance and outcome is primarily a subjective one. Willingness to make or increase one's effort is based on the belief that it will result in improved performance, and that the subsequent outcome will be a rewarding one. Understanding belief cycles and how to stimulate positive beliefs in others is therefore an essential part of the motivational process.

Vroom's two-factor theory

Victor Vroom, an American psychologist, explored the relationship between a person's goals and expectations (Vroom, 1964). He suggested that levels of motivation are determined by the individuals' expectation of a particular outcome resulting from their behaviour. If the expected outcome is regarded as positive and welcome, motivational levels are likely to be high. Conversely, if the most likely outcome is perceived negatively, motivation is likely to be low. Vroom called this strength of preference for a particular outcome 'valence', and the perceived likelihood of this outcome 'subjective probability'. These two factors can be given numerical values and can be shown in the form of a simple equation through which the level of motivation can be worked out.

$$\text{Motivation level} = \text{valence} \times \text{subjective probability}$$

Vroom stated that valence could be scored as a positive or negative number, or even zero, as the anticipated outcome can be viewed positively, negatively or with indifference. Subjective probability could be given a score between 1 (certainty) and 0 (impossibility). The formula can become quite complicated as there are often several outcomes with associated probabilities to be considered with any new task. These might include consideration of time factors and extra work, improving status or increasing promotional prospects, maintaining or improving relationships with colleagues.

Vroom's work was not meant to imply that people consciously carry out such equations to determine their level of motivation. Clearly they do not. However, Vroom did maintain that people go through this process in a subconscious manner, comparing the number of positive and negative outcomes and their relative significance and probability.

McGregor's Theory X and Theory Y assumptions

Writing in 1960, McGregor suggested that much managerial action derived from assumptions about human behaviour. He presented Theory X and Theory Y assumptions, arguing that most people tend to support one theory more than the other. Theory X is based on the assumption that human beings have an inherent dislike of work and need to be controlled, coerced, directed or threatened to ensure sufficient effort. Most people, the theory goes, actually prefer to be directed and seek to avoid responsibility. Theory Y reflects the opposite assumption: that human beings do not inherently dislike work and, depending on the circumstances, work may be a source of satisfaction or punishment. Providing the goals set are regarded as valuable and worthwhile, people will exercise self-control and self-direction, and will learn to seek responsibility.

Activity 1.18   How do you regard McGregor's two theories? Which do you favour? Why?

Can you think of any individuals who, by their actions, appear to agree wholeheartedly with Theory X? Can you think of anyone who would be as supportive of Theory Y?

Clearly, a person who naturally tends towards a belief in Theory X will create working environments, structures, systems and motivational styles that are very different from the person who tends towards Theory Y. Who is right? Neither theory encapsulates the full range of human motives, experience and personality. Indeed, one of the great values of McGregor's work is to remind us of the possible dangers of basing our behaviour on assumptions – our personal views about the nature of reality, determined by deeply ingrained mindsets and beliefs – rather than objective study. Different people will behave in the same way but for different reasons. Similar actions need not imply similar motives, although, according to Maslow (1970) and Alderfer (1972), human behaviour is driven by a series of common, hierarchical needs that have to be satisfied if levels of motivation are to be high.

Maslow's hierarchy of needs

Maslow (1970) classified human needs, ranging from the most basic to the subtle and complex, in a hierarchy that is most often drawn as a triangle (see Figure 1.7). According to Maslow, physiological needs are those most basic

Figure 1.7
Maslow's hierarchy
of needs

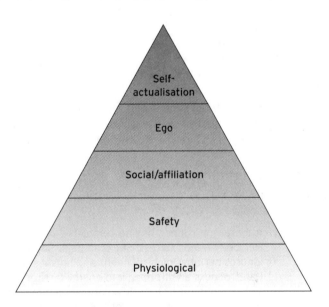

needs that override all others whenever they are not met. They include the need for food, water, air and pain avoidance. Most of us, in our day-to-day lives, are able to meet these needs as a matter of course. On the rare occasions we are unable to do so, they immediately take priority. Physiological needs represent the first tier of Maslow's hierarchy of needs. Safety needs (the second tier) represent another basic requirement, but they are addressed only when our physiological needs have been satisfied. The need to feel safe is significant, but a person who is starving to death, for example, will be driven to risk his/her safety if that is required to get food. On the third level of Maslow's hierarchy is the need to belong. With our physiological and safety needs met, we focus on meeting those with whom we can bond in some way. Ego needs follow next. These satisfy the requirement to be recognised as an individual; for others to acknowledge our special talents or expertise, or the unique contribution we have made to the group. The final level represents self-actualisation needs. These are the highest order and the most personal needs. They reflect the desire to fulfil our potential, to become the person we most want to be.

Important points to bear in mind are that needs cease to be needs once they have been satisfied and, as soon as one level of need is met, the next level then becomes the most important. Need satisfaction is often transitory. A good meal will satiate hunger but it will not prevent the person from becoming hungry again. Likewise, a manager can satisfy ego needs by praising a person's work but this will only have a short-term effect if not repeated at appropriate intervals. Few people enjoy situations in the workplace where all their needs are constantly met.

Maslow himself acknowledged weaknesses in his theory, not least the fact that it applies primarily to middle-class, English-speaking, first-world cultures. Hackman and Lawler (1971) identified four core job dimensions that provide scope for satisfying those who are driven by higher-level needs. These are:

- ☐ Variety
- ☐ Autonomy
- ☐ Task identity
- ☐ Feedback on performance.

Aldefer (1972) developed the ERG Theory – an abbreviated, needs-driven approach using three levels instead of Maslow's five. Alderfer discussed needs in terms of Existence, Relatedness and Growth.

Activity 1.19   Consider Maslow's hierarchy of needs critically in the light of the following two examples:

1. A marathon runner, having completed 22 miles, is drained of physical energy. Her body needs to rest. She is in pain. She cannot win the race. However, she ignores her physiological needs and finishes the race.
2. Paratroopers are dropped into enemy territory. Throughout the operation, their survival depends on their ability to maintain high levels of performance and motivation without many of their physiological and safety needs being met. They do so.

Can you think of other examples in which individuals and/or teams are highly motivated (that is, they satisfy higher-level needs) when their more basic needs are not being met? What are the implications in terms of:

1. Maslow's theory that physiological needs override all others when they are not met?
2. The key drivers of motivation?

Herzberg's motivators and hygiene factors

Frederick Herzberg, a writer and consultant, asked the following questions:

- ☐ 'What single thing at work gave you the most positive satisfaction in the last twelve months?'
- ☐ 'What single thing at work gave you the most negative dissatisfaction in the last twelve months?' (Herzberg et al., 1959)

He discovered that the factors which cause satisfaction in the workplace are not the same as those which cause dissatisfaction. Satisfiers were different elements of work from dissatisfiers. Herzberg referred to them as motivators and hygiene factors. Motivators are those factors which, if present, provide satisfaction. Examples include:

- ☐ Achievement
- ☐ Recognition
- ☐ Opportunities for learning and personal development.

Hygiene factors are those which, if absent, create dissatisfaction but, when present, are not in themselves motivators. An example would be a good canteen. While people would quickly become dissatisfied if they were unable to enjoy adequate food and drink while at work, few people if any select their workplace because of the quality of the cooking available. Other hygiene factors include bureaucracy, company policies and relationships with managers. Salary can be either a motivator or a hygiene factor, or both. As a recognition of status and skill, it is a motivator. As a means of removing certain dissatisfiers associated with living conditions, it is a hygiene factor.

Herzberg's work has also been criticised. Other researchers were not always able to confirm his results, and he has been accused of being too rooted in middle-class professional American values.

Activity 1.20   Review your last 12 months at work. What single thing gave you the most positive satisfaction? What single thing gave you the most negative dissatisfaction?

Self-motivation

Anthony Robbins states that: 'Change is usually not a question of capability; it's almost always a question of motivation!' (Robbins, 1992: 124). Certainly, most of us are aware of what we want to achieve in both our personal and professional lives, and many of us are acutely aware of the gulf that exists between knowing what needs to be done and actually doing it. The concept of aligning the five elements shown in Figure 1.1 (see page 11) – identity, beliefs and values, capabilities, behaviour and environment – to create rapport with oneself is central if levels of self-motivation are to be high and the gulf between 'knowing' and 'doing' is to be bridged. Try motivating yourself to do something that contradicts your sense of identity, or denies one of your primary beliefs, and see how difficult it is.

Robbins also argues that the language many people use decreases motivation, providing an emotional opt-out clause rather than creating the sense of urgency that spurs effort. Talking or thinking in terms of what 'should' be done is not as powerful or demanding as acknowledging what 'must' happen, although accepting that something must change is not always sufficient either. Individuals who are highly self-motivated are capable of creating a sense of urgency and immediacy. They know what must be done and are compelled to follow it through *now*. For them there is no possibility of waiting for a more suitable time. They are not limited by thoughts of what they can or cannot do, but focus strongly on what they *will* do. A primary step in creating this overwhelming need is to associate massive pain with not taking immediate action. As with managing negative beliefs, recognising and then *feeling* the pain caused by failure to change is the starting point for establishing new thoughts and behaviour. The feeling that 'something must happen now, because I cannot possibly tolerate this situation any longer' is a powerful motivator.

Motivation: key points!

☐ Managers need to motivate themselves and others.

☐ They also need to be aware of the danger of assuming that all people are motivated by the same things.

☐ Motivational theories and models include:

  ☐ The expectancy theory

  ☐ Vroom's two-factor theory

  ☐ McGregor's Theory X and Theory Y assumptions

  ☐ Maslow's hierarchy of needs

  ☐ Herzberg's motivators and hygiene factors.

☐ Some theories, no matter how well known, can be challenged in a variety of ways.

☐ Highly motivated individuals create a sense of urgency to perform tasks that:

  ☐ Are congruent with their identity, beliefs and desired behaviours

  ☐ Develop their capabilities

  ☐ Contribute to their environment.

☐ Stress and pressure management

By learning to utilize pressure and make it your friend instead of your foe, you can truly hone it into a tool that assists you in living life to the fullest. Besides, we need to remember that our stress level is self-induced. So let's induce it intelligently.

(Anthony Robbins, 1992: 280)

In its simplest form, stress is a pressure on an object. It is neither positive nor negative. The value of its effect is determined by the object's response and level(s) of resiliency. The human skills of observation, recognition, intuition and learning provide us with the potential to withstand, adapt to and even enjoy a variety of pressures and stressors. Why is it, then, that so many people suffer from stress-related illnesses? The answer lies partly in the fact that people's coping strategies are not always on a par with their levels of awareness – stressors are identified but not managed appropriately – and partly in the rapid rate of change that is at the core of the Communication and Information Age. Ideally, coping strategies – the ability to manage a variety of pressures – are based on an understanding of our biological responses to perceived pressure and the prompt identification and classification of the stressors we face.

The biology of stress

The threats facing primitive man were primarily physical, with predators, enemies, and poor weather conditions being among the most obvious. The threats facing the modern manager are primarily intellectual and emotional. We may fail to meet a deadline, to motivate a colleague appropriately, or to create the best relationship with our team, but the odds of us being eaten, attacked or freezing to death are low in the extreme! Despite this, our essential biological responses to a perceived threat mirror those of our primitive ancestors. Sophisticated though we are in many ways, our bodies cannot differentiate between a threat to our ego and a threat to our physical well-being. While the level of threat can be identified – clearly defending yourself against a wild animal would create a higher-level response than, say, attending a potentially awkward meeting – the so-called 'fight or flight' syndrome comes into play whether the danger is to our body or our mind.

The first thing to bear in mind about this syndrome is that it is *not* a fight or flight response. Think of a situation in which you have experienced a nervous feeling in your stomach and a quickening of your heartbeat. Perhaps your palms dried, your voice began to shake or you began to sweat. At that time, did you feel capable of managing the problem in a relaxed, confident, determined manner, or did you experience an urge to avoid it altogether? In all probability you felt the latter, because the sensations described reflect a chemical response that is primarily designed to aid rapid flight, not confrontation. A more appropriate way to think of this reaction is the 'flight, freeze or fight when there's absolutely no alternative' syndrome. In the workplace, of course, managers facing numerous pressures do not have the luxury of either running away or hiding. People, issues and projects have to be faced and managed irrespective of the stress involved. Professional responsibility (and ego) mean that managers have to override their innate desire to avoid potential stressors and, quite simply, get on with their job. The science of PsychoNeuroImmunology (PNI) explains some of the potential dangers of doing this without appropriate coping strategies.

Imagine James, our unconfident presenter, being told by his manager to deliver a significant presentation to a very important client in two weeks' time. While forewarned is forearmed and, in theory, James has the time to structure, prepare and practise his presentation, he also has two weeks in which to worry about the event. As the day nears his nervousness increases and the desire to avoid the situation is hard to resist. The 'flight, freeze or fight' syndrome is at work. But what is actually happening inside James? The instant James was given the task, he identified it as a major stressor and felt extremely nervous.

At that point, his hypothalamus produced a chemical called corticotrophin (CRF). This travelled to the pituitary gland, causing the release of two adreno-corticotropic hormones, TSH and ACTH. TSH is responsible for an increase in James's metabolic rate. ACTH travelled via the bloodstream to his adrenal glands. James's cortex produced cortisol, while the medulla produced adrenalin and noradrenalin. They are responsible for speeding up his heartbeat and raising his blood pressure. Cortisol increased James's blood sugar and also increased his metabolism. Because this event is such a major stressor for James, his body, unaware that the threat is only to James's professional pride and ego, is preparing itself for a physical, possibly life-threatening encounter.

In the time leading up to the presentation, James thinks about it a great deal. It comes into his thoughts even when he doesn't want it to. He wakes up at night thinking about it. And with every thought the syndrome is stimulated again – the body cannot know that the threat is not imminent – and James spends most of the two weeks with his body inching into overdrive. His heartbeat and blood sugar are up, his metabolism is racing, there are higher levels of glucose in his system than is normally the case.

On the actual day of the presentation, James is feeling such intense pressure that his body makes its final pre-conflict preparation: blood drains away from his extremities and pools in the centre of his body. During the presentation itself James suffers from tunnel vision – an inability to monitor his environment and, in this particular case, his audience sufficiently. He also has a distorted sense of time. The 20-minute talk seems, to him, to last for hours. Both are symptoms of the chemical changes that are dominating James's body. When the presentation ends the 'flight, freeze or fight' syndrome does not automatically stop. It will take several days, even if the presentation was a success, for the syndrome to work its way through his system.

Colonel Jeff Cooper of the American Pistol Institute devised an approach to managing levels of awareness and associated stress which he called 'Colour Coding'. Intended for use primarily by armed personnel working in the most stressful situations, Cooper's approach can be adapted for use by managers. There are four colour codes, each representing a specific level of awareness. These are:

☐ Code White
☐ Code Yellow
☐ Code Orange
☐ Code Red.

Code White

This is a time of rest and relaxation, with no awareness of the environment. It is not relevant in a professional context, but is essential for the maintenance of health and a balanced lifestyle.

Code Yellow

This is a time of calm, relaxed awareness, when changes in attitude and behaviour are observed. This is the working state.

Code Orange

This is a time when a specific threat or stressor has been identified. Responses and options need to be identified and evaluated. The 'flight, freeze or fight' syndrome will begin with the gradual release of adrenalin and cortisol into the system.

Code Red

This is a time of emergency. The situation is now so stressful and/or threatening that it cannot be tolerated for extended periods; it must be resolved with urgency and commitment. Adrenalin and cortisol flood the system. As a consequence, individuals may experience a sudden burst of energy or the inability to move. Their perception of the environment will probably be distorted (notice how survivors of a serious accident or crime give different accounts to the police). Emotions may run riot or seem to disappear. Bodily functions may be difficult to control.

James spent most of the two weeks prior to his presentation in Code Orange. On the day itself, he may have experienced aspects of Code Red even though he was in no physical danger. James's perception of his situation determined his physical response. Interestingly, this relationship, if not understood and managed, can be responsible for ill health.

PNI is a relatively new medical science, having been formally named in the 1970s. Early research made sense of some common work-related experiences and highlighted the potential health risks for people who are often involved in Code Orange (or Code Red) situations. The constant release of adrenalin into the system damages heart tissue and T cells, thus weakening the immune system. The constant release of cortisol further weakens the immune system, but has also been closely linked with the increased likelihood of depression.

Although exposed to many Code Orange situations, James's determination to be a successful professional drives him on. He works to the best of his ability until his holiday arrives – and then he becomes ill. Thankfully, he recovers in time to return to work, and the cycle begins again. James is neither weak-willed nor sickly. If he was, he would have avoided the presentation and fallen ill before his holiday. Rather, he is a normal human being experiencing natural, age-old responses to modern pressures.

Activity 1.21   This exercise will enable you to identify the degree of pressure you are currently experiencing. Make a note of all the Code Orange situations/events you experience in both your personal and professional life during the next week. How many of these happen on a regular basis?

An understanding of the 'flight, freeze or fight' syndrome does not, however, explain James's instinctive nervous reaction when first told of the presentation. This is caused by the amygdala – two almond-shaped, interconnected structures situated above the brainstem on either side of his head. The amygdala acts as an emotional memory storehouse. Although it is not essential for survival – James would live if his amygdala was removed – it is essential for maintaining the emotional meaning and value – the passion – of his life. Unfortunately, that also includes those negative emotions associated with stress and fear. The key role the amygdala plays in our emotional brain was first discovered by Joseph LeDoux (1986), a neuroscientist at the Centre for Neural Science at New York University. His research demonstrates how the amygdala causes an emotional response to a stimulus before the neocortex, or thinking brain, comes to a decision.

James's fear of presentations is not wholly rational. As discussed earlier, deep-rooted assumptions and negative beliefs prevent him from calmly evaluating his performances and assessing his skill development. There are indications that James is already competent at presentations and is improving, but his mindset is so firmly established to the contrary that he is incapable of seeing these. In James's mind – specifically, within his amygdala – presentations are intimately linked with feelings of fear, incompetence and failure. This connection is so powerful that simply being given the task creates the emotionally negative reaction that triggers the 'flight, freeze or fight' syndrome before he can create any logical thoughts that might increase his confidence and keep him calm and focused. If James combines an understanding of the biology of stress with a programme of skill development, and the evaluative support of experienced colleagues, his chances of changing his established neural associations regarding the delivery of presentations will increase significantly. He may always feel the release of adrenalin into his system prior to a presentation. Indeed, it is preferable that he does. However, with practice he will come to use it to enhance his performance.

Stressors

While different people experience the negative effects of stress in different situations, common stressors can be placed into four categories. These are:

1. Encounter stressors.
2. Situational stressors.
3. Anticipatory stressors.
4. Time stressors.

1. Encounter stressors

Conflicts within relationships, or *encounter stressors*, grow out of role incompatibility, disagreements and/or shared feelings of antagonism. Managers who are responsible for people rather than equipment, and who therefore interact frequently with others, may experience high levels of encounter stress. Prerequisites for avoiding, or minimising, encounter stressors are:

☐ Excellent communication skills
☐ Information-sharing
☐ Relationships built on trust and mutual respect
☐ Well-developed problem-solving capabilities.

2. Situational stressors

The second most significant category contains *situational stressors*. These result from the environment in which a person lives or works. Poor working conditions, long unsociable hours, and a sense of isolation are all examples of situational stressors.

Another powerful factor in this category is rapid change. The world of work is changing faster than ever before. The only certainty with some aspects of work-related learning, for example IT, is that by the time we have improved our equipment and developed the corresponding skills we are already out of date. Research such as that by Holmes and Rahe (1970) and Miller and Rahe (1997) has done much to clarify the impact and possible consequences of a variety of life changes. In 1967 the Social Readjustment Rating Scale (SRRS) was introduced to monitor the changes experienced by over 400 individuals during a 12-month period. As some events are clearly more significant than others, a scaling method was used to reflect the levels of stress caused by different changes. Its validity has been confirmed by subsequent studies across a range of cultures, age groups and professions. The events identified as most stressful are:

☐ Death of a spouse
☐ Divorce
☐ Marital separation
☐ Death of a close family member
☐ Serious injury or illness
☐ Imprisonment.

Other changes, such as beginning or ending formal education, trouble with the boss, and major changes in working hours or conditions, have also maintained their place over the years as significant stressors.

Statistically, the more life changes individuals experience in a relatively short time (and therefore the higher their SRRS score), the greater their chances of illness. For example, a score of 151–300 increases the probability of a serious illness occurring in the following year by approximately 50 per cent, while a score of over 300 increases the risk by 80 per cent. Viewing this relationship through the so-called 'Emotional Gateways to Change' (see Figure 1.8) provides an additional insight into these findings, reinforcing the role of rapid change as a major stressor.

Figure 1.8
The emotional gateways to change

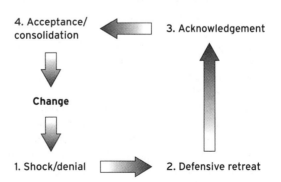

The first two gateways are 'Shock/denial' and 'Defensive retreat'. During these stages a person experiences an inability to accept the truth of his/her situation ('I don't believe it!'), followed by a desire to avoid, ignore or escape it. These are the most limiting and potentially harmful gateways. A Code Orange state, with the associated biological responses and a keen awareness of any relevant negative beliefs, is the norm, although Code Red can also be triggered, depending on the suddenness and significance of the change and the degree of threat it poses.

A person trapped for an extended period in the gateways of 'Shock/denial' and 'Defensive retreat', possibly as the result of several, overlapping changes, is at risk of becoming another statistic in the increasing number of people suffering from so-called stress-related illness.

For a manager, the value of thinking in terms of 'Defensive retreat' rather than resistance is that it avoids the language of conflict. This is a useful ploy in stress-charged times driven by rapid change, particularly when some displays of defensive retreat can appear to be quite aggressive.

The third gateway, 'Acknowledgement', represents the time when the individual is able to acknowledge the reality of the situation. He/she may not yet see any value or potential for future growth within it, and may still be experiencing feelings of uncertainty and doubt, but he/she is now able to accept the reality and/or inevitability of the change. At this point, managers might provide relatively simple tasks designed to increase their colleague's confidence and ability to manage the new situation. However, a mistake at this point – a task that proves too difficult, for example – can send the individual concerned scurrying back into 'Defensive retreat' – his/her worst fears confirmed by his/her failure.

The final gateway is 'Acceptance/consolidation'. Now the individual has adjusted fully to the change. While he/she may not regard it as perfect, he/she can see some value in it, and is confident of his/her capability to manage it successfully. Theoretically, the person is now emotionally ready to face another change, if necessary, and repeat the cycle. In the real world, however, changes do not wait patiently in line. Professional and personal changes often occur in unison, which is one reason why stress-related illness is so prevalent.

The four emotional gateways are experienced by people whenever they experience change, whether it is welcome or not. If the change is minimal or welcome, the transition from feelings of shock to those of acceptance can be swift and barely noticeable. If the change is significant or perceived as negative, the transition can be slow and, without the employment of appropriate coping/learning strategies, may never be complete.

People demonstrate these emotional responses in their own ways, and progress through them at their own pace. It would be a mistake for a manager to assume that because colleagues quietly confirm their acceptance of a change that they have reached 'gate three' and are calmly acknowledging the situation. It may be that they are still in shock and cannot yet begin to demonstrate their concerns. The challenge for modern managers lies in knowing the members of their team enough to recognise the gateway each person has reached. The goal is to move every member of the team through all four gateways as swiftly and as safely as possible.

It should also be borne in mind that those who initiate change also go through these gateways. Managers leading a specific change have not necessarily reached the point of acceptance and consolidation; sometimes managers have to assume a role that is not at one with their emotional state.

The emotional gateways have much in common with a bereavement cycle; people have to mourn what is lost before they can create a new reality. Sometimes, however, stress is caused by an awareness of what is likely to happen in the future rather than loss in the present.

Activity 1.22   Think of three people you have seen go through life- or work-related changes. How did each demonstrate Shock/denial, Defensive retreat, Acknowledgement and Consolidation?

If you manage a team, develop this exercise further by identifying each of the team's responses at the four different stages. For each team member, identify one change they would welcome and one they would regard negatively. Repeat this activity focusing on yourself.

---

3. Anticipatory stressors

This category includes:

☐ Fear of failure or embarrassment, particularly in front of one's peers
☐ Fear of inevitable life changes, such as retirement
☐ Fear of the unknown.

Some anticipatory stressors are caused by emotional memories stored in the amygdala, the result of negative neural-association experienced whenever specific situations, objects or topics are considered. Other anticipatory stressors can be the product of an over-active imagination.

4. Time stressors

These are often the greatest sources of pressure for managers and result from having too much work and too little time, or the precise opposite. Kotter (1987) showed that managers suffer frequent interruptions and rarely engage in long-term planning. Time stressors can be caused by individuals' lack of time management skills and/or their superior's inability to create realistic schedules and deadlines, combined with inadequate communication between the two.

Activity 1.23   List the most common stressors you face under the following headings: encounter; situational; anticipatory; and time.

Time management

Effective time management is founded on the ability to manage time in both the short and long term. Sondhi (1999) offers the DOPE model as a focus for developing control and minimising overload, the four key principles being:

1. Discipline
2. Organisation
3. Prioritisation
4. Expediency.

1. Discipline

Discipline relates to the self, environments and others. Self-discipline is demonstrated, for example, in the willingness to make a daily list of tasks *and* to follow it through, or the scheduling of personal 'Code White' time to allow relaxation and reflection, or the ability to operate to time limits. Unnecessary, continual worry indicates a lack of self-discipline and distracts from the essentials. However, a simple instruction to 'stop worrying' or to 'forget about it' is unlikely to have much effect – the biological and emotional realities of stress are too powerful for that. A more useful approach to managing state change is an NLP technique called the SWISH (see Activity 1.24).

Activity 1.24 **SWISH**

1. Identify a particular state, or response, you wish to change.
2. Determine what triggers this state. Identify the specific details that precede your shift into this state. Visualise yourself in that situation; recreate it in your mind exactly the way it happens. See precisely what you would see if you were experiencing the situation for real.
3. Determine which elements of this trigger have the most significant effect upon you. Again, be specific. Visual triggers are most commonly used in the SWISH. So, for example, if a certain person, object or place triggers your most powerful response, explore what happens when you imagine him/her/it bigger. Then return the image to its normal size and imagine him/her/it brighter. Practise changing the elements of the trigger until you discover those that maximise its effect.
4. Break your mental state by thinking about something completely different.
5. Now imagine how you would like to feel and behave in response to this previously negative trigger. It may be that you need to replace feelings of uncontrollable worry with calm, confident action. Again, create a detailed visualisation of the new, ideal you. Spend time exploring all the implications of making this change. Will it support or increase your sense of rapport with yourself? Will there be any potentially negative effects? Ensure that this change will satisfy your needs without disrupting the balance of your life, relationships and goals.
6. Break your mental state by thinking about something completely different.
7. Recreate the image of the initial trigger, using the factors that enhance its effect.
8. Place a small, dark image of the 'new' you in a corner of this bigger image.
9. Now make the large image small and dark and, at the same time, make the small image of you large and bright. Do this very quickly. Make the sound 'SWISH!' to accompany the transition. If this sound isn't appropriate, use one with which you are more comfortable.
10. Break your mental state.
11. Repeat the process five times. Evaluate its success. It is working when you either imagine or are confronted by the trigger situation and automatically SWISH into your new, desired state. If this isn't happening, revisit the earlier steps and experiment with other elements until you find the ones that make the most significant difference.

A disciplined environment is one in which everything has its place, working spaces are kept clear, paperwork is either thrown away or responded to. Discipline of others is not meant to imply an authoritative approach, but rather clearly established, universally-understood relationships. Delegation principles and skills are of such significance in this regard that they are examined in detail in Chapter 3.

2. Organisation

Organisation relates to the same three elements. Examples of good organisation include:

☐ The setting of realistic time-scaled targets
☐ Agreed long-term goals
☐ Meetings always starting on time, whether or not everyone is present
☐ Meetings being cancelled when they are not needed.

Activity 1.25   List four more examples of good organisation.

---

3. Prioritisation

Prioritisation means differentiating between vital tasks that only you can resolve and urgent tasks that can be delegated or left to others. Too often managers are seduced by the urgency of a situation that takes them by surprise. Although the urgent problem is then resolved, the time that had been allocated for a vital task is lost. Failure to correct this tendency creates a vicious circle in which urgent issues are managed and an ever-increasing number of vital tasks are put on hold. Developing the awareness to distinguish the vital from the merely urgent, and the self-discipline to avoid urgent distractions, is not easy, but it is essential.

Prioritisation also means combining trivial tasks that require minimal thought (for example, signing documents while talking on the phone) but doing important tasks one at a time. Managers who set clear priorities for themselves and/or their staff can also limit time wasted through unnecessary perfectionism by specifying a required standard. Not every task has to be completed perfectly. An email to a colleague confirming a meeting does not need to be checked several times for grammatical accuracy. A letter of application does.

Activity 1.26   Review your experience at study/work today. How many vital tasks did you perform? How many urgent tasks did you delegate, put on hold, or ignore? If the balance is wrong, how will you correct it?
Tomorrow, if the phone rings and you are engaged in a vital task, what will you do?

---

4. Expediency

Expediency, being willing and able to take advantage of situations, requires a creative, flexible approach, increases the likelihood of opportunities being taken and, ideally, is demonstrated within the confines of well-established beliefs and values. The key questions managers need continually to address are:

☐ Is this task necessary, urgent or vital?
☐ Is this a task that only I should do?
☐ If so, when should I do it and what standard is required?
☐ If not, to whom should I delegate it?
☐ When should they do it and to what standard?

Activity 1.27   List examples of the DOPE criteria you currently employ. Do examples that you don't use spring to mind? What is stopping you? Score yourself against the DOPE criteria. Ten signifies faultless ability; zero no ability.

Discipline

1 ----------------------------------- 10

Organisation

1 ----------------------------------- 10

Prioritisation

1 ----------------------------------- 10

Expediency

1 ----------------------------------- 10

Identify one target (a behavioural change you can make) for the criteria in which you scored least. Implement it and observe the impact it makes. When this behaviour has become the norm, identify the next target.

The 80/20 principle

In his book, *The 80/20 Principle* (1998), Richard Koch explores the Pareto principle, arguing that 80 per cent of results come from only 20 per cent of causes. As only a few activities ever produce significant results, it follows therefore that most efforts fail to create the desired outcome. This doctrine of 'the vital few and the trivial many' – that most good results stem from a minority of forces and that most activity is essentially a waste of time – led Koch to offer five rules:

1. Only approximately one in 20 decisions are important, so don't waste time analysing and worrying about the unimportant ones. Delegate them if possible.

2. Many important decisions are forced upon managers because of the ways situations change. When this occurs, don't spend time collecting and collating information. Use your intuition and insight instead.

3. When making an important decision collect 80 per cent of the required data and carry out 80 per cent of the required analysis in the first 20 per cent of the time available. At that point *always* make your decision and *always* act upon it with absolute certainty. (Koch called this his 80/20/100/100 rule.)

4. If what you are doing isn't working, change your mind and your behaviours sooner rather than later. Be willing to experiment.

5. When something is successful, when the 20 per cent is really working for you, don't hesitate to capitalise on it.

Value

Recognising the true value of your time is at the heart of good time management. Today cannot be repeated. Time cannot be held, bought or saved, but it can be wasted. What is of greater importance than spending your time in a manner that is true to your identity, beliefs and values, while using your capabilities in environments of your choosing? Remind yourself repeatedly of the value of your time. Use your awareness of that value as a motivating tool. Remember also that good time management is a two-sided coin. Being late or failing to complete tasks or meet deadlines are the most common areas of focus – and rightly so. However, there are times when being *too soon* is also an error. An idea introduced into a culture that is not yet ready to accept it or an idea too far ahead of its time is unlikely to be accepted. A surprise sprung too soon is no surprise at all. As the song reminds us, there is a time and a place for all things. Getting them both right is the measure of successful time management.

Symptoms of poor time management

These include:

- ☐ Failure to delegate
- ☐ Little or no leisure time
- ☐ Failure to meet deadlines
- ☐ Hasty decision-making
- ☐ Feeling out of control
- ☐ Inability to refuse requests from others
- ☐ Selecting the interesting tasks before the uninteresting ones
- ☐ Waiting until a deadline nears before taking action
- ☐ Selecting the easiest tasks first
- ☐ Mismanagement of information
- ☐ Ignoring one's internal clock.

This last symptom refers to the need to recognise the times of day when we naturally work best. As a general rule, tasks that require the most concentration and/or creative thinking are best dealt with in the early morning, while our minds are uncluttered from the day's events. When this is not possible, the ability to summon a powerful sense of self-motivation and enthusiasm comes into its own.

It is possible to exercise creative energy at the end of a busy day, however. Relevant techniques and strategies include:

☐ NLP state-changing techniques (this chapter)
☐ Exercises designed to promote divergent thinking (Chapter 5)
☐ Creating an inspiring learning environment (this chapter)
☐ Maintaining a clear awareness of the value of the task at hand.

Coping strategies

These can be of both a specific and general nature. Specific strategies are those designed to manage particular stressors, while general strategies ensure a balance between the various aspects of our lives, incorporating quality 'Code White' time.

Coping strategies for encounter stressors

Powerful, close-knit relationships not only provide meaning and value to life, but they also promote emotional and physical well-being. While the stress caused by unfulfilling relationships can be great, the benefits derived from a strong sense of community can be quite amazing.

Thirty years ago it was discovered that the residents of Roseto, Pennsylvania, were without heart disease or any other stress-related illness. Research determined that this was not due to a particularly healthy diet or to an effective community-wide exercise programme. Indeed, the people of Roseto were average in both respects. What distinguished them was an unusually strong sense of social cohesion and support – a powerful awareness of family and community. This was a community which, individually and collectively, had a clearly defined identity and shared well-established beliefs and values that promoted supportive, caring behaviour in an environment that was nurtured and respected. The entire population were descendants of Italians who had moved to America 100 years earlier from Roseto, Italy. Few people married outside the community, children were often named after their forebears, and signs of social superiority were discouraged. In this sense, the town of Roseto was a world apart, removed from the rapidly-changing, competitive world around it. But not forever. By the mid-1970s twentieth-century America, with its large houses and seemingly even larger cars, had invaded Roseto, bringing with it an urgency to be more successful than anyone else. The result was a loss in the sense of community and in the people's connection with the past. This change created precisely the health problems the Rosetons had previously managed to avoid. The rate of heart disease quickly became the same as in any other town.

To be loved, respected and to *belong* is, for most people, more important than professional status and success. The inhabitants of Roseto remind us that caring, loving relationships, combined to create community spirit, are good for the heart in every possible way. In the workplace, specific interpersonal skills are needed to establish positive relationships and so limit encounter stressors. Those we will discuss later include:

☐ Establishing rapport (Chapter 2)
☐ Coaching and Counselling (Chapter 3)
☐ Delegation (Chapter 3)
☐ Conflict management (Chapter 2)
☐ The use of Power (Chapter 4).

Coping strategies for situational stressors

It is worth remembering Robbins's observation that while there are short- and long-term strategies for managing specific stressors, much of our stress is 'self-induced' and therefore we ought to take responsibility for creating and managing it appropriately. Pressures and the dangers of negative responses to them – negative stress – are real, but there is also the danger that it is becoming fashionable to be 'under too much pressure', to ensure that we are busier than everyone else, to work longer and harder whether the job requires it or not, because this is how we need to be perceived. It is because the dangers of negative stress are so real that Robbins offers his advice. If encouraging work overload as a means of highlighting one's ability, commitment and value is, indeed, the new management game, it is a dangerous one.

Strategies for managing situational stressors depend to some extent on the nature of your situation. The basic principle would be to implement creative measures for managing your own stress, before trying to help others, this being along the lines of the airline instruction to ensure that, if required, you fit your own oxygen mask before turning to those in your care.

The aim of all coping strategies is two-fold: to establish an appropriate degree of control; and to create and maintain a sense of balance. Workplace strategies could include:

☐ Job and/or environment redesign
☐ System recognition: understanding the value of specific tasks, how they combine with, and relate to, others; knowing the value of your work in the big picture.
☐ Increased decision-making capability
☐ Combining appropriate activities
☐ Ensuring the end-product is visible: experiencing customer satisfaction is rewarding and motivating; the tangible awareness of a 'job well done' and the role 'we' played to achieve it can do much to develop personal and team pride
☐ The development of accelerated reading, recording and remembering skills: these are essential for ensuring the swift understanding and transmission of information.

Coping strategies for anticipatory stressors

These coping strategies are designed to eliminate anxiety rather than to improve environments or systems. Emotional concern caused by an awareness of future challenges demands a measured response based on the identification of clearly defined goals, incorporating the setting of CSMART

(Challenging, Specific, Measurable, Agreed, Realistic and Time-scaled) objectives, supported by a prompt reward system. Aim for small, progressive successes. In combination they represent significant change.

The 'Personal Safety Pyramid' (see Figure 1.9), although designed originally as a model for managing conflict and threat(s), provides an approach through which all stressors can be addressed. The foundation of the pyramid defines Attitude as a combination of awareness ('I cannot manage what I'm unaware of') and evaluation ('How significant is this opportunity/issue/problem?' and 'What is the time-scale?'), supported by a willingness and determination to take appropriate action.

The next level, Strategy, can be summarised by the question 'What is a win?'. Although in itself a simple question, the complexity of some issues can make it difficult to answer. Mindmaps can be used to identify and weigh the relative merits of a limited number of options, while systems thinking is an excellent tool for regarding more complex situations with clarity (see Chapter 5 for both mindmaps and systems thinking).

Tactics and Skill are the methods by which we achieve our 'win'. If we are lacking in this area, three alternatives are available:

1. Design a new strategy.
2. Develop the required skill(s).
3. Enlist the necessary support.

Even if your strategy is based on existing skills, it may still require assistance to be successful.

The final level of the pyramid encourages a consideration of the technical and/or human support that may be required. Once identified, it is necessary to ensure that it will be available when needed. This process can be repeated if a contingency plan is to be made.

Figure 1.9
The Personal
Safety Pyramid

Awareness --- Evaluation --- Willingness to take action

General coping strategies

As previously stated, these are the methods by which we ensure that the various elements of our lives are in balance. The 'Balanced Learning Performance' system (Figure 1.10) is one example of a framework for that evaluation, as is the five-step model for creating rapport with oneself (see Figure 1.1 on p. 10). The Balanced Learning Performance system was originally designed by Parker to enable part-time MBA students to monitor and manage their study in conjunction with the other aspects of their lives. It emphasises management of learning environments, study times, mental states and motivation, alongside work demands, family life, social and leisure activities. The aim is to achieve high-level balanced performance in all areas. This is in recognition of the fact that peak performance is a limited activity and cannot be maintained for great lengths of time. High-level balanced performance is a realistic daily target. Peak performance should be reserved for times of greatest need.

Holidays are, for most people, the ultimate example of 'Code White' time – the perfect opportunity to escape from everyday pressures and unwind. However, holidays alone are not sufficient. We need opportunities for rest, relaxation and reflection on a far more regular basis. Yet planning 'Code White' time into a busy schedule can be difficult; sometimes it just seems as if we have too much to do. If that is the case, remind yourself of your core values. Imagine how these may be affected if you do not allow yourself suitable rest and relaxation. Explore the pain that can be caused if you fail to maintain your well-being. Give yourself powerful reasons for having 'Code White' time. Be as committed to that as you are to all the other activities in your diary.

Activity 1.28   Identify ways in which you would spend the following amounts of 'Code White' time:

☐ 3 minutes only
☐ 5 minutes only
☐ 10 minutes only
☐ 30 minutes only
☐ 60 minutes or more.

Look in your diary at your coming week's commitments. Write in your '3 minute only' activity every day. Now commit yourself to your '5 minute only' activity three times in the coming week. Commit yourself to your '10 minute only' activity twice and the '30 minute activity' once. Plan in the longer activities on a less frequent basis according to your schedule.

What are your family's 'Code White' strategies, tactics and skills?

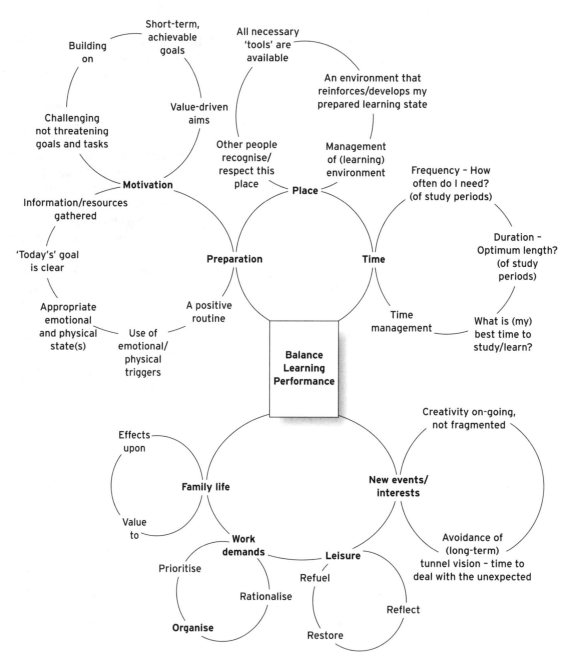

The first question
Is this the right time (in my life) to begin this study? ...Do I have (just) enough time to 'succeed'?

Figure 1.10 The Balanced Learning Performance system

Stress and pressure management: key points!

☐ Stress is neither positive nor negative.

☐ Stress is simply pressure on a person or object.

☐ The value of its effect is determined by the person's response and resiliency.

☐ Stressors fall into the following categories:

   ☐ Encounter stressors

   ☐ Situational stressors

   ☐ Anticipatory stressors

   ☐ Time stressors.

☐ Coping strategies are founded on an understanding of the biology of stress. This includes knowledge of:

   ☐ The flight/freeze/fight syndrome

   ☐ The emotional gateways to change

   ☐ The role of the amygdala.

☐ Coping strategies can be:

   ☐ Specific - for example, Sondhi's DOPE model for time management

   ☐ General - for example, the Balanced Learning Performance system.

Summary: managing self and self-image

☐ The successful management of self and self-image is founded upon:

   ☐ A clearly defined sense of personal identity

   ☐ Positive beliefs and values

   ☐ Behaviour(s) within environments that both reflect and support those beliefs and values.

☐ The core skills are those associated with:

   ☐ Emotional Intelligence

   ☐ Self-presentation

   ☐ Self-motivation

   ☐ Stress and pressure management

   ☐ Assertiveness.

☐ The aim is to achieve synergy between one's personal beliefs and values and one's behaviour and goals, while maintaining healthy physical and mental states.

A final thought

Dr Takeshi Mitarai was the chairman of the Japanese organisation Canon from 1947 until his death in 1984. Reforming the company after the Second World War, he emphasised a code of ethics highlighting the company's obligation to improve society, particularly through job creation. In a culture that rarely rewarded people solely on their merits, Mitarai broke with tradition; at Canon individuals were promoted because of their ability rather than simply because of their seniority or connections. Mitarai's philosophy included an absolute commitment to the notion of managing self and self-image. Known as the Three Js, it encapsulates the key elements of this chapter. Takeshi Mitarai's three Js are:

☐ *Ji-hatsu* – Self-motivation
☐ *Ji-kaku* – Self-awareness
☐ *Ji-chi* – Self-management.

References

Alderfer, C. 1972. *Existence, Relatedness and Growth: Human Needs in Organizational settings.* Glencoe, IL: Free Press.

Friedman, M. and Rosenman, R.H. 1959. 'Association of a specific overt behaviour pattern with blood and cardiovascular findings', *Journal of the American Medical Association*, 169: 1286–96.

Gardner, H. 1999. *Intelligence Reframed.* New York: Basic Books.

Goffman, E. 1959. *The Presentation of Self in Everyday Life.* New York: Doubleday.

Goffman, E. 1972. *Interaction Ritual: Essays on Face-to-face Behaviour.* Harmondsworth: Penguin.

Goleman, D. 1996. *Emotional Intelligence.* London: Bloomsbury.

Greenberg, J. 1987. *Comprehensive Stress Management* (2nd edn). Dubuque, LA: Wm.C. Brown Publishers.

Guilford, R.R. 1959. *Personality.* New York: McGraw-Hill.

Hackman, J.R. and Lawler, E.E. 1971. 'Employee reactions to job characteristics', *Journal of Applied Psychology*, 55: 259–86.

Herzberg, F., Mausner, B. and Synderman, B.B. 1959. *The Motivation to Work.* New York: Wiley.

Holmes, T.H. and Rahe, R.H. 1970. 'The Social Readjustment Rating Scale', *Journal of Psychosomatic Research*, 14: 121–32.

Jones, E.E. 1964. *Ingratiation.* New York: Appleton-Century Crofts.

Kobasa, S.C. 1979. 'Stressful life events, personality and health: an inquiry into hardiness', *Journal of Personality and Social Psychology*, 37: 1–12.

Koch, R. 1998. *The 80/20 Principle.* London: Nicholas Brealey.

Kotter, J. 1987. *The General Managers.* New York: Free Press.

Kunce, J.T., Cope, C.S. and Newton, R.M. 1991. 'Personal Styles Inventory', *Journal of Counselling and Development*, November/December: 334–41.

LeDoux, J. 1986. 'Sensory systems and emotions', *Integrative Psychiatry*, 4.

Maslow, A.H. 1970. *Motivation and Personality* (2nd edn). New York: Harper and Row.

Mayer, J.D. and Stevens, A. 1993. 'An emerging understanding of the reflective (meta) experience of mood'. Unpublished manuscript.

McGregor, D.M. 1960. *The Human Side of Enterprise.* New York: McGraw-Hill.

Miller, M.A. and Rahe, R.H. 1997. 'Life changes scaling for the 1990s Social Readjustment Rating Scale', *Journal of Psychosomatic Research*, 43 (3): 279–92.

Myers, A.P. and Briggs, I.B. 1962. *The Myers–Briggs Type Indicator.* San Diego, CA: Educational Testing Services.

Robbins, A. 1992. *Awaken the Giant Within.* New York: Simon & Schuster.

Rokeach, M. 1973. *The Nature of Human Values.* New York: Free Press.

Senge, P. 1993. *The Fifth Discipline.* London: Century Business.

Sondhi, R. 1999. *Total Strategy.* Bury: Airworthy Publications.

Vroom, V.H. 1964. *Work and Motivation.* New York: Wiley.

Further reading

Robbins, A. 1992. *Awaken the Giant Within*. New York: Simon & Schuster.
Senge, P. 1993. *The Fifth Discipline*. London: Century Business.
Goleman, D. 1996. *Emotional Intelligence*. London: Bloomsbury.
Molden, D. 1996. *Managing with the Power of NLP*. London: Pitman.

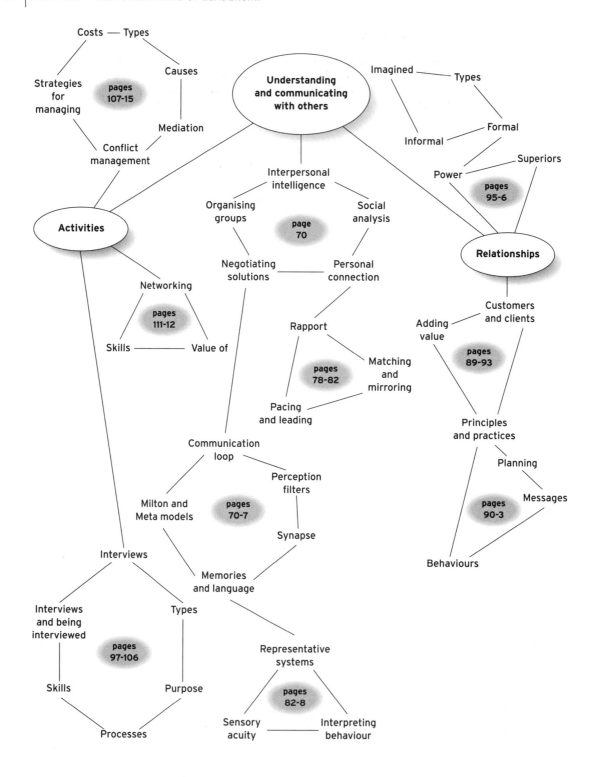

Managing one-to-one relationships

We can only grow as people by living in relationships, by in-depth communication.

(Catharina J.M. Halkes)

This chapter will develop your:

Awareness of:	Knowledge of:	Capability to:
The concepts of interpersonal intelligence and the communication loop.	Perception filters and the communication synapse.	Understand others.
The concept of representation systems.	Matching, mirroring, pacing, leading.	Create rapport with others.
The concept of customer service.	Key customer service principles and practices.	Add value to relationships with clients, suppliers and superiors.
The concepts of enquiry and whole-body listening.	Types and purposes of interviews. The interview process from preparation to feedback. Types of question.	Plan and manage interviews. Prepare for and be interviewed.
The concept of conflict management.	Causes of conflict. Types of conflict. Costs of conflict. Strategies and tactics for avoiding and/or minimising conflict.	Stop conflicts happening. Minimise the duration and costs of those that do.
The concept of networking.	The value of networking. Networking skills.	Create, maintain, and develop a network.

☐ Communication and perception filters

Gardner and Hatch (1989) identified four distinct skill areas as key components of interpersonal intelligence. These are:

1. *Social analysis*. This is the ability to identify, and have accurate insights into, other people's feelings, motives and concerns. It is a crucial element in creating rapport.
2. *Personal connection*. This is the ability to empathise, to make connections with others. People who have this skill adapt their responses to enable the development of appropriate relationships. They are regarded as easy to get along with.
3. *Negotiating solutions*. This is the ability to prevent or resolve conflicts, to mediate in disputes, to make deals. People with this skill are excellent at maintaining harmonious relationships, at ensuring interpersonal 'win–win' solutions. The more formal aspects of negotiation will be discussed in Chapter 7.
4. *Organising groups*. This is the ability to overcome what Senge (1993) calls 'the myth of the management team' – or the team that breaks down under pressure. To create teams in which skills are aligned with vision and energy is not wasted is a primary leadership skill and will be discussed in Chapter 4.

These interpersonal talents presuppose the ability to manage self and self-image, and have at their core highly developed communication skills. They can be applied in a multitude of ways. The following list, therefore, is indicative rather than exhaustive:

- ☐ Selling
- ☐ Managing suppliers
- ☐ Developing client relationships
- ☐ Networking
- ☐ Managing your boss
- ☐ Interviewing
- ☐ Conflict management
- ☐ Introducing new ideas.

Activity 2.1   List five other applications of interpersonal skills.

The communication loop

As discussed previously, human beings communicate through a combination of words, the tone, pace and clarity of their voice, and body language. Words can be regarded as the content of our message, while tonality and body language signal the context. The aim of all communication is not simply to transmit a message, but to have the meaning of your message recognised and understood as intended and then, in turn, to recognise the meaning of the reply. Communication, then, is a two-way process, and is best thought of as a loop rather than a straight line. The four elements of the communication loop (see Figure 2.1) are:

☐ The originator
☐ The message
☐ The receiver
☐ The feedback.

That there are several elements, which can be influenced by distractions within the environment ('noise'), is an indication of the complexity of the process.

Figure 2.1 A communication model

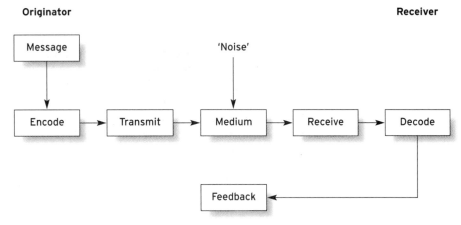

How can you be sure the meaning the 'receiver' places on your message is the one you actually meant? How can you be sure the meaning you place on his/her message is the one he/she actually meant?

Activity 2.2   Take a few minutes to identify potential blockages in communication. In your experience, what causes communication breakdowns?

Review different forms of communication you have shared in the last week. How accurately were the meanings of your messages received? How do you know?

If a person misinterprets the meaning of your message, where does the responsibility lie?

The most positive answer to the final question is: 'The responsibility is mine.'

NLP practitioners operate on the principle that communication is measured by the response we get. This response, whether as hoped for or not, is regarded as feedback or information that can be used to evaluate success and direct the content and style of our next message. To accept the responsibility for being understood is a challenging task – the easy option is to blame the other person when misunderstandings or confusion arise – but it is one that all great teachers and trainers accept. They are experts at constantly changing the content and delivery of their message until everyone has received it as intended. Managers are problem-solvers, decision-makers, information gatherers and disseminators, motivators, role models, teachers, story-tellers and more. These roles all require the ability to communicate effectively, to take responsibility for their messages being understood.

Perception filters

Why is it that sometimes the message we are sure we have given with absolute clarity is misinterpreted? How is it possible to be misunderstood by a person who is only a few feet away? The answer may be due to our inability to manage personal image; a failure to ensure synergy between words, voice and body language. It may also be because of cultural differences that are not recognised or understood by either party. (We examine cultural stumbling blocks in Chapter 8.)

Information filters are a part of our everyday existence. We experience the external environment through our senses of sight, hearing, smell, taste and touch, yet we do not experience every potential stimulus. If we did, our minds would suffer from information overload, with more than two million pieces of information bombarding our senses at any one time. How do we make sense of such a sensual environment? Simply by selecting the information we focus on. It is filtered through for our attention; the rest passes us by unnoticed. The filters we use to determine the importance of our experiences are the following:

- ☐ Beliefs
- ☐ Values
- ☐ Memories
- ☐ Language
- ☐ Perception of time
- ☐ Habitual thoughts and behaviours.

Perceptual filters operate like invisible spectacles, through which we experience and make sense of the world. As people have different beliefs, values, memories, language, perceptions of time and personal habits, the effect of these 'spectacles' is to increase the likelihood that we will see and interpret the same event, speech or situation differently from those around us. Every message we send passes through the perceptual filters of those we are communicating with. Every reply they make is filtered by us in a similar way. The filters influence the way we decode every message.

Figure 2.2(a)
The communication synapse (i)

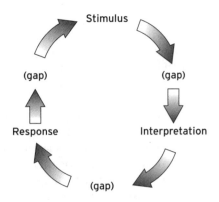

Figure 2.2(b)
The communication synapse (ii)

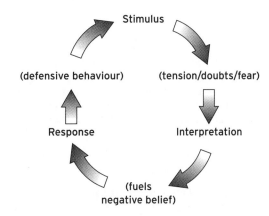

Being an effective communicator means creating messages that are most likely to be received as intended, while monitoring our own responses to ensure that we do not suffer from 'filter distortion'. We need to remember that in every form of communication there is a gap in transmission – the communication synapse (see Figure 2.2(a)) – during which time the information is filtered according to the other person's current perceptions and expectations. The manager's choice is simple. He/she can either (i) construct messages that fill the gap with positive, encouraging, exciting connections that inspire the desired reaction, or (ii) run the risk that his/her communication is distorted through others' perceptual filters (see Figure 2.2(b)). A consideration of each filter highlights the part it plays in determining how the communication synapse is filled and the message is interpreted.

Beliefs and values

The potential of beliefs and values to limit or empower was discussed in Chapter 1. Their role as filters is most easily demonstrated through the consideration of a simple scenario (see Activity 2.3).

Activity 2.3   Read the following story. How would you explain the result?

The Faith Healer
You receive a phone call informing you that a close friend, Paul, has become paralysed from the waist down. When you ask what has caused this, you are told that it is not clear. Paul woke one morning and could not move his legs. His doctor has been unable to find a medical explanation, but is equally incapable of making him walk again. As Paul is not known as the most emotionally stable person, some people whisper that the problem is 'all in his mind'.

Six months pass. Paul is resigned to life in a wheelchair. One day, as he is being pushed through the town centre by his wife, Marie, a woman stops them. She explains that she is a faith healer and, without further comment, she places her hands on Paul's legs. He reports later how he felt an incredible heat emanating from her palms. Within sixty seconds, he has stepped out of the wheelchair and declared himself cured. The woman smiles and disappears into a crowd of shoppers. Both Paul and Marie describe the event as a miracle.

Activity 2.3   *Continued*

The point of the story is this: if you don't believe in miracles, it is highly unlikely that this story will change your mind. You will have automatically filtered out those details that might support the 'miraculous' and focused on those that suggest psychosomatic influences. On the other hand, if you do believe in miracles, you will at least be prepared to consider the possibility that Paul experienced one. Either way, your beliefs will be acting as filters.

Activity 2.4   List four beliefs you hold about the nature and purpose of your study or work. Consider how they filter alternative perspectives and ideas.

Memories

The human brain is excellent at making connections. Indeed, it would be fair to say that this is one of its core competencies. Those individuals with great recall invariably use systems that are based on association. If they want to remember the names of ten people, they won't write the names down on a list and read it repeatedly. Rather, they will create a mental link between each person's name and a bright, often exaggerated, image that will always spark the association they require. Our memories work in much the same way, helping us make sense of new information by providing links to past experiences and meanings. These links with the past also create expectations about the future. (Consider how James's memories of past presentations influence his thoughts about his next attempt.) Memories also carry with them an emotional attachment. We remember not only what happened, with whom, where and when, but also how it made us feel. (James cannot review his experiences and skills as a presenter in a detached manner. It always upsets him.) Memories are an important part of our psychological and emotional make-up. They are also powerful perceptual filters, influencing not only the information we acknowledge but how we interpret it and/or what we expect from it.

Language

Language is a code used by humans to exchange information. Unlike many other codes, it is open to misuse and misunderstanding. People can lie – in detail or by omission – or offer their interpretation of an event under the guise of reporting the facts. People can listen to the same proclamation by their CEO and arrive at a variety of interpretations. In many ways, language can be cumbersome and inefficient. For most of us, the words we use to describe an event provide an oversimplified representation of what we actually experienced. There are two reasons for this:

1. Few people have the skill to create universally powerful images with minimal words.
2. Most of us, therefore, would have to use literally thousands of words, and devote a great deal of time, to recall events in the detail necessary to evoke their full complexity and meaning. This is not feasible.

For these reasons, there is an implicit acceptance that people, for the most part, use language to generalise, simplify, distort or delete. By doing so, they can change the very meaning of their original thoughts. Consider the following extract from a conversation:

'How did your meeting go with the new MD?'

'It was productive and to the point. He's going to make some changes, but nothing that you wouldn't expect. There are things he likes, issues we have to address, and new targets to aim for. He's realised that we're over-staffed, but I'm sure I made an impression.'

Is the questioner any the wiser? Probably not. Was her colleague generalising and simplifying? Of course. To what extent did he distort or delete information, and was he doing so deliberately? It is difficult to say. What we can say with certainty is that he was selecting specific language to reflect and share his view of reality: a unique perspective revealed in his own, unique style. David Molden describes language as: 'The surface structure of our experience, and the thoughts that produced the language are the deeper structure. Words can never be the original experience they seek to represent – they are too far removed from it' (Molden, 1996: 148). This distance can be shown in a simple chart.

Experience -------- Interpretation of ---------- recall ------------- language use ----------▶ (Original thoughts
the experience   (Of memory) (Delete, distort,   changed by
(Through senses   generalise)   repetitive
and existing   language use)
perceptual filters)

The conclusion we can draw is this: if there were no other filters in operation, language alone would be reason enough for frequent breakdowns in communication.

One group of people who, it seems, have always appreciated how language acts as a filter on human experience, and who know how to use it to their own advantage, is politicians. They are particularly skilled at using two specific language models:

1. The Milton Model.
2. The Meta Model.

1. The Milton Model

Some people prefer to talk about specific details, while others more naturally discuss and consider the bigger picture. As a general rule, senior managers and those with the highest levels of responsibility within an organisation tend to 'chunk up' information, to use the NLP term: they talk globally, take an overall view and need to understand the big picture. When making presentations to their subordinates or stakeholders, they will often use sweeping, generalised statements that, while not providing specific detail, are easy to believe and can motivate, encourage, or even warn their audience of impending difficulties. This is the Milton Model. It is the use of language devoid of detailed content but with a clear sense of mission, needs and/or accomplishment. It is a powerful style, much favoured by great orators. Vague, artful and often inspiring, it can be used to create unity within teams, organisations and countries. The Milton Model is the language of leaders.

2. The Meta Model
The Meta Model cuts through the vagueness of the Milton Model by demanding a focus on detail. People using the Meta Model recognise and then question the assumptions and generalities of those using the Milton Model. The questions posed tend to be:

☐ How ... exactly?
☐ Who ... exactly?
☐ Where ... exactly?
☐ When ... exactly?
☐ Why ... exactly?
☐ What ... exactly?

Activity 2.5	Read what was actually said by the new MD in the conversation on page 75. He is clearly using the Milton Model. Notice the generalisations, the vagueness. Make a note of the Meta Model responses the listener could have made to gain a clearer insight into what was meant. MD: 'I have great respect for my predecessor. I feel that she created a standard of performance from which we can take this department forwards. There are people in this team with very obvious skills and experience; some who have been here for a long time and understand the way the company works. Our task is to maximise our potential, to achieve excellence in every aspect of our work, to meet the new challenges that will soon confront us. I am confident that, if we all do what is required of us, we will be successful. Of course, I am expecting managers to set the example... .'

The most adept communicators, including politicians, shift from one model to the other according to the demands of their situation. The next time you watch a political interview, notice how the politician responds to a potentially dangerous question about specific details by shifting the discussion to a more global perspective. Or conversely, if he/she wants to turn attention away from the big picture, he/she will produce specific examples of how successful his/her policies have been.

Perception of time

As will be discussed in Chapter 8, attitudes towards time are to some extent culturally driven, although individual differences are also evident. Some people are excellent at planning for the long term, others focus more easily on the short term. Indeed, what is meant by the concept of long-term planning can vary from person to person. For one, the long term is anything 'after this week'. For another, it means preparing for retirement.

Perception of time also influences recall. Some people 'live more in the past', paying great attention to, and placing great importance on, what has gone before. Consequently, they remember myriad events with great clarity. Others 'live more in the moment', placing all their attention on the 'here and now'. Such different perceptions of time influence how people interpret certain situations, and their subsequent behaviour.

Habitual thoughts and behaviour

Some habits are essential for survival (for example, you don't want to have to think about which pedal is the brake if a child steps out in front of your car),

---

Activity 2.6   Below are five examples of habitual behaviours/attitudes. Where on each line would you place yourself? Consider how these behaviours/attitudes act as deletion filters. Repeat this exercise considering two other people you know well.

Activity preference

Things --- People

(Focus on machines; less aware of people's needs)   (Sensitive to others' needs; customer service focus)

Work preference

Options --- Procedures

(Prefer variety and choice; good ideas people)   (Prefer clearly defined procedures to follow)

Reference standard

Internal --- External

(Accurately and instinctively judge your own performance)   (Need feedback from other sources)

Language preference

Global --- Specific

(Milton Model; need to see the 'big picture';   (Meta Model; focus on details;
connects different topics randomly)   a sequential speaker)

Group focus

Task --- Maintenance

(Primary focus: successful completion of task)   (Primary focus: team maintenance functions)

but they also act as filters, deleting information and possibilities that do not fit automatically into our established patterns, encouraging us to focus our attention on the beliefs, behaviours and processes we are used to.

Communication and perception filters: key points!

☐ Interpersonal intelligence comprises:
- ☐ Social analysis
- ☐ Personal connection
- ☐ Negotiating solutions
- ☐ Organising groups.

☐ The four elements of the communication loop are:
- ☐ The originator
- ☐ The message
- ☐ The receiver
- ☐ Feedback.

☐ Perception filters determine the ways we interpret, and the importance we place upon, our experiences.

☐ Key perception filters are:
- ☐ Beliefs
- ☐ Values
- ☐ Memories
- ☐ Language
- ☐ Perception of time
- ☐ Habitual thoughts and behaviours.

☐ Two language models are:
- ☐ The Milton Model
- ☐ The Meta Model.

☐ Skilled communicators switch from one model to the other as the situation demands.

☐ Rapport and representation systems

Rapport can be thought of as a 'natural communication dance'. The more two people share rapport, the closer the match and the more obvious the 'dance'. When people do not share rapport, their bodies reflect this also. The ability to recognise people's unique communication patterns and to understand the totality of their message is what NLP practitioners refer to as 'whole body listening'.

Activity 2.7   Take the opportunity to observe strangers interacting in a bar, restaurant, airport lounge, etc. Estimate the degree of rapport by observing their body language and eye contact. Notice the differences between those sharing a 'communication dance' and those who cannot even hear the music!

While rapport is a natural skill (newborn babies move in rhythm with voices they hear, for example), it is also one that can be consciously refined through the use of:

☐ Matching
☐ Mirroring
☐ Pacing
☐ Leading.

Matching and mirroring

The purpose of matching and mirroring is to communicate with other people's unconscious minds by getting into the same state as them. It is possible to match people's gestures, eye contact, the tone, rhythm, speed or volume of their voices, even their preferred representation language. Matching is far more than the exaggerated, indiscriminate copying of other people's behaviour – which is likely to be noticed and deemed offensive. Matching requires sensitivity and respect. For example, expansive gestures with the arms can be matched by smaller hand movements. You can match posture or distribution of bodyweight, always bearing in mind that if you match too precisely you are likely to be asked, 'Why are you mimicking me?' And rapport will be lost, not gained.

Physiology is probably the easiest element to match. Breathing is certainly the most subtle and, arguably, one of the most powerful. Gestures are best matched when you are talking, not while the other person is. A slow speaker, wanting to create rapport by talking at the naturally faster pace set by a potential client, can increase his/her speed by breathing more quickly and making it more shallow, focusing on the upper chest. Conversely, a naturally fast talker needing to slow down can breath more deeply and slowly. Mirroring is, as the name suggests, when you create a mirror image of the other person, matching a right-handed gesture with a left-handed one, for example.

Matching is a form of communication demonstrated unconsciously by people who have deep rapport. However, it can be used deliberately, with sensitivity and respect, to speed up the process of establishing trust and mutual interest. As Joseph O'Connor and John Seymour observe: 'Successful people create rapport. ... When people *are* like each other, they like each other' (1993: 19–20).

Activity 2.8   Practice matching and mirroring. Begin by observing the communication styles of people you meet on a casual basis. Match and mirror these in a subtle, gradual manner.

(*Note*: As a basic principle, reserve *any* skill practice for the 'training ground' - i.e. situations where failure is not costly. Do not apply them in the workplace until you are confident of your ability.)

As a final point on this topic, it should be noted that the ability to mirror and match also teaches us how to bring unwanted conversations to a speedy conclusion. If you want the other person to lose interest, simply observe his/her physiology, tonality and language preferences, and reply using opposites. People who are dancing to a different tune are usually not partners for very long.

Pacing and leading

Matching and mirroring enable you to recognise and share another person's 'communication dance'. Pacing and leading is the ability gradually to change the dance to one you deem more appropriate. It is the shift from following to leading. Great teachers know they cannot force behavioural change on their students. They match and mirror to create rapport (pace), and then set a new direction (lead). As with matching and mirroring, pacing is a natural rapport skill – we change our behaviours, communication styles, dress, etc. according to the situations we are in and the people we are with. Pacing is also the essential precursor to leading.

Imagine that you need to have a conversation with a man who is walking along a street. If he has no intention of stopping, what is the first thing you do? Do you tell him to slow down, or stop? Maybe. But the person has his own destination and schedule, so why should he take any notice? Actually, the best way – the *only* way – to be sure of getting his attention is to *match his pace*. If you do not keep up with him, you cannot hope to communicate effectively in the short term. You cannot afford to walk too quickly or too slowly. There is only one ideal pace – his. If you do not match it perfectly, the impact of your message will be lost. Only when you have matched the person's pace (created rapport) can you hope to set a new speed or direction.

Some situations or relationships, however, might require an autocratic leadership style in which the ability to understand others and create rapport is less important than the ability to direct behaviour. This is discussed further in Chapter 4.

Pacing emotions

Most people naturally pace emotional states. For example, if a friend is unhappy, we would probably match his physiology, the pace, volume and tone of voice. To do otherwise – to approach him in a powerful manner and tell him in a loud voice to 'Snap out of it!' – is likely to have as much success as instructing a bald man to grow hair. If anything, it will make your friend feel even more miserable, because your manner has reinforced how 'out of sorts' he is. By pacing his tonality and body language (without feeling miserable yourself), rapport is established. Once you are at the same pace, you can begin to gently take the lead. As you begin to talk in a more confident tone, and to sit in a more confident manner, watch closely for signs that your friend is following, that he is now matching you. If he is not, slow down. Re-establish the match and, when the time is right, try again.

Pacing values

In a business context, the ability to pace values is an important skill. Examples of relevant professional values include:

- Organisational values
- Cultural values
- Group values
- Role values.

Business leaders often express the beliefs and values that underpin their organisations. Anita Roddick, founder of The Body Shop, wrote:

We absolutely believe in the power of community economic initiatives to affect and change lives. Our trade with these communities is our way of participating in and encouraging these initiatives.

(Roddick, 1995)

And the company motto of the Dallas-based Mary Kay Cosmetics Company reads: 'God first, family second, and business third. In that order, everything works, and out of that order, nothings works' (quoted in Brown, 2000: 46). If you are not able to pace the values of an organisation, you will almost certainly experience difficulty in creating rapport with the CEO.

Likewise, learning about the cultural values of the country you are going to work in is a much more productive use of your time than trying to remember a thousand and one new social behaviours. It is the difference between understanding *why* something is done and knowing *how* it is done. For example, showing an understanding of, and respect for, a Chinese person's view of the world is far more likely to lead to rapport than simply knowing how to eat with chopsticks.

Rapport or manipulation?

Occasionally people argue that high-level communication skills increase the ease with which managers can manipulate others. Whole-body listening, an understanding of belief and value management, and knowing how to create rapport, they argue, all enable the manager to have even more power and exert even more influence. This is true. After all, that is the point. More knowledge, more skills, more power. Right? As long as power is understood to be the ability to take appropriate action. Making decisions, and seeing them through, has always been the crucial management task. The issue at the heart of this argument is not that managers make decisions that affect others, it is the moral dilemma. After all, what is to stop communication experts presenting a false image, pacing values they secretly reject, creating rapport, and then leading their unsuspecting victims to a conclusion they would otherwise have avoided? The answer is two-fold. First, people who have aligned their personal beliefs and values with their behaviour, capabilities and environments are unlikely to use any skills they possess for a selfish, harmful purpose. Secondly, skills such as whole-body listening and matching and pacing, create empathy – not antipathy. As Daniel Goleman reports: 'The empathic attitude is engaged again and again in moral judgements. ... Empathy researcher Martin Hoffman ... argues that the roots of morality are to be found in empathy' (Goleman, 1996: 105). Given that, we will continue with a consideration of representation systems.

Representation systems

When information has passed through our perception filters, it is represented internally as pictures, sounds, feelings, smells or tastes. These are representation systems (see Figure 2.3). They shape the reality we experience in our mind and, consequently, influence our thinking and our language. Over a period of time, people develop preferences for the ways they use these systems. Most people from the western world use visual, auditory and kinesthetic representation systems as their primary choice. For that reason, we will concentrate on them.

Figure 2.3
Representation
systems

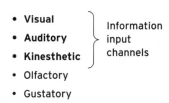

- **Visual**
- **Auditory**   } Information input channels
- **Kinesthetic**
- Olfactory
- Gustatory

There are two distinct types of representation system. These are:

1. The preferred representation system.
2. The lead representation system.

1. The preferred representation system

Although people use all three of the primary representation systems, most develop a preference for a particular one which, over time, becomes more developed. Film directors, for example, tend to favour the visual system, sculptors the kinesthetic system, and singers the auditory one. Pitch a storyline to a director by asking him 'to picture this ...' and, if you use the right language, he may tell you that he can 'see where you're coming from'. Talk to a sculptor about how you plan to 'shape the future' and she may well 'get a feel for the idea'. Ask a singer how a particular proposal 'sounds' and he may confirm that it 'strikes a chord'.

Recognising people's preferred representation system enables you to use language and images that encourage rapport. It also provides insights into their experiences and capabilities when learning new skills or managing change. Ask a person with a preference for the visual system to learn how to touch-type and she will probably struggle to stop looking at the keyboard. Give the same task to someone who favours the kinesthetic system and you can expect quicker results.

2. The lead representation system

People's lead representation system is that which is used to recall past experiences. Once the memory is recalled, the preferred system directs their focus. A person might lead with the visual system before changing to the kinesthetic, for example. Behavioural cues indicate how a person is thinking.

The visual system

People who prefer this system focus more on pictures than on feelings or sounds. Visual thinkers tend to make skyward gestures and to breathe in a shallow, fast manner. They often look upwards or towards some point ahead of them as they visualise. Visual thinkers tend to speak quickly – they have to in order to keep up with the flow of pictures in their mind – and in a relatively high pitch. Examples of visual language include:

- ☐ 'I can't see where this conversation is leading'
- ☐ 'Your work shows potential'
- ☐ 'Let's look at the options.'

The kinesthetic system

People who prefer this system focus on feelings. Their gestures are usually limited to the lower part of their body, and they tend to breathe deeply from low within the abdomen. They often look down and to their right when accessing this system. Kinesthetic thinkers talk quite slowly, pausing often to evaluate how they are feeling about what they are going to say next. Examples of kinesthetic language include:

- ☐ 'I have a bad feeling about this'
- ☐ 'The pressure is building'
- ☐ 'Let's keep in touch.'

The auditory system

People who prefer this system focus on sounds, including the words they hear. Their gestures are usually rhythmic in nature. They may habitually touch their ears or hold their heads to one side, as if listening to something. People who think in sounds often move their eyes laterally. Breathing tends to fill the entire chest, and they demonstrate good tonal range when talking. Examples of auditory language include:

- ☐ 'I hear what you are saying'
- ☐ 'It sounds to me as if we have a problem'
- ☐ 'That suggestion is music to my ears.'

Another popular thinking style is to talk to oneself. People who favour internal dialogue often rest one hand along the side of their face, as if their hand is a telephone receiver. They tend to look down and to their left, and can be silent, and seem distant, during a conversation.

No single representation system is better than any of the others. People simply learn how to access, interpret and describe the world in different ways. Awareness of preferred representation systems can be of value in a variety of ways:

- ☐ To create rapport
- ☐ To match individuals with tasks
- ☐ To determine areas of training and development for others (Chapter 3)
- ☐ To determine the most appropriate teaching/training styles (Chapter 3)
- ☐ When making presentations (Chapter 6)
- ☐ When campaigning (Chapter 6).

Activity 2.9   What is your preferred representation system? Determine the preferred system for three people you know well. Match their preference. Repeat this for people you need to influence.

Rapport and representation systems: key points!

☐ Rapport, or empathy, is essential in creating successful relationships.

☐ Rapport can be developed through:

  ☐ Matching

  ☐ Mirroring

  ☐ Pacing

  ☐ Leading

  ☐ Whole-body listening.

☐ When information has passed through our perception filters, it is represented internally in one or a combination of the following systems:

  ☐ Visual

  ☐ Auditory

  ☐ Kinesthetic

  ☐ Olfactory

  ☐ Gustatory.

☐ People develop a preference for a particular system, which influences their language and the images they use.

☐ The lead representation system is that which is used to recall the past.

☐ Interpreting behaviour

This lies at the heart of understanding others. In a survey of 150 American and UK executives, the 'ability to understand people' was identified as the most important of 16 management skills by the US contingent, and second in importance by those from the UK. Maureen Guirdham, in her excellent book, *Interpersonal Skills at Work* (1995), writes that managers looking to improve their skills at interpreting other people's behaviour need to:

> *increase self-awareness and self-control in each of the five processes of interpretation:*
>
> *1. Hearing and seeing the cues.*
> *2. Identifying the cues with attributes.*
> *3. Associating the attributes with other attributes.*
> *4. Deciding the cause - the person or the situation.*
> *5. Judging.*

(Guirdham, 1995: 175)

Cues, attributes and causes

As previously discussed, NLP provides a framework for understanding certain cues. This presupposes the ability to see and hear those cues. Perceptual filters lead to the development of mental models that can blind us to certain cues, or lead us to interpret them inaccurately. Factors that can influence our ability in this regard include:

☐ Self-perception: how I regard myself, my value and potential
☐ The other person: how they look, move and communicate
☐ The relationship: shared experiences, established or required roles
☐ The situation: goals, levels of comfort and expectations.

In other words, interpreting behaviour is dependent upon an awareness of self, situation, other people, roles, relationships, desired outcomes and expectations. No wonder it is a risky business. There are five key errors that managers can make:

☐ Grasping the quick answer
☐ Painting the perfect picture
☐ Expectations
☐ Expectations
☐ Expectations.

Grasping the quick answer

If only politicians would allow teachers to spend time teaching youngsters how to identify the most useful questions! As it is, students are often rewarded for getting the most correct answers in the shortest amount of time. Little wonder they grow up to be managers who too often seek out and hold on to the quickest acceptable interpretation or solution, ignoring Senge's (1993) warning that there is rarely a single, simple answer or a single, simple cause.

As will be discussed more fully in Chapter 4, the tendency to hunt for the quick answer encourages another potential management error, which is to interpret current behaviours in the light of previous experiences. This syndrome is best reflected in the line: 'We've faced this problem before and the best solution is ...' Its equivalent in terms of managing relationships is: 'I've seen this behaviour before and what it means is ...'

Painting the perfect picture

Also known as the halo effect, this is the desire to draw general conclusions from specific observations. Managers need to assess accurately the specific skills, knowledge and qualities of subordinates, colleagues, suppliers and even bosses, while resisting the temptation to accord abilities that do not exist. No individual is good at everything, and the wise manager knows that specific skills do not imply general excellence.

Expectations ... Expectations ... Expectations

In some respects, this factor underpins the previous two. We create mental models of the world to help us simplify and make sense of our experiences. Mental models encourage us to see what we expect to see. Our expectations can therefore blinker us to new realities or lead us to interpret behaviour in a certain way. If managers are convinced of their colleagues' expertise – if they *expect* good results – they are likely to view all their work positively. Similarly, if managers' expectations are low, they are more likely to notice every indication of under-achievement. Guirdham reports:

> *Researchers have shown that teachers' beliefs about pupils' abilities and performances strongly influenced their marking. When the work of pupils of whom they had high expectations was submitted under the names of pupils of whom they had low expectations, consistently lower marks were awarded, while high marks were given to work submitted in the names of pupils of whom much was expected, regardless of who did it.*

(Guirdham, 1995: 151)

Assumptions

Assumptions also reflect the way we simplify and make sense of our world. Two assumptions that can limit our ability to manage relationships are:

☐ Assuming similarity
☐ Assuming an intention.

Similarities

Although, as human beings, we have many things in common, we are not all the same. To attribute characteristics to others because we possess them ourselves can lead to awkward and sometimes confused relationships. Worse still is the assumption that people automatically share the same motives – that we do the same things for the same reasons.

Intentions

Directors spend much time talking to actors about their characters' motivation. Actors are encouraged to understand where their characters have come from and are going to, and what their reasons are for talking and behaving in a particular way. The more actors understand their characters' intentions, it is argued, the more realistic their performance will be. But to what extent does that reflect the real world – the one beyond the stage?

Activity 2.10 Review your interaction with people yesterday. How many times was your language and behaviour a precise reflection of a carefully formulated intention? How many times did you have a general intention that was reflected in general terms by your language and behaviour? How many times did you say and/or do things without any planning or intention?

You probably realised (from doing Activity 2.10) that your day was a mixture of all three, and that at times you said and did things almost by accident. Why are we not always driven by a precise intention that is translated into the most appropriate language and action? Because, unlike actors, we do not have the luxury of a script. Life is more an ongoing improvisation than a two-act play. We can only act with clear intentions when we are in control of ourselves and our situation. This is equally true for those with whom we share a relationship. How often do we – and they – have such control? The moral is to be aware of the dangers of assuming a specific intention.

All of this highlights the potential pitfalls in judging other people's behaviour.

Judging

In Chapter 1 we made reference to Eysenck's Personality Inventory. Actually this lists 24 levels of extroversion, but we offered only the two that were necessary for Activity 1.9 (see p. 26). However, the powerful human inclination to judge others does tend to focus attention on extremes. As mentioned in the 'Personality' section in Chapter 1 (pp. 25–30), people are described in a variety of ways, such as 'competent' or 'incompetent', 'reliable' or 'untrustworthy', 'hard-working' or 'lazy'. Such judgements create either positive or negative expectations about the people concerned, yet human characteristics are not polar in nature – they have degrees. Neither are they necessarily permanent.

Managers have to make judgements. The above is not meant to imply that they should shirk that responsibility, only that they should do so with care, monitoring their own assumptions and expectations, evaluating the nature, purpose and significance of the relationships involved, and interpreting accurately the messages being given and received. This ability is known as sensory acuity.

Sensory acuity

Sensory acuity is best demonstrated by people who are totally alert to what is going on around them, and who are receptive to messages and meaning no matter how subtle. They see contradictions when they occur between words they hear and the body language of the speaker. They recognise when 'Yes' actually means 'No', then take appropriate action. Sensory acuity is one of three key skills in understanding and managing others. The other two are:

☐ *Outcome* – knowing what you need to achieve
☐ *Flexibility* – changing the content and style of your input as necessary until you achieve your desired outcome.

Activity 2.11   Identify one relationship in which you are involved that could be improved. Analyse it using the following ten steps:

1. Write down your desired outcome(s).
2. How do you measure these?
3. Make brief notes outlining the nature of the situation, the roles you both play, any responsibilities you both hold, and any other influences.
4. Identify the other person's preferred representational system.
5. Remind yourself of your own.
6. Make brief notes outlining the content and style of your input.
7. What specific responses/feedback does this approach attract?
8. Identify an alternative approach that may have more success.
9. Consider if you need an alternative method of assessment.
10. Make a commitment to develop your sensory acuity and flexibility until the relationship has improved.

Interpreting behaviour: key points !

☐ The ability to understand other people is regarded by many executives as the key management skill.

☐ To understand people, managers need to develop their ability to:
  ☐ Hear and see cues
  ☐ Identify the cues with attributes
  ☐ Associate the attributes with other attributes
  ☐ Determine the cause
  ☐ Judge.

☐ This ability is influenced by:
  ☐ Self-perception
  ☐ The other person
  ☐ The relationship
  ☐ The situation.

☐ Expectations and assumptions can lead to behaviour being misinterpreted.

☐ To understand others and create positive relationships with them, managers need to focus on and develop:
  ☐ Outcome(s)
  ☐ Acuity
  ☐ Flexibility.

☐ Managing customers, clients and superiors

70 per cent of lost customers hit the road not because of price issues but because they didn't like the human side of doing business with the prior provider of the product or service.

(Tom Peters, 1995: 5)

Activity 2.12   Think of five different types of business that depend upon providing excellent customer care. Now think of one that does not. Which did you find easiest to do? Why?

Managers can ensure awesome customer service by:

☐ Adding value through the quality of the relationships they are personally engaged in
☐ Adding value through the quality of the relationships colleagues are engaged in.

Both examples are dependent upon excellent communication skills, including a high level of sensory acuity, and an acknowledgement of the absolute importance of providing the best possible customer care. In the first instance, the manager is responsible for his/her own development. In the second, the manager is responsible for both staff training (Chapter 3) and the creation of an explicit culture that values customer relations above all else.

Glen McCoy, in his highly entertaining and practical book *Extraordinary Customer Care*, writes: 'If you get the customer care completely right in any business, the future sales and marketing would just about look after themselves' (McCoy, 2000: 10). David Bond, current owner of Health Works Inc, surprised a group of students enquiring about his marketing practices, by discussing the skills of his waiters and waitresses. The point he was making was that people talk about quality of service; word of mouth is a great advertising medium and front-line staff are directly responsible for much of what is said about a business. Everyone who works for David Bond and has direct contact with customers understands the importance he places on excellent service and his view that they play an essential part in his marketing strategy.

Activity 2.13   Imagine you are a manager in the following three businesses. Write a memo for your front-line staff reminding them of the behaviours, responses and messages that constitute excellent customer care.

1. Restaurant and bar.
2. Call centre.
3. Fashion outlet.

When was the last time you were the recipient of outstanding customer care? When was the last time you were on the wrong end of poor customer service? Which was easier to remember?

There are four key elements in ensuring successful customer relationships – the springboard for excellent service. These are as follows:

1. Perimeter planning.
2. Matching messages.
3. Completing the circle.
4. Walking the talk.

1. Perimeter planning

This is the process by which excellent service is guaranteed at every level and in every part of your business. The underlying principle is that there is no time or place in which customer care is not of paramount importance. While the nature and style of your service may change according to the needs of the customers and their current place within the perimeters of your business, your overall aim does not: the customer will experience excellence every step of the way.

The first stage in this process is to draw a simple diagram identifying the perimeters – virtual and physical – that exist around and within your business. In its most simple form, the diagram might look like that shown in Figure 2.4.

Figure 2.4
Perimeter planning

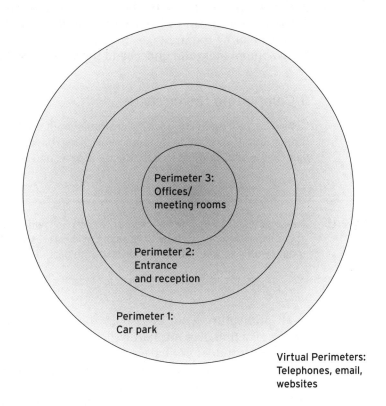

Perimeter 3:
Offices/
meeting rooms

Perimeter 2:
Entrance
and reception

Perimeter 1:
Car park

Virtual Perimeters:
Telephones, email,
websites

Once the perimeters are identified, take each one in turn and determine how excellent customer care is best demonstrated at each place. With this done, consider your customers' transition from one perimeter to the next and decide ways in which your high-level service can be maintained during these phases. The next three elements provide a useful focus for this.

Activity 2.14   When you are sure that your perimeter planning is perfect, improve it.

2. Matching messages

This builds on the ability to create rapport. The purpose of matching messages is to ensure that your customers experience a consistent, positive approach from all staff irrespective of which perimeter they work in or within. The nature and style of the messages given will vary according to the business focus and the needs and expectations of the customers. Common practices, though, incorporate the use of only positive language, including body language in the case of face-to-face communication, mirroring and matching, and the use of customers' names. Remember, it is impossible to interact with others without giving out messages. Part of a manager's responsibility is to ensure that the messages given out by his/her teams are agreed and delivered as intended.

Organisations can only present consistent, positive messages if all staff members know the messages they have to give, have the skills to present them appropriately and understand the value of doing so.

3. Completing the circle

Consider every interaction with a customer as an individual film or play. Both need three things if they are to be memorable. They have to start well, have an engaging plot that moves along at exactly the right pace, and have a terrific ending.

Activity 2.15 Take a moment to review your favourite film. Consider how it grabs your attention at the very beginning, how it engages and interests you throughout, how the ending works so well. Which is your favourite part of the film?

In all probability, your answer to the question in Activity 2.15 was 'the ending'. If a film does not start well, the audience will run out of patience and dismiss it. If it does not have a good 'middle', the audience will lose interest. However, if the director, actors and technicians get those two elements right but fail to deliver a great ending, the audience will invariably feel let down. The purpose of the first two elements is to set up a brilliant finish. People remember endings. A film that promises much throughout but fails to end well is like a joke that has a great story but an awful punch-line. It is a disappointment. Excellent customer care has the same three parts:

- ☐ Great beginning
- ☐ Great middle
- ☐ Awesome ending.

Figure 2.5
Completing the circle

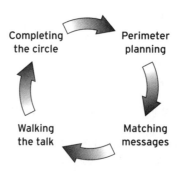

In the final analysis, the quality of the relationships created with customers, and therefore the standard of customer care, are measured by the quality of the conclusion. Of course, steps one and two need to be perfect, but if the conclusion is not at least comparable, the 'customer care film' will be deemed a failure. Whatever else you call it, a curved line that does not connect beginning and end is not a circle (Figure 2.5).

4. Walking the talk

This is the flip side of matching messages. Walking the talk simply means ensuring that your behaviour always matches any messages, promises and so on that you make explicitly or implicitly. Simply put, the base line in customer care is: if you say you'll do something, do it even better than the customer expects.

The value of great customer relationships

In many industries buyer power is increasingly high, and the ability to establish great customer relationships through excellent service is an essential way of creating a meaningful difference. Perhaps the best example of a growth industry in which the quality of customer relationships and care can make the difference between success and failure is that of sport and leisure.

Changes in work patterns, earlier retirement ages and an increasingly healthy and active older generation combine with greater public awareness of health and related issues to create an environment that spawns new businesses in rapid fashion. This, in turn, offers consumers great choice. There are myriad ways in which we can now spend our leisure time and our disposable income. For many businesses in the sports and leisure industry the threat of substitution is high. The key to creating customer loyalty is in building a valued relationship through outstanding service.

Relationships and power

As mentioned above, recognising levels of power can influence behaviour. We would argue for the value of customer care regardless of the level of buyer power, but any business in an industry with high buyer power that does not commit itself to creating a significant meaningful difference deserves everything it gets. Power plays a role to a greater or lesser degree in all relationships. It appears in three guises:

- ☐ Formal
- ☐ Informal
- ☐ Imagined.

Formal

Formal power is evident primarily in formal, or structured, relationships. Such relationships are the focus for the remainder of this chapter, in which we consider the skills needed to manage:

☐ Relationships with superiors
☐ Interviews
☐ Conflict
☐ Networking.

In formal relationships people interact as equals or as superior and subordinate when functioning within certain environments. However, sometimes these boundaries stretch beyond usual limits. As Maureen Guirdham writes:

> *Sometimes power is treated as a property of certain individuals, such as the rich or heads of governments and businesses. According to this approach ... powerful individuals can exert power in any of their relationships, while other, powerless individuals can exert none.*
>
> (Guirdham, 1995: 372)

The relationship between power, influence and control has been widely debated, and a variety of theories regarding the nature and purpose of power exist. The power/dependence theory proposes that power is closely linked to dependence. The subordinate is dependent on their superior for praise, reward and progression, and the superior is dependent to some degree on the required responses from the subordinate. The deterrence theory focuses on the ways in which the perceived power balance limits or encourages hostility and aggression. In formal structures, levels of professional power are signposted through the use of role titles and other indicators, such as the type of car provided to employees at certain levels in the hierarchy, and office placement and design.

Informal

Informal power is evident primarily within informal relationships and situations. Such relationships more obviously reflect one aspect of the balancing of power than formal ones, that is the way power shifts according to the nature of the situation and the corresponding levels of individual expertise and experience. In informal relationships, power differentials are not signposted as in formal structures, but are demonstrated through the nature and purpose of interaction.

Imagined

Is power an objective reality or a product of the imagination? Can power be held and wielded by one person without the implicit agreement of another? Is power as much a product of people's beliefs and assumptions as it is of status, knowledge and authority? In other words, where power is concerned, is perception everything?

Certainly there are situations in which power is demonstrated through what is *held* by one party alone. In a business context this may be specific knowledge or the ability to award a pay rise. In a physically threatening situation it may be a gun. However, in every relationship and situation, the apparent subordinate accepts that role to some extent because of his/her belief in the other person's willingness to *use* his/her power. For example, if I am convinced that my boss will never offer me a promotion, I will probably change organisations; his power to reward will not motivate me to stay and work hard unless I believe he will use it.

While it is necessary to recognise and respond appropriately to the nature and balance of power in relationships, it is also necessary to ensure that the power we attribute to others is real, not imagined. The relationship we share with our boss is influenced primarily by his/her identifiable powers, but incorporates also a degree of interdependency. It is one of our most important professional relationships. Which is why, as managers, we need to manage it with care.

Activity 2.16   Analyse the nature and balance of power in three relationships you share by answering the following questions:

1. Is the power structure formal or informal?
2. What is the degree of dependency?
3. Is *all* the power you attribute to the other person real or imagined?
4. How does he/she use the power he/she holds?
5. Is *all* the power attributed to you real or imagined?
6. How do you use the power you hold?
7. What changes would you make in the balance of power?
8. Why?
9. How could you achieve this?

Relationships with superiors

Managers need to pay as much attention to managing their relationships with superiors as they do to customer care. The nature of this relationship is determined to a great extent by the preferred leadership style of the boss. An autocratic leader, for example, is unlikely to encourage the degree of discussion and debate that a more participative leader would welcome, although it is not necessarily a wise move to take even a participative leader at his/her word if he/she tells you that he/she wants to be informed if he/she is making a mistake. And this reinforces the point made earlier: the relationship we share with our boss needs to be managed by us with the aim of creating a win–win situation. How is this achieved?

☐ By recognising and responding appropriately to the boss's preferred leadership style
☐ By recognising and then matching the boss's preferred representation system
☐ By sharing the boss's organisational vision and aims and demonstrating that through your professionalism
☐ By maintaining your personal integrity.

It is also important to be aware of any differences that exist between your superior's purported leadership and communication styles, and the realities of how he/she actually behaves. As with organisational strategy, there can be a gap between what is formally acknowledged to be happening and what is really going on. So base your evaluation on what you actually experience, rather than what your superior, or someone else, tells you.

Finally, it is best to work on the principle that your boss will only ever have limited time to spend with you. Therefore, when meeting with your boss:

- ☐ Have your messages prepared and streamlined
- ☐ Stress the key points or issues
- ☐ Provide sufficient supporting data
- ☐ Emphasise organisational benefits
- ☐ Show how risk can be minimised
- ☐ Use the language and images that will be most appealing
- ☐ Essentially aim to be more prepared for every meeting you have with your boss than he/she is.

The first time we are likely to meet our boss is at interview and, without prior research, it will be all but impossible to determine accurately his/her style within the limited confines of that potentially stressful situation. Without good interview skills, then, the relationship will not develop further.

Managing customers, clients and superiors: key points!

- ☐ Customer service is one important way organisations can establish a meaningful difference.
- ☐ Some experts argue that excellent customer care impacts positively on marketing and sales.
- ☐ To achieve excellence, managers and their teams need:
  - ☐ Excellent communication skills
  - ☐ A high level of sensory acuity
  - ☐ An absolute commitment to the importance of customer care.
- ☐ Techniques that can be used include:
  - ☐ Perimeter planning
  - ☐ Matching messages
  - ☐ Completing the circle
  - ☐ Walking the talk.
- ☐ The aim of the techniques is to provide a quality of service that exceeds customer expectation.
- ☐ Power is a factor in all relationships. It can be:
  - ☐ Formal and structured
  - ☐ Informal
  - ☐ Imagined.
- ☐ Recognising and managing the balance of power is an essential part of establishing successful relationships.
- ☐ In relationships with superiors, power is formal and structured. It is strongly influenced by the superior's preferred leadership style.
- ☐ Managers can take responsibility for managing this relationship by:
  - ☐ Using appropriate language structure
  - ☐ Demonstrating a commitment to the leader's vision and aims
  - ☐ Maintaining their personal integrity.

☐ Interviews

There are different types of interview, including:

☐ Selection
☐ Assessment
☐ Fact-finding
☐ Feedback
☐ Reprimanding
☐ Firing
☐ Counselling.

While these clearly have different aims, they also share key characteristics. First, however apparently informal the style, an interview is not a simple conversation. Rather it is a *planned interaction at work characterised by objectives*. Secondly, all interviews centre around a sharing of information upon which decisions are made. Thirdly, interviews are planned and, ideally, prepared for. Finally, interviews involve a question-and-answer process that is intended to provide insights and/or clarify issues or situations.

Beyond the everyday conversation, interviews are one of the most common forms of interaction in the workplace. Despite this, they can provide a significant skill challenge, create a good deal of nervous tension and lead to conclusions that are not universally acceptable. We will concentrate our attention on managing two types of interview: (i) selection interviews and (ii) information gathering. We will also look at the skills needed to be a successful interviewee.

The selection interview

The onus is on the interviewer to maximise the benefit of the interview for all concerned and to set the most appropriate style, setting and atmosphere. Power is overtly in the hands of the interviewer – the success or failure of the interview is measured against the objectives he/she has set – but, as we will discuss later, the power balance is a little more complex than it might first appear.

Expressed most simply, the interviewer is responsible for four things:

☐ Defining and sharing the objectives
☐ The style of the interview
☐ The content
☐ Feedback.

To do this effectively, the interviewer needs to be clear about his/her role and associated task, and the relationship to be established with the interviewee.

Activity 2.17 Create sets of objectives for the following types of interview:

	Interviewer's objectives	Interviewee's objectives
Grievance		
Appraisal		
Information-gathering		
Selection		

The skills required by an effective interviewer are determined by the type and purpose of the interview. Overall, though, interviewers need a high level of people-perception, communication and image-management skills. These are particularly important when assessing the suitability of candidates for a job.

The purpose of a selection interview is invariably understood by both parties: it is to create the most appropriate match between a job and an individual. There are, therefore, considerable potential gains for all concerned. Other objectives, relating to, for example, the practical organisation of the interview and the desired nature of the experience can be made clear to the interviewee in writing prior to the day and, again, at the start of the interview.

Assuming that the interviewer has selected the most suitable physical environment and is able to manage his/her own image, the two most significant skills are whole-body, active listening and questioning. These are interdependent. The style and quality of the questions asked either encourage and enable the interviewee to disclose significant information about his/her abilities, motives, attitudes and intentions, or make it difficult for him/her to do so. Clearly, the benefits to the interviewer of whole-body, active listening are minimised if he/she fails to question appropriately. For that reason, we will begin with questioning.

Questioning

The core elements of good questioning are:

1. Determining the focus of enquiry.
2. Sequencing and framing questions.
3. Flexibility.

1. Determining the focus of enquiry

☐ Identify the topics for discussion and the information needed to achieve your objectives. This is an essential part of pre-interview planning.

2. Sequencing and framing questions

☐ Create natural connections between questions. Aim to create a sense of flow throughout the interview.

☐ Recognise the interviewee's preferred representational system and frame your questions using that.

☐ Avoid asking key questions too early. Give the interviewee a chance to 'warm up' and gain confidence. Neither party benefits if the sequencing and framing of questions do not encourage the best possible responses.

☐ Ask open questions if you want the interviewee to respond freely and fully. Bear in mind that the more open questions you pose the longer the interview is likely to take.

☐ Keep questions as short and as simple as possible. Long, complex questions can become a test of the interviewee's memory rather than an inducement to share his/her knowledge and thoughts.

☐ Avoid double-barrelled, bipolar and leading questions. The former incorporates at least two questions at the same time and can confuse an inexperienced interviewee who will be unsure which question to answer first. Some double-barrelled questions can appear as simple, single questions (for example: 'What are your reasons for seeking a new job at this time?') and can elicit an unwanted, or unexpected, response which then becomes a challenge for the interviewer to manage. Bipolar questions offer the interviewee two choices ('Do you prefer to work alone or as part of a team?') and can also cause confusion and indecision. Bipolar questions should only ever be asked when there are only two distinct alternatives – in many situations the lines are not so clear-cut. (For example: 'I do enjoy working alone, but also value interaction and learning from others, and am aware that some tasks cannot be done alone.') Leading questions imply the desired answer and so have minimal value in encouraging disclosure.

☐ As a basic principle assume that, if the interviewee asks for clarification, you have not framed the question correctly.

3. Flexibility

☐ Be willing to change your planned sequence and/or to ask unplanned questions in response to the interviewee's comments. Keep in mind the thoughts 'What question can I ask now that will help the interviewee and/or help me at this moment? and 'What is the most useful way for me to think about what I've just heard or seen?'

☐ Flexibility is the hallmark of a great interviewer. It reflects attentiveness, a willingness to go with the flow of the interview and a commitment to discovering as much as possible about the interviewee. The most flexible interviewers are excellent, active, whole-body listeners.

Whole-body, active listening

As previously discussed, this is the skill of accurately interpreting all the messages – explicit and implicit, verbal and non-verbal – that another person sends, while encouraging further disclosure through the management of the messages we send in return. The use of supportive, reinforcing statements like 'I understand', 'Thank you for that' and 'I see', combined with encouraging gestures and expressions, shows attentiveness, interest and respect and helps develop rapport.

Resist the temptation to interrupt, even if you are particularly excited, interested or even annoyed by what is being said. Always allow the speaker to complete his/her answer. You may use a mind map (see Chapter 5) to record his/her comments or your own thoughts during the course of the interview. If you do, share your intention with the interviewee before you begin questioning. Done in a positive way, this will also encourage the interviewee to speak freely and in detail as he/she will regard your note-making as a sign of your interest in what he/she is saying. Ensure, of course, that your notes are brief. It is dispiriting and difficult to talk with enthusiasm and in detail to someone who is continually looking down and writing. Those experienced at mind mapping should have no problem in this regard.

Silence is an acceptable part of the interview process and can, to a degree, be encouraged and used by an active listener. A few seconds of silence in response to an interviewee's answer, if accompanied by appropriate body language and expression, can indicate interest and thought, whereas rapid-fire questioning can create the sense of an interrogation. Likewise, a brief silence before the interviewee responds need not indicate lack of certainty, but rather a marshalling of his/her thoughts.

Realising what has *not* been said by the interviewee, and evaluating the significance of that, is another important benefit of active listening. Essentially, a well-prepared, flexible questioner using whole-body, active listening skills will be seen to offer the interviewee that most important of all gifts – undivided attention.

Activity 2.18   Arrange to interview a friend or colleague for 15 minutes about an agreed subject. Decide your objectives. Plan and sequence your questions using the guidelines above. Commit yourself to being flexible in your questioning.

Record or, ideally, film the interview and use the recording to evaluate the quality of your questioning. How many open, closed, double-barrelled, bipolar and leading questions did you ask? Did you ever interrupt? Why? Did the interviewee have to ask for clarification? Did the interviewee speak freely and confidently, and did he/she tell you more than he/she had intended?

If you filmed the interview, how did you use your body language to set the tone for the session, to create rapport and/or show control? What aspects, if any, do you need to work on?

Questioning and active listening skills, although important, are only one part of a six-step process that begins before the interviewer and interviewee meet, and continues after it.

The interview process

1. Preparation

This includes evaluating preliminary responses against an agreed standard, and short-listing and contacting those invited with appropriate information. The nature of this contact, the language and style of written communications and/or telephone conversations, the decision whether or not to provide the opportunity for an informal visit, etc., all set the scene for the tone of the forthcoming interview.

Final preparations on the day of the interview will centre upon checking that the environment is as required, the schedule and style of the day is known by all involved, the interviewees will be greeted and treated appropriately, necessary information is at hand and, finally, that you are in control of any nervous tension you may be feeling. (As this is likely to affect interviewees more than interviewers, we will discuss it more fully in the next section.)

2. Introduction
Use the interviewee's first moments in the interview room to:

☐ Welcome him/her in a manner that sets the required tone
☐ Introduce yourself and other panel members
☐ Remind him/her of the purpose and style of the interview
☐ Make clear how you will treat any information the interviewee shares.

Be aware at this point of the power of first impressions – and that it is a two-way process! If you are leading a panel of questioners, everyone needs to behave in a manner consistent with the agreed approach.

3. Gathering and sharing information
This is the main body of the interview, in which questioning and whole-body, active listening skills are paramount. Aim for a listening/talking ratio of approximately 80/20. The information you are willing to share with the interviewee will have been decided as part of your preparation.

4. Closure
Flag up the impending closure of the interview so that the interviewee:

☐ Is not surprised by an apparently abrupt ending and is left wondering if closure was caused by an error on his/her part
☐ Has a chance to review his/her performance, add any additional details, and pose any unasked questions of his/her own.

End the interview by thanking the candidate for his/her involvement and effort, and by stating precisely the timing and nature of the feedback he/she will receive. The interviewee's departure needs to be as well managed as his/her arrival.

5. Evaluation
Even though this will be carried out against a previously agreed specification, personalities and performances on the day will often create a degree of debate. As the ideal candidate almost certainly does not exist, there may well be a need for some flexibility – a re-evaluation of the most appropriate mix of experiences, skills, attitudes and intentions – in your thinking. Be aware of the potentially negative influence of perception filters, reflected through the expression of a particular bias, at this stage. Equally, do not allow the halo effect to exaggerate an applicant's qualities. In the final analysis, if none of the candidates is deemed suitable, resist the temptation to appoint the one who is closest to the mark and start again, although, if that is the case, you may want to review your initial selection process.

6. Feedback

Of value to all interviewees, feedback needs to be:

☐ Positive
☐ Relevant
☐ Prompt.

Interviews need to be a learning experience for both interviewer and interviewee. Feedback therefore needs to identify what the interviewee did well and provide guidelines for what he/she could do better. Constructive, timely appraisal signals the end of the selection interview process.

The information-gathering interview

More common than selection interviews and with less apparent structure, the information-gathering interview may imitate a conversation to such an extent that, on occasion, the interviewee may not even realise he/she is being interviewed. The interviewer, however, still has to be prepared – selecting environments that encourage free responses, determining questions and style, choosing the best time, etc.

When needing information to increase understanding about a specific issue or to aid in problem-solving, the interviewer has the opportunity to choose an expert who has:

☐ A willingness to talk
☐ The time available.

To question a person who is lacking either of these qualities is to limit the potential value of the interview.

Sometimes it may be necessary to interview a number of people about the same topic. Consistency of approach, environment and timing are needed here to enable a reasonable comparison to be made. Talking to one colleague for 30 minutes over a relaxed lunch and to another for five minutes as you walk to a meeting does not provide the equality of experience from which sound judgements can be realised.

A useful technique when gathering information is to funnel question sequences from the general to the specific. Asking interviewees to talk in general terms about a particular issue enables them to review the situation and organise their thoughts without feeling any pressure; this prepares them mentally for the specific questions which will follow. Of course, in most interview situations interviewees are well aware of what is happening. They arrive with their own agenda and are suitably prepared and skilled. It is important, therefore, that managers conducting information-gathering interviews are aware of the interviewees' bias or personal agendas, and can interpret their responses accordingly.

Being interviewed

Successful interviewees also manage the six-step interview process. They are aware of what makes a good interviewer and are skilled at managing those who are not so good and, importantly, they recognise the power they hold –

namely the capability to refuse an offer if terms and conditions are not acceptable. Good interviewees, like good interviewers, have well-developed communication and image-management skills.

1. Preparation

The three steps in pre-interview preparation are:

☐ Research – organisation, job, interviewers
☐ Self-analysis – personal SWOT analysis
☐ Managing nervous tension.

Learn as much as possible about the organisation's history, culture, present focus and performance, and future plans. Consider how these may impact upon the position for which you will be interviewed. Find out about the experiences, roles and attitudes of the interview panel. This allows you to present a style and messages that meet their expectations. The key issue here, as ever, is to maintain personal integrity – presenting a false impression of yourself will not lead to a win–win resolution. If the organisation welcomes informal visits, take up the offer, but do your research before you go. However informal the preliminary visit, you are still on show and people will discuss you afterwards. So be prepared.

Analysis of the organisation and the job specification will enable you to frame the interviewer's most likely questions and to structure your answers. Some interviewers allow the use of cue cards during the interview. Clarify this beforehand. If you do decide to take some form of notes in with you, a mind map is again the most useful format. A personal SWOT analysis, in which you identify your strengths, weaknesses, opportunities and threats, is a useful way of determining your appropriateness for specific jobs and identifying training needs. The SWOT analysis should be an ongoing document that is updated in the light of your learning and experience. When considering your suitability for a job, consider also the style and culture of the organisation. Having a skills and experience 'fit' is only one part of the equation. Beliefs and values need to match to an acceptable degree. Environments need to be appropriate at worst, and inspiring at best. There needs to be a clear indication of how your capabilities will be developed and over what time period. Most of all, the new job needs to match your sense of personal identity.

When all preparation is complete, ask a friend or colleague to put you through a trial run. You can provide him/her with the job specification, some key points about the organisation and the questions you regard as the most likely. Encourage your friend or colleague also to make up questions of his/her own – however outrageous or absurd! Practice at dealing with the unexpected helps prepare you for the shock of the question you had not thought of, and for the inexperienced interviewer who constantly asks double-barrelled, bipolar, leading or other unnecessarily awkward questions. Treat the experience with the seriousness of a real interview. In any area, good performance is the result of the graduated practice of skills in situations that increasingly reflect the real thing. Being successful at interviews is no different. Finally, if at all possible, film your performance. This will enable you to analyse your body language.

Nervous tension is a natural – in some respects, an essential – part of being interviewed. In Chapter 1 we explained the biological chemistry of stress and discussed negative and positive emotional responses to it. A personal SWOT analysis that acts as a constant reminder of your suitability for the post, combined with a clearly defined cultural match, an awareness that the job fits your personal and professional identity, and well-developed interview skills, can do much to ensure that nervous tension becomes a performance enhancer. Recognition of nervous tension can also be reframed. Rather than thinking or talking of it as fear, stress or pressure, regard it as *creative tension*, which is an essential element in the development of something new.

Activity 2.19   Produce your personal SWOT analysis.

Strengths	Weaknesses
Opportunities	Threats

Update this every three months.

---

2. Introduction

First impressions count, so ensure that your dress, body language and greeting(s) match the interviewer's expectations. Greet and make eye contact with everyone present. Resist the temptation to judge the interviewer(s) on the basis of your first impression. If facing a panel of questioners, do not assume, for example, that the emotionless, stern-faced man has decided against you while the smiling, encouraging woman is on your side. The reverse could be true. Direct your comments equally to all present and remember that looks can be deceiving.

As a general rule, it is best to sit in a relaxed, alert manner, with feet flat, back slightly erect and hands resting on your lap. Hands and feet often betray excessive nervousness, so avoid clenched fists, unnecessary movements, nervous twitches and the like.

3. Sharing and gathering information

When answering questions, be prepared to:

☐ Be silent for a moment, organising your thoughts, before replying
☐ Summarise the key points you have made at the end of lengthy answers

☐ Address all members of the interviewing panel equally
☐ Listen for statements or hidden questions behind the questions being asked
☐ Address the assumptions behind closed questions rather than answer the questions themselves
☐ Ask for a summary of an unclear or rambling question
☐ Determine whether it is best to 'chunk up' or 'chunk down' in response to questions
☐ Use concrete examples to support your views and claims
☐ Reply using the language of the interviewer. If facing a large panel, use all three primary representation systems to ensure that you 'strike the right note', 'show your potential' and 'make an impact' on everyone present.

Although you will have several questions of your own already prepared, have the flexibility to identify new questions during the course of the interview. Regard this part – it is usually at the end – as an opportunity to demonstrate insights that you have gained from your research and to clarify any uncertainties you still have. Questions about future job development, for example, are more likely to impress than asking when the holiday entitlement increases.

4. Closure

Good interviewers will flag impending closure. When the interview is complete, simply thank all present, maintain the relaxed, confident image you arrived with, and the same degree of mental focus, and leave. Do not relax your vigilance. Do not say any more than you have to. Work on the principle that your task is not complete until you have left the premises.

5. Evaluation

Objective evaluation of one's own performance is difficult. Immediately after an interview, most people experience an emotional 'gut' sense of how well they did. This should not be dismissed. Sometimes we can accurately sense a standard without having measured it against objective criteria. The great actor Laurence Olivier once performed Othello to such a high standard that his fellow actors joined the audience with their applause. Immediately afterwards Olivier flew into a rage. When asked 'What's the matter – don't you know you were brilliant?', he replied, 'Of course I know – but I don't ******* know *why*!' Intuitive evaluation can be supplemented later with a more objective analysis, using the criteria identified previously as a guide.

6. Feedback

Regard constructive, prompt feedback as your right. Even if you get the job, you need to know how and why you impressed the interviewer(s), and what aspects of your performance could have been improved upon. If you did not get the job it does not automatically follow that you interviewed badly. Compare the constructive criticism from the interviewer with your own evaluation. Note the similarities and try to identify reasons for the differences. Use the two to direct the ways you will manage your next interview.

The value of interviews

The value of interviews is determined by the respective skills and attitudes of the people involved and, to some extent, by the purpose of the interview itself. For example, selection interviews that do not include a skills or aptitude test provide no accurate gauge of the abilities of the interviewee. One measure of the value of interviews is the degree to which they influence the future performance of all involved.

Interviews: key points!

☐ An interview can be defined as 'a planned interaction with objectives'.

☐ The different types of interview all share key characteristics. These are:
  ☐ Prior planning and preparation
  ☐ Sharing information
  ☐ A question-and-answer process.

☐ The key skills that are needed to managing a selection interview are:
  ☐ Questioning
  ☐ Whole-body, active listening.

☐ Effective questioners:
  ☐ Determine the focus of enquiry
  ☐ Pay attention to the sequencing and framing of their questions
  ☐ Have the mental flexibility to ask new questions in response to the interviewee's comments.

☐ Whole-body, active listening is the skill of interpreting both verbal and non-verbal messages accurately and, when appropriate, encouraging disclosure through the use of supportive gestures and comments.

☐ The interview process can be divided into six steps:
  ☐ Preparation
  ☐ Introduction
  ☐ Gathering and sharing information
  ☐ Closure
  ☐ Evaluation
  ☐ Feedback.

☐ When being interviewed for a new job:
  ☐ Research the organisation thoroughly
  ☐ Use a personal SWOT analysis to measure your suitability for the post
  ☐ Pay attention also to the degree of cultural 'fit' – the extent to which the job and the organisation reinforce your sense of identity.

☐ Information-gathering interviews may appear more conversational and informal than others. The selection of 'experts' is determined by:
  ☐ Their willingness to talk
  ☐ The time they have available.

☐ If talking to more than one expert, it is important to ensure consistency of environment and time allocation if meaningful comparisons are to be made.

☐ Conflict management

There are essential differences between competition and conflict. The former is entered into willingly, operates within agreed parameters, employs specific rules to which all parties adhere and is monitored from the outset. Many people who compete still argue that 'taking part in the correct manner is more important than winning'. A race is an obvious example of a form of competition. The primary purpose of conflict is to win at all costs, even if this means causing harm in the process. Conflicts have few, if any, rules, occur without the appointment of a referee and tend to grow out of tension. War is the ultimate example of conflict. Sun Tzu, the great Chinese military strategist, famous for his book *The Art of War* (Wing, 1989), identified four types of conflict and the costs (emotional, financial or time) associated with each. The conflicts are:

☐ *Conflict with oneself.* This reflects a lack of alignment in one's beliefs, values, behaviours, capabilities and environment. The costs are primarily emotional.

☐ *Conflict in the environment.* This can be caused by external forces necessitating changes in organisational structure, systems or strategy. The costs can be high in terms of emotional stress, finance and time.

☐ *Conflict with another.* This is often the result of differences in perception and/or objectives. The costs are primarily emotional, but can also include finance and time.

☐ *Conflict among leaders.* This can be caused by different perceptions and/or opposing strategies. The costs can be high in all regards.

John Hunt's definition reinforces Sun Tzu's observation regarding the role of perception in conflict: 'Interpersonal conflict occurs between two or more persons when attitudes, motives, values, expectations or activities are incompatible and if those people perceive themselves to be in disagreement' (Hunt, 1982). There is a body of opinion, however, that argues that conflict can be a necessary and positive force. Proponents of *constructive conflict* take the view that without the expression of different perceptions, open challenges to ideas and practices and passionate disagreements little valuable change will occur. Teams that recognise the value of such deliberately created tension will engage in constructive conflict confident in the benefits they will share as a consequence. This concept has much in common with the atmosphere of creative tension which will be discussed more fully in Chapter 5.

By contrast, *destructive conflict*, which will be our focus for the rest of this section, has no such mutually agreed, positive goals. Behaviours are driven by self-interest, with little or no regard for any negative outcomes experienced by others. Destructive conflicts are typified by the fact that, irrespective of the resolution, there are always costs to be paid rather than benefits gained. Destructive conflict wastes time, money and emotional energy. Constructive conflict can help build a valuable new reality (see Table 2.1). Tom Peters focuses on destructive conflict and its costs when he writes:

I hate conflict. Avoid it like the plague ... I don't think conflict makes much sense. Your scintillating personality and brilliant analytical skills rarely turn enemies into allies. And win or lose, you waste a hell of a lot of time training for the battle and cleaning up the mess.

(Peters, 1995: 51)

Table 2.1
Comparison of destructive and constructive conflict

Destructive conflict	Constructive conflict
Acknowledged as damaging	Acknowledged as positive
Unwanted by the organisation	An approved change of management technique
Instigated by one party, usually without warning	Planned and prepared for by all involved
Mediator may be needed to end the conflict	Facilitator may be appointed to ensure balance and progress
Creates costs	Creates benefits
Motivated by self-interest	Reflects shared commitments
Continues until a resolution is agreed or forced	Occurs within an agreed time span
Reflects lack of respect	Reflects a highly developed team
Leads to group disintegration	Strengthens teams
Agreed goals are subverted	Is intended to help achieve agreed goals

Activity 2.20 Review an example of a professionally (or personally) destructive conflict you either witnessed or were engaged in. List the costs under the following headings: time; money; and emotional energy.

Causes of conflict

Interpersonal conflicts have four main causes:

1. Personal and/or perceptual differences.
2. Information breakdown.
3. Environmental pressures.
4. Role incompatibility.

1. Personal and/or perceptual differences

The ways people filter and interpret information and events can create differences of opinion so severe they result in conflict. The power of personal beliefs, as discussed in Chapter 1, is such that they can unite and inspire or fuel disintegration and create distrust. Primary beliefs, such as in the essential nature of existence and the purpose of life or in the need for structure and order or in the most important human qualities, help people to make sense of the world and their reasons for being in it. Often these same beliefs cause varying levels of bias which, in turn, create a form of perceptual blindness – an inability to see, or accept, the possible validity of other points of view. The

Titanic was unsinkable and no debate could possibly have persuaded its designers otherwise. When people's belief systems crash into each other, one view rarely sinks without trace. If anything, the opposite is true and beliefs harden, with the antagonists equally convinced that they are morally right. Such conflicts are perhaps the most difficult to resolve. The damage is often extensive and the effects long-lasting.

2. Information breakdown

This often reflects a weak link in an organisation's communication system, although it can also be the result of misinterpretation. Conflicts caused by information breakdown are quite common but, as they are factual in nature and beliefs are not being challenged, they are relatively easy to resolve. Once the breakdown has been identified, and accurate information made available, the parties involved have no reason to continue with the conflict. The ending is normally abrupt with minimal 'fallout'.

3. Environmental pressures

There are two environmental pressures that can incite conflict: uncertainty and minimal resources.

Uncertainty
Uncertainty can result from any of the following:

☐ The leader's inability to create a shared vision
☐ Rapid environmental change
☐ Communication breakdown
☐ The behaviour of major competitors.

Uncertainty raises personal stress levels, causes anxiety and increases the likelihood of conflict. Responses to uncertainty are, to some extent, culturally driven and will be examined more fully in Chapter 8. As a general principle, though, there are types of uncertainty that few people find positively stimulating. For example, the sudden revelation that an unnamed number of staff will be laid off or having to wait several days for the results of a selection process are not experiences that excite many people.

Conflicts that grow out of uncertainty tend to be intense, emotional and, at first glance, often appear to have been sparked by a trivial incident or problem. This is usually an example of 'the straw breaking the camel's back', with a deep-rooted anxiety being forced into the open by what in more certain times would have been regarded as an event of little consequence. Frequent change in the workplace is one of the primary causes of uncertainty and the conflicts associated with it. Resolution of such conflicts is achieved by successful change-management strategies – once the new reality is regarded as the accepted routine, uncertainty dissipates and conflicts dissolve.

Minimal resources

Minimal resources can lead to territorial disputes between departments and teams as each stakes its claim to the limited resources available. Divisions can develop on a personal as well as a functional level, and relationships that appear well founded can be threatened. Minimal resources also create uncertainty, eventually being seen as a reflection of organisational weakness or failure and, as doubts about the future grow, conflicts arise as people sense the need to protect their own position.

4. Role incompatibility

Individuals within organisations have responsibilities, deadlines and goals which are largely determined by the roles they are expected to play. While organisational activities are interdependent, with each function relying on the timely completion of tasks in related areas, roles can often appear to be incompatible precisely because of the different agendas associated with each. The goals of a research and design department, for example, are very different from those of marketing.

Conflicts that stem from role incompatibility can also be influenced by differences in personality and perspective. This, in turn, is influenced by the fact that different departments may be supplied with different information and report to different managers using different systems.

Activity 2.21   Identify the causes of the conflict you considered in Activity 2.20.
Determine what are the most likely causes of interpersonal conflict within
the following organisations:

☐ A political party in government
☐ A comprehensive school
☐ An infantry regiment.

Avoiding or minimising conflict

Tom Peters recommends: 'Forget your enemies. Work around them. Work instead on developing friends, turning people who agree with you (a little bit or a lot) into passionate advocates and adherents. That is, surround your enemies with your friends' (Peters, 1995: 51). The best conflict resolution is, as Peters implies, to create environments and situations that minimise the possibility of conflict occurring. This can be done positively by establishing good communication throughout the organisation, a sense of ownership of problems, solutions, successes and vision, and the development of supportive and creative teams. It can also be achieved by minimising uncertainty and creating a flexible, adaptive culture in which change, however challenging, is recognised as an opportunity for personal and professional growth. Conflict resolution can be done negatively by creating and maintaining appropriate, high-profile deterrents.

Networking

Peters's recommendation to 'work on developing friends' highlights the role networking can play in helping to avoid or minimise conflict. Building up networks of contacts is essential for the manager who needs to:

☐ Influence others
☐ Gather up-to-date information
☐ Have a wide range of expert support available.

In short, networking improves the manager's power base by providing him/her with sources of information and the resources to take action. Peters says: 'The most potent people I've ever known have been the best networkers' (Peters, 1995: 36). Daniel Goleman reports how a study of star performers at Bells Labs, a famous American scientific think-tank, revealed that what distinguished the stars from the merely competent was their level of emotional IQ, reflected in their ability to motivate themselves and create *ad hoc* teams out of informal networks.

> After detailed interviews, the critical differences emerged in the internal and interpersonal strategies 'stars' used to get their work done. One of the most important turned out to be a rapport with a network of key people. ... Star performers ... do the work of building reliable networks before they actually need them.
>
> (Goleman, 1996: 162)

Networking skills

These are the intra- and interpersonal skills discussed earlier. Networkers hold positive beliefs about their ability to influence others, and are confident in their capacity to create change. They cultivate relationships through their sensitivity to other people's motivation, perceptions and needs. Networkers know how to create rapport and, of equal importance, they recognise the timeless value of the networking process. Managers who have created a reliable network will probably be forewarned of impending or possible conflict and, through their network, have access to support and resources that may help them head off or minimise the problem. According to Tom Peters: 'It has always been the age of "networkers"; and in an era where organisations depend more and more on tenuously connected outsiders to get the job done, it will only become more so' (Peters, 1995: 36).

For those conflicts that are not prevented, several responses can be considered. These are:

☐ Accommodation
☐ Confrontation
☐ Compromise
☐ Collaboration.

Activity 2.22 Ensure that the record of your existing network is up to date. Commit yourself to:

☐ Increasing it every week
☐ Making occasional contact with everyone in your network – do not always wait until you need something!

Accommodation

Accommodation is a resolution achieved by meeting the demands of the other party, sometimes at the expense of our own. Accommodation is a strategy often born out of weakness, a failure to value one's own position and needs, and an inability, or unwillingness, to manage and balance the other person's power. Having said that, it can be employed as a measured strategy when one party determines that there are more important issues at risk if the conflict escalates. In such situations, an accommodating response ensures a swift resolution and in doing so safeguards more important values. Overall, though, this is an approach that should be used with caution and generally avoided.

Confrontation

The opposite of the accommodating approach, confrontation is the explicit use of power to satisfy one's own needs without regard for the effect on the other person. This always creates a sense of defeat, and often humiliation, in the other party, particularly when accompanied by a demand for recompense of some kind. Authoritative leaders who use the power of their position, including when necessary the influence of their allies, give out messages that are easy to identify and tend to experience few challenges while their power base is strong. Although some onlookers admire this approach, it brings with it the risk of a gradual, sometimes secretive, increase in opposition, resulting in a powerful backlash when the time is deemed right. The forceful approach may be appropriate in certain situations, for example when it is vital that a hierarchical structure is maintained or when subordinates take immediate action, but it is only rarely the best option.

Compromise

A popular approach to conflict management, compromise can lead to the combatants automatically demanding far more than they need in anticipation of the request to make concessions. It can also be viewed as a 'quick fix', caused by a lack of interest in the issues involved. Compromise, when it is done well, leaves both parties feeling a sense of shared benefit. Done badly, however, the sense is of shared pain. It is most applicable in situations where there are no serious time demands and the issue is of only moderate importance.

Collaboration

This is a genuine problem-solving approach based on a desire to identify and then address the concerns of all involved. Objective in nature, its purpose is to create a win–win resolution, from which both parties feel they have bene-fited. Collaboration works well when peers are in conflict over what are perceived as critical issues and when long-term relationships need to be main-tained, as it seeks to ensure that neither party publicly loses face. Requiring more skill to implement than either accommodation or confrontation, it is overall the most valuable approach, although there are occasions, for example when there are very severe time pressures, when it may not be favourable.

Other tactics that leaders can employ to resolve conflict within their team are:

☐ Divide and rule
☐ Suppressing or working through differences
☐ Employing a mediator.

Divide and rule

Managing the conflicting factions separately and discouraging communication between them enables the leader to control the situation through the management of information and often encourages the various parties to solicit the leader's atten-tion and support. This approach damages overall team spirit and cohesiveness.

Suppressing or working through differences

Leaders can suppress differences of opinion by demanding objectivity alone. As there are invariably emotional levels of involvement in all conflicts, the concept of ignoring anything other than 'the facts' is simply a refusal on the leader's part to acknowledge the realities of the situation. This either drives the conflict under-ground or, at best, creates passive acceptance. Neither result improves team-working. Working through differences is a more positive, structured response that aims to increase self-awareness in all parties concerned, encouraging a speedy resolution while limiting the likelihood of future, extended conflicts. A willingness to work through differences is a sign of a culture in which team learning is valued.

Employing a mediator

The success of this strategy is dependent upon: (i) the skills of the mediator; and (ii) how the mediator is perceived by the opposing factions.

The skills of the mediator
Mediators need to begin with realistic objectives. They need to know what will constitute an acceptable outcome. They need to understand the type of con-flict in which they have become involved. Effective mediators are skilled at:

☐ Recognising each party's commitment to the conflict, the emotional, finan-cial and time costs they are willing to pay, and letting that influence their style, the type of meetings they convene – joint or separate – and their goals
☐ Using appropriate language
☐ Acknowledging the seriousness of the situation

- ☐ Determining the different ways the problem is perceived
- ☐ Understanding the relationship between the two parties
- ☐ Ending the conflict, rather than necessarily correcting the causes
- ☐ Encouraging both parties to focus on only the most productive issues
- ☐ Preventing attention turning to the most potentially damaging areas of disagreement
- ☐ Exploring solutions rather than judging responsibility
- ☐ Creating options by encouraging a focus on interests, not positions
- ☐ Ensuring that both parties understand and support the agreed solution
- ☐ Ensuring that procedures are in place to support the implementation of the solution.

Mediators demonstrate these skills most obviously by managing the content and style of the communication between the two parties, enabling them to negotiate their own resolution. Mediators are experts in the processes of social interaction (see Table 2.2).

Table 2.2 The mediator's role

Preparation	Understanding	Style	Follow-up/Support	Solution
☐ Knowledge ☐ Reputation ☐ Impartiality	☐ Type of conflict. ☐ Relationship(s) ☐ Costs both sides willing to pay to continue ☐ Motivation to stop	☐ Meetings: type and timing. ☐ Communication styles	☐ Agreed procedures ☐ Agreed time scale	☐ Win-win ☐ Understood by all
		☐ Productive focus: solutions not judgements; interests not positions		
	☐ The problem and perceptions of it			

Unskilled mediators, unaware of hidden agendas and conflicts of interest, are liable to encourage open, detailed discussion on emotionally-charged topics in the mistaken belief that this will lead to rational debate and a mutually acceptable resolution. Acknowledgement of the emotional context *is* important, but only the most skilled mediators establish a process through which significant emotional standpoints are revealed but not allowed to block dialogue. A second error made by inexperienced mediators is to identify, with a view to correcting, the causes of the conflict. In complex situations, this would entail significant organisational change and would therefore be beyond the scope of the mediator's role and power.

How the mediator is perceived

Not only must the mediator employed have the appropriate skill-level, but the conflicting parties must recognise this to be so. They should also perceive the mediator to be knowledgeable of the situation, but without bias.

Cross-cultural conflicts

Solving the problem when the antagonists are from different cultures is even more difficult, requiring an understanding of the culturally-driven variables in behaviour and expectation that both parties bring to the conflict. (See Chapter 8.)

Activity 2.23 Select a conflict with which you are familiar. Based on your knowledge of the situation and the parties involved, determine how you would approach the role of mediator. Justify the style and strategies you would employ. How easy would it be for you to remain impartial?

Conflict management: key points !

- ☐ Conflict and competition are not the same. Some writers argue that there are essentially two sorts of conflict:
  - ☐ Constructive
  - ☐ Destructive
- ☐ The costs of destructive conflict can be measured under the headings:
  - ☐ Emotional
  - ☐ Financial
  - ☐ Time.
- ☐ Conflicts are caused by different interpretations of a situation, which in turn can be the result of:
  - ☐ A breakdown in communication
  - ☐ Role incompatibility
  - ☐ Different personal beliefs
  - ☐ Environmental pressures, including a lack of resources and uncertainty.
- ☐ Conflicts can be avoided or minimised by:
  - ☐ Establishing good communication throughout the organisation
  - ☐ Establishing a sense of ownership of problems, solutions, successes and vision
  - ☐ Developing supportive and creative teams
  - ☐ Reducing uncertainty
  - ☐ Creating a flexible, adaptive culture
  - ☐ Creating appropriate, high-profile deterrents.
- ☐ Networking is also valuable in this regard.
- ☐ Depending on the type of conflict and its associated factors, resolution strategies can focus on:
  - ☐ Accommodating
  - ☐ Confronting
  - ☐ Compromising
  - ☐ Collaborating.
- ☐ Leaders may also choose to implement procedures that enable opposing factions to work through their differences. Failing this, a knowledgeable, respected mediator may be employed.
- ☐ Working on the principle that prevention is better than cure, managers should aim to create structures, cultures and systems that limit the likelihood of conflict breaking out.

Summary: managing one-to-one relationships

☐ The successful management of one-to-one relationships is founded upon:
  ☐ An understanding of communication styles, models and processes
  ☐ Understanding expectations
  ☐ An understanding of the nature and purposes of different relationships.

☐ The core skills are those associated with:
  ☐ Managing self and self-image
  ☐ Communication and creating rapport
  ☐ Customer service
  ☐ Interviewing and being interviewed
  ☐ Managing conflict
  ☐ Networking.

☐ The aim is to create appropriate relationships that have meaning and value and, whenever possible, exceed the expectations of others.

A final thought

By way of conclusion, we turn not to a giant of the business world but to a poet, Mary Oliver, who in her poem 'Mockingbirds' reminds us of the single quality that unites all the communication skills we have discussed and practised:

> In Greece,
> a long time ago,
> an old couple
> opened their door
> to two strangers
> who were,
> it soon appeared, not men at all,
>
> but gods.
> It is my favourite story –
> How the old couple had almost nothing to give
>
> but their willingness
> to be attentive –
> but for this alone
> the gods loved them
> and blessed them.
> (Mary Oliver, 1994)

References

Brown, A. 2000. *The 6 Dimensions of Leadership*. London: Random House.
Gardner, H. and Hatch, T. 1989. 'Multiple intelligences go to school', *Educational Researcher*, 18(8).
Goleman, D. 1996. *Emotional Intelligence*. London: Bloomsbury.
Guirdham, M. 1995. *Interpersonal Skills at Work* (2nd edn). Hemel Hempstead: Prentice Hall.

Hunt, J. 1982. *Managing People in Organizations*. New York: McGraw-Hill.

McCoy, G. 2000. *Extraordinary Customer Care*. Chalford, Gloucestershire: Management Books.

Molden, D. 1996. *Managing with the Power of NLP*. London: Pitman Publishing.

O'Connor, J. and Seymour, J. 1993. *Introducing NLP*. London: The Aquarian Press.

Oliver, Mary 1994. 'Mockingbirds', *The Atlantic Monthly*, Vol. 273.

Peters, T. 1995. *The Pursuit of WOW!* London: Macmillan.

Roddick, A. 1995. 'Training with communities in need', The Body Shop corporate video.

Senge, P. 1993. *The Fifth Discipline*. London: Century Business.

Wing, R.L. 1989. *The Art of Strategy*. A translation of Sun Tzu's *The Art of War*. Wellingborough, Northamptonshire: The Aquarian Press.

Further reading

Molden, D. 1996. *Managing with the Power of NLP*. London: Pitman Publishing.

O'Connor, J. and Seymour, J. 1993. *Introducing NLP*. London: The Aquarian Press.

Guirdham, M. 1995. *Interpersonal Skills at Work* (2nd edn). Hemel Hempstead: Prentice Hall.

McCoy, G. 2000. *Extraordinary Customer Care*. Chalford, Gloucestershire: Management Books.

Part Two

Essential leadership skills 1: creating value

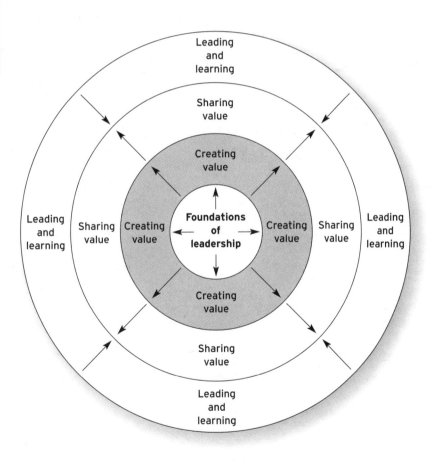

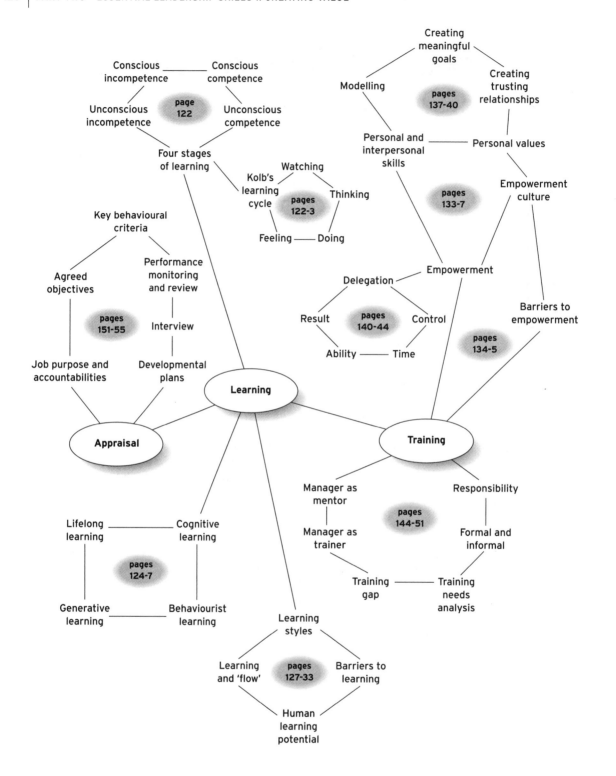

03

Developing others

Chapter

Training is a sacred trust.

(US Navy Seal instructor)

This chapter will develop your:

Awareness of:	Knowledge of:	Capability to:
The concept of learning.	Learning styles, cycles and environments.	Learn more effectively and efficiently. Teach more effectively and efficiently.
The concept of empowerment and associated issues.	How to empower others.	Create empowering environments and situations. Empower yourself.
Delegation.	Delegation principles and practices.	Delegate appropriate tasks and control them in an appropriate manner.
Assessment and appraisal.	Methods of assessment and appraisal styles and purposes.	Establish standards and criteria for evaluation. Choose the most appropriate methods of assessment and/or appraisal. Provide feedback.
Mentoring.	The role of 'mentor'.	Perform these roles effectively. Receive support.
The relationship between these topics and the skills in Chapters 1 and 2.		

☐ Learning

In Chapter 1 the difference between 'reactive learning' and 'generative learning' was introduced. Now we will explore it more fully. Reactive learning is a response to a problem that has already happened. It is certainly better than no learning at all but, as a last-minute survival tactic, it often comes with an unacceptable price. However, it is true to say that adults are motivated to learn primarily to solve problems – and, in solving problems, they learn.

The four stages of learning

Skill development can be broken down into four stages. These are:

1. Unconscious incompetence. This is the stage of blissful ignorance, when you have neither experience of nor ability in a particular skill. Unconscious incompetence is a childlike state. There are mysteries that have not yet been discovered.
2. Conscious incompetence. This is experienced in the very early stages of learning when students first become aware of how much they do not know and cannot do. Depending on the attitudes of the students and the ability of the trainer, this awareness can become either a motivating or a demotivating factor.
3. Conscious competence. This is the stage at which the skill can be demonstrated and applied, but only with great concentration and attention.
4. Unconscious competence. This is the stage when the skill finally becomes a subconscious reflex, performed in a natural and relaxed manner.

Activity 3.1   Review a skill you have learnt, identifying what you experienced in, and how you progressed through, each of these four stages of learning. What could act as a barrier to learning at each stage ? What could be done to inspire learning at each stage?

While the four stages above identify the mental and physical changes experienced during the acquisition of a new skill, the learning process itself has been described and explained in a variety of ways.

Kolb's learning cycle

D.A. Kolb suggests that learning involves four interrelated activities, any one of which can begin the cycle (see Figure 3.1). These are:

☐ Watching
☐ Thinking
☐ Doing
☐ Feeling.

Watching

Observing how other people carry out tasks can provide a benchmark against which to evaluate and improve our own performance. Such observation might occur in a formal setting, with a trainer or mentor providing a demonstration, or informally during the course of the day.

Thinking

Thinking about problems, issues or behaviours can lead to the development of new ideas and theories, and an increased awareness of what does or does not work.

Doing

Being willing to experiment, to try new methods and to practise is the most obvious demonstration of involvement in the learning process. By doing, we test our theories and our skill levels in the pursuit of improvement.

Feeling

Learning requires – and creates – an emotional involvement which can be a guide to our progress or needs, either as a motivating factor or as a hindrance.

Figure 3.1
Kolb's learning
cycle

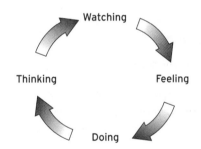

There are implications in Kolb's learning cycle for trainers and mentors as well as for students. For learning programmes to engage and motivate students they need to incorporate all four elements of the cycle. According to Kolb, learning that does not stimulate the senses, promote thought, require action and provoke emotional responses is not learning at all.

Activity 3.2   Imagine that, engaged in further study, you have been given an assignment to identify and justify the most important management skill. Your tutor sets a time limit of only one hour. As you sit in the library pondering your essay, you **watch** a fellow student engaged in the same assignment walk past carrying a video camera. You **think** ... what? Then **do** ... what? It makes you **feel** ... what?

Activity 3.3   Think of a skill at which you have achieved unconscious competence. Think of a colleague or friend who has, at best, only conscious competence in this skill. Design a training programme to raise his/her standard, based on Kolb's learning cycle. How would you incorporate each element? Use your knowledge of the other person to determine which of the four elements you would begin with.

Not only are there different elements to the learning process, there are also different approaches. We will consider:

1. Cognitive learning.
2. Behaviourist learning.
3. Generative learning.
4. Lifelong learning.

1. Cognitive learning

This is the type of learning most commonly associated with schools. It is the mental processing of information, which is interpreted through perception filters before being stored in the memory. Cognitive learning is dependent for its value on the individual's ability to recall as required, whether in the short or long term. The two elements that promote good recall are meaning and association.

Meaning

Information assumes meaning if the student determines that it:

☐ Aids problem-solving
☐ Supports existing perceptions and/or ideas
☐ Raises personal status and power.

Figure 3.2
Meaning and
motivation

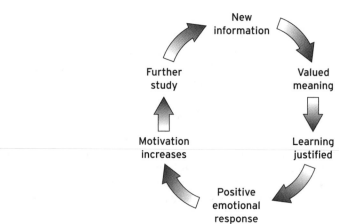

New
information

Further
study

Valued
meaning

Motivation
increases

Learning
justified

Positive
emotional
response

Information that is perceived to have meaning arouses interest and increases motivation. As shown in Figure 3.2, it justifies the learning process and increases the likelihood of further study or training. Mentors and trainers therefore have a responsibility to show the meaning of the information they present or the activities they encourage.

Association

The most effective way to remember something is to associate it with an already known item in the most imaginative way possible, engaging all aspects of the brain's capability and using what have traditionally been referred to as left and right brain functions. The most successful cognitive learners also demonstrate a sense of playfulness. They enjoy gathering information and are excited by their ability to retain and recall knowledge. The best cognitive learners get a buzz from developing their understanding of a topic.

2. Behaviourist learning

This focuses on the relationship between an external stimulus and its effect on the learner, which is revealed through an observable response. At the heart of behaviourist learning is:

☐ The importance of repetition
☐ The need for reward or punishment.

Perhaps the most famous example of research in this area was that carried out by Ivan Pavlov, the creator of conditioned learning theory.

3. Generative learning

Learning can be described as a system, a process through which we change ourselves and our capabilities. Simple learning is shown in Figure 3.3. Generative learning (see Figure 3.4) differs from simple learning because it includes a willingness on the students' part to challenge and/or change their current mental models in the light of their experience.

Generative learning, or double-loop learning as it is sometimes known, develops:

☐ A focus on the learning process – generative learners are concerned with learning *how* to learn
☐ The ability to identify and question personal assumptions
☐ The ability to adopt different perspectives when evaluating a situation or creating solutions.

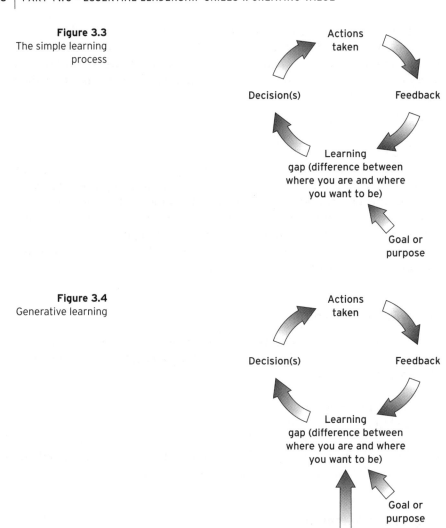

Figure 3.3
The simple learning
process

Figure 3.4
Generative learning

4. Lifelong learning

Today, lifelong learning and professional and personal development go hand in hand. Acquiring a job that meets most, if not all, our objectives is now the starting point, not the finishing post. Learning that leads to an increased knowledge and improved performance, and that challenges our existing mental models and *never ends*, is the cornerstone of success.

Tips for lifelong learning

- ☐ Constantly review the lifeline you drew in Activity A on p. 5. If you are not on schedule, take the appropriate action. Be willing to change your life objectives in response to your learning.
- ☐ Make a point of learning one new thing every day.
- ☐ Practise reviewing your experiences. There is always something to learn from them.
- ☐ Always get feedback on your work or behaviour. Without feedback, there can be no learning.
- ☐ Develop good time and pressure management skills. Without them, it will be practically impossible to maintain the correct life balance.
- ☐ Build up a portfolio of evidence to demonstrate your level of skill, knowledge and experience. This will help you apply for jobs that will further your learning.
- ☐ Understand different learning styles. Know and apply the style that suits you best.

Learning styles

Most people develop preferred learning styles in much the same way as they develop preferred representation systems: subconsciously. However, for generative lifelong learners, recognition and application of their preferred styles will increase their learning efficiency and effectiveness. For trainers and mentors, the ability to recognise learning preferences is essential if they are to develop and deliver programmes and activities that are regarded as meaningful and engaging by all students. Trainers also need to be aware of their own preferences, to avoid the trap of using only the style that best suits them. When explaining a new concept to a group of students, for example, a skilled trainer will use a combination of visual, auditory and kinesthetic language to accommodate the full range of preferences within the group. The same flexibility needs to be shown when considering learning styles. In *The Learning Styles Questionnaire* (1992), Honey and Mumford discuss four different approaches. They identify these as:

- ☐ Reflectors
- ☐ Theorists
- ☐ Pragmatists
- ☐ Activists.

Activity 3.4   If, as part of your study, you were required to research the public's view of the qualities that make a great leader, would you:

1. Begin by considering and evaluating the different ways you could approach the task?
2. Begin by identifying the basic assumptions that underpin the task?
3. Begin by questioning the relevance and value of the task?
4. Simply get started?

While Activity 3.4 provides only a snapshot of your learning style, the indications are as follows:

Answer 1

This is the response you would expect from a *Reflector*, a person who considers all possible points of view before making a decision. Reflectors tend to say little in discussions, are cautious about committing themselves and resist the temptation to jump to conclusions. They are often good at providing feedback.

Answer 2

This is the *Theorist's* approach: a logical, rational, step-by-step analysis of the situation. Theorists tend to be uncomfortable with uncertainty, but will enjoy solving complex problems providing they have all the information they need, and a clearly defined structure within which to work. As the title implies, Theorists prefer the theoretical rather than the practical aspects of study.

Answer 3

This suggests that a *Pragmatist* is at work, a person driven by the need to find practical solutions, to determine better ways of doing things. Pragmatists are best motivated when they see the practical value of an activity or when study relates to real-life events. At times they may ignore necessary research and/or conceptualisation in their rush to implement a solution.

Answer 4

This indicates an *Activist*, an out-going, energetic and open-minded person. Activists thrive on lively group discussions and a variety of short-term, intense tasks. Confident, sometimes to the point of foolhardiness, Activists tend to rush into things with minimal planning or thought. Extended tasks that require sustained effort can demotivate Activists, leaving them bored and in need of a new challenge.

Activity 3.5 Refer back to Activity 3.3 (see p. 124) in which you devised a training programme for a friend incorporating the elements of Kolb's learning cycle. How would you change the structure and content of the programme if your friend was:

☐ A Reflector?
☐ A Theorist?
☐ A Pragmatist?
☐ An Activist?

Such classifications provide a simplified overview of what is, in reality, a complex process, but they do focus our attention on the need to understand the advantages and disadvantages of different learning styles. Individuals who tends towards the pragmatic approach, for example, could improve their learning ability by consciously developing the skills and routines of the Reflector, Theorist and Activist. The same is true, of course, for the other preferences. Exercises to encourage this might include:

Reflector

1. Spending some time every day observing interaction between others, thinking about the manner and content of any feedback you can offer.
2. Reviewing your behaviour and experiences each day, making a note of the important lessons learnt and the ways you can improve your performance in different settings.

Theorist

1. Watching debates on television, identifying the assumptions upon which different points of view are based and the weaknesses in both the structure and content of the arguments.
2. Developing your questioning and/or research skills in pursuit of answers that are rational and logical.

Pragmatist

1. Doing at least one practical activity every week.
2. Discussing problems or issues with the sole purpose of identifying a way of improving the situation.

Activist

1. Engaging in a variety of disconnected activities in the same day.
2. Forcing yourself to behave in a manner that is completely out of character on a regular basis.

Barriers to learning

Even people committed to lifelong learning have to overcome occasional barriers. These can be the result of either external or internal factors (see Tables 3.1 and 3.2).

Table 3.1
External barriers
to learning

Barrier	Solution
Lack of feedback	Seek out feedback by asking trainer, mentor or observer(s) Learn to review and evaluate performance
Feedback delayed	Be aware that, in some situations, time delays occur between the experience and the feedback. Identify the likely delay. If possible, agree feedback time with trainer, mentor, etc.
Feedback is unclear, confusing, inappropriate	Ask trainer/mentor for clarification Personal review and evaluation
Inability of trainer or mentor	Change trainer or mentor
Inappropriate relationship with trainer or mentor	Identify causes of relationship problem and use communication skills to correct the problem Change trainer or mentor (see Chapter 2)
Inappropriate learning environments	Increase personal motivation (see Chapter 1) Create personal learning environment (see this chapter)
Increase of other life demands; unexpected events	Time management skills (see Chapter 1) Pressure management skills (see Chapter 1) Ensure personal approach is based on the Balanced Learning Performance system (see Chapter 1)

Table 3.2
Internal barriers
to learning

Barrier	Solution
Ignoring aspects of feedback	Identify limiting mental models and acknowledge them as assumptions/interpretations, not facts Commit to exploring new perspectives
Inability to achieve positive learning state	Apply SWISH technique (see Chapter 1)
Inability to respond appropriately in the light of feedback received	Decision-making skills (see Chapter 4) Time management skills
Lack of motivation	Review personal goals Place a tangible reminder of the value of continued learning – a picture or phrase, for example – in your learning environment Take a rest (see Code White in Chapter 1)
Fear (of mistakes, change, even success!)	Create positive beliefs and mental models Highlight the value of the learning process and of your personal and professional goals, and apply state-changing techniques (see Chapter 1)

As discussed in Chapter 1, fear is a limiting and debilitating state if not understood and managed appropriately. The best generative learners understand that the purpose of learning is to create valuable new realities. They talk and think in terms of *learning* and *growth* rather than change. They also perceive mistakes in a more positive manner than most.

Mistakes

As no one can maintain a perpetual state of flow, mistakes are inevitable. Learning is littered with them. Mistakes can be embarrassing and costly in a variety of ways. The most positive way of managing mistakes is to:

☐ Accept their inevitability as part of the learning process
☐ Avoid a culture that connects mistakes with blame
☐ Create a positive definition of the concept
☐ Learn something of value from every mistake.

Acceptance of mistakes is not an excuse for lack of care or attention to detail. The manager's task is to ensure the very best professional standards, but the reality is that mistakes will sometimes occur. The key word here is 'sometimes'. Mistakes should not be a frequent occurrence, and the same mistake should not be repeated frequently.

The learning process can be stifled if the fear of making a mistake, and the subsequent loss of face and blame, prevents experimentation. Creating an agreed, positive definition of a mistake can do much to reduce that fear. Such a definition might be: *A mistake is an unintended outcome from which something of value can be learned.* Some of the world's most significant discoveries have been the result of so-called mistakes, identified because the discoverer had an inquisitive and positive approach to unintended outcomes. Penicillin is just one such example. In the final analysis, people who are not making the occasional mistake are probably not learning much either.

Activity 3.6   Create your own positive definition of 'mistake'. Identify three important discoveries that were the results of a mistake.
      Consider the last mistake you made. What are you able to learn from it ?

The human potential for learning

In many respects, this would appear to be limitless. Ongoing research into the functioning and capability of the brain reveals a complexity and a capacity that are staggering. Generative learners are excited and inspired by their potential for success, not afraid of it.

The work of Roger Sperry (1968) and Robert Ornstein (1977) led to the conclusion that the right cortex of the brain is responsible for the development of imagination, rhythm, spatial awareness and colour, while the left cortex deals with logic, number, sequence and analysis. Consequently, people began to think of themselves as either 'right-brain' or 'left-brain' dominant (artists or scientists, with little connection between the two) because of the ease with which they developed particular skills. However, when Eran Zaidel continued this study in the 1980s, his findings challenged that view. Zaidel (1983) discovered that each side of the brain contained a more complete mix of abilities than Sperry and Ornstein previously thought. While the great scientists appeared at first glance to be 'left-brain' dominant and the great artists 'right-brain' dominant, a more careful study revealed that the division was not so clear-cut. For example, Einstein said that he never learnt anything of value with his rational mind. The man who gave us the Theory of Relativity acknowledged the role his powerful imagination played in the development of his scientific theory. Einstein was a musician and an artist, a man with 'whole brain' capability.

Zaidel's work demonstrated not only the connections that exist between 'left' and 'right' brain skills, but also the value of developing both simultaneously. Indeed, because of the brain's inherent completeness, you cannot develop one without the other. People who argue that they are naturally artistic and not scientific are simply revealing that they have developed certain skills more than others. We may not develop our 'whole brain' skills to the extent of Leonardo da Vinci, but if we reject the notion that we have a particular learning bias and balance our activities more equally to engage both 'left' and 'right' brain skills, we can make significant progress.

Activity 3.7   How would you have previously defined your learning bias: 'right' brain or 'left' brain? Write one sentence justifying your choice.

During the coming week list everything you do that requires skills from the other brain hemisphere. (By the end of the week it should be an extensive list.) Use this list to remind you of the need for whole brain capability. Make a commitment to develop more fully your whole brain skills. Plan regular activities that encourage this.

Learning and flow

As discussed in Chapter 1 (Figure 1.4) flow is the state of optimum performance that is stimulated by an activity that is challenging but not oppressive. A person operating in a state of flow is unlikely to experience debilitating fear. The likelihood and frequency of flow can be increased through:

☐ The creation of an inspiring learning environment
☐ A commitment to developing whole brain capability
☐ Recognition of the value of what is being learned and of the learning process
☐ Self-motivation
☐ Clearly defined, achievable goals
☐ The application of good time and pressure management skills.

As Daniel Goleman writes: 'Pursuing flow through learning is a more humane, natural, and very likely more effective way to marshal emotions in the service of education' (Goleman, 1996: 95).

Learning: key points!

☐ There are four stages of learning:
  ☐ Unconscious incompetence
  ☐ Conscious incompetence
  ☐ Conscious competence
  ☐ Unconscious competence.

☐ And, according to Kolb, there are four interrelated activities:
  ☐ Watching
  ☐ Thinking
  ☐ Doing
  ☐ Feeling.

☐ Cognitive learning is that which is associated with schools, and is most obviously demonstrated by the ability to recall relevant information.

☐ Behaviourist learning creates learned responses to specific stimuli through the repetitive use of reward or punishment.

☐ Generative learning focuses on learning as a system, sometimes called a 'double-loop', through which existing mental models can be challenged or changed.

☐ People favour different learning styles, although the best learners adapt their style to suit the task and demonstrate 'whole brain' capability.

☐ All barriers to learning can be overcome through the application of appropriate skills and the adoption of appropriate perspectives.

☐ Empowerment

Perhaps too frequently, empowerment has been portrayed as an option available to enlightened management to create healthy, happy and productive organisations. For many organisations, however, empowerment may be a necessity to be disregarded at their peril, rather than a luxury to be dispensed in moments of generosity.

(Neil Glass, 1996: 203)

The concept of empowerment is not new, even though it has become one of the best-known examples of what cynics would call 'management jargon'. The reason for such cynicism may well be that empowerment is discussed and recommended more often than it is demonstrated. So what does 'empowerment' actually mean? What are its roots and why is it so difficult to accomplish?

The *Collins Dictionary* says that empowerment is: 'To give someone the power or authority to do something'. In one sense, this book is an empowerment tool, in that its purpose is to increase individual knowledge and capability and to expand your personal and professional power. In a broader context, empowerment has been an issue from the time people first realised they had rights that were not being met. Social, and on occasion military, campaigns most graphically reflect the human need for equality of opportunity and, perhaps even more importantly, the capability and freedom to control one's own destiny. Empowerment, then, in a social and a business context can be thought of as the ability and freedom to make decisions that are appropriate to the circumstances, needs and aspirations of oneself and others.

Business companies in the western world perhaps first became aware of the need to empower employees at all levels in 1979, when Konosuke Matsushita of Matsushita Corporation explained to a group of western managers:

> *The reasons for your failure are within yourselves. ... With your bosses doing the thinking while the workers wield the screwdrivers, you're convinced deep down that this is the right way to run a business. ... For you, the essence of management is getting the ideas out of the heads of the bosses into the hands of labour. We are beyond the Taylor model ... For us, the core of management is precisely this art of mobilizing and pulling together the intellectual resources of all employees in the service of the firm.*
>
> (quoted in Dearlove, 1998: 147–8)

Given the growing success of Japanese business and methods at that time and in subsequent years, Matsushita's message was heeded and acted upon. Empowerment was seen by many as the solution to most, if not all, business ills. However, as previously acknowledged, it was found to be much easier to talk about than to establish. As Peter Block noted: 'Many managers have tried repeatedly to open the door of participation to their people, only to find them reluctant to walk through it' (Block, 1987). To empower others, therefore, it would seem that managers first of all need to understand those things that stand in their way.

Overcoming barriers to empowerment

The personal freedom to make decisions and take action is dependent upon a supportive environment and culture, and an appropriate level and mix of personal and interpersonal skills, both of which can be broken down into different elements.

Empowerment and culture

Ultimately, all cultures reflect the deep-rooted beliefs and assumptions, the 'social proof', agreed and accepted by the majority of those operating within them. The beliefs and assumptions that most obviously influence the levels of empowerment within an organisation are those:

☐ Held by leaders about
    ☐ The best ways to manage and motivate subordinates
    ☐ The best ways to demonstrate and apply control
    ☐ The best ways to ensure their own recognition and status.
☐ Held by subordinates about
    ☐ The leaders' motivation for empowering them
    ☐ Their own capability to manage their new freedom and responsibilities.

Leaders who subscribe to McGregor's Theory X (see Chapter 1, pp. 44–5) are likely to support the view that their subordinates lack the inherent desire for empowerment and the responsibilities that come with it. This type of belief leads managers to argue that, while they are willing to offer empowerment, their subordinates are unwilling to accept it; the responsibility for a culture that does not empower workers at every organisational level lies, in their eyes, in the failings of the workforce rather than the management.

Beliefs about the use of control are often closely connected with concerns about maintaining personal value and status, and the lowering of standards. Some managers associate empowering others with losing their previous level of control, and with the risk of no longer being regarded as an essential role player. Others hold firm to the belief that without clear and precise directions from a single leader confusion and failure will increase. The degree of truth in each of these perspectives is open to debate. What is certain is that managers who use beliefs to ignore the challenge of empowerment are not only failing to recognise that they are promoting a belief as if it were a fact, they are also limiting the degree of success their team or organisation could achieve. Equally, though, managers who leap on to the empowerment bandwagon without an understanding of how to overcome potential barriers often cause unwelcome levels of negative stress, leaving people struggling to live up to the new demands placed on them without the support of an appropriate environment, culture and training.

Personal and interpersonal skills

The skills and attitudes discussed throughout this book increase a person's capability to accept new challenges and the freedom to make decisions and implement them. Lifelong learners are wedded to the concept of empowerment. However, in an organisational setting, these personal skills can be frustrated if a genuine commitment to empowerment is not demonstrated through the appropriate provision of:

☐ Training
☐ Resources
☐ Rewards
☐ Information
☐ Authority.

Organisations in which empowerment initiatives fail often demonstrate a lack in their provision of the above. They may provide the training, but not the adequate resources; they may give authority but insufficient information; they may increase responsibility but offer no additional reward. Whatever the weak link in the empowerment chain is, the end result will often be the same: dissatisfaction and disenchantment, increased levels of negative stress, and a potential breakdown in relationships.

Managers who regard themselves as facilitators, and who see empowerment as a key function of their role, focus on the creation of:

☐ Personal values and competencies
☐ Meaningful goals
☐ Relationships built on trust.

The creation of personal values and competencies
Training plays a primary role in supporting and developing the personal values and professional competencies of others. Without the provision of meaningful and timely training and a clearly defined support system, the concept of empowerment cannot become a reality. The relationship between individuals' sense of self-worth, the value they place on their professional role and their capability to perform that role to their own satisfaction is synergistic (Figure 3.5). Training therefore plays an integral part in ensuring that this value chain is strong, and that self-esteem is reinforced by self-efficacy.

Figure 3.5
Values and competencies

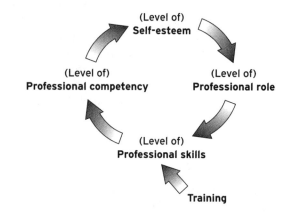

Activity 3.8   Review an activity that reinforces your self-esteem. Take a moment to consider the nature of the role you play, the level and variety of your skill and your overall competency. Notice how just thinking about this makes you feel good.

Now consider an activity that challenges your sense of self-worth. Review the role. Identify the attitudes and skills you need to develop to increase your overall competency to a level that would reinforce your self-worth. If this activity is important to you, plan how your training needs can be met, then put the plan into operation. If this activity is not important to you, consider why you are letting it have a negative effect on your self-esteem.

In essence, empowerment needs to support the sense of personal alignment discussed in Chapter 1. An essential aspect in the development of values and competencies, and therefore empowerment, is modelling.

Modelling

There are two sides to the modelling 'coin': (i) the ability to present oneself as an appropriate role model; and (ii) the ability to model others.

To act as a role model requires an understanding of the skills and attitudes associated with 'self-presentation' (see Chapter 1), and a sense of self-discipline and control. Although the demands of being an appropriate role model are significant, the example the manager sets does much to create a context, and desire, for empowerment. The benefits therefore outweigh the demands. Role models can have a profound influence, inspiring people to set ever more challenging goals and to surpass their expectations. Managers who accept the responsibility of being role models are committing themselves to the continual development of their own professional, communication and image-management skills.

Activity 3.9   Think of one person you regard as a role model. What are the qualities you admire? To what extent do you consciously copy them?

Think of one person who might regard you as a role model. To what extent are you conscious of this when that person is with you? How does it affect your behaviour?

Modelling others is a core NLP skill, defined by Sue Knight as 'a means of celebrating excellence' (Knight, 1999: 32). As children we are born with the ability to model. We learn how to communicate and develop our first awareness of right and wrong by modelling adults. For many of us, though, the passing of time erodes our innate ability. Essentially, modelling has three elements:

☐ Selecting the role model. This needs to be done with care. It is important to ensure that the beliefs and values of your role model are not in opposition to your own. For modelling to be most successful, it needs to support your existing sense of personal alignment, not contradict it.

☐ Modelling physiology. This means observing and reproducing the breathing patterns, voice, posture and rhythms that your role model displays when performing at his/her best.

☐ Modelling mental states. This means identifying the key beliefs and values and the state of mind that, according to your role model, enables him/her to achieve excellence.

Excellent performers are not always conscious of the physical and mental processes that drive their success. Modellers therefore often need acute observation, questioning and whole-body listening skills. Also, the ability to visualise their desired outcomes will be greatly enhanced if they understand their own preferred representation system(s).

Activity 3.10   Make a commitment to model either the role model you identified in Activity 3.9, or someone else who possesses skills you need.

The creation of meaningful goals

Activities and goals that are seen to be meaningful create a sense of purpose which, in turn, raises self-esteem, encourages self-control and commitment, promotes a sense of team unity, and fuels a desire for learning. The greater the meaning, the greater the energy levels and, often, the creativity of those empowered to achieve the goal. In short, managers who understand how to create meaning in the goals they set and the tasks they delegate are setting the conditions which encourage empowerment.

However, this is not the sole responsibility of those who manage us. The concepts and skills discussed in Chapter 1 enable individuals to build their own sense of meaning into every aspect of their life. Writing in 1966, J.B. Rotter put forward the concept of 'locus of control' (Rotter, 1966), distinguishing between people who, like W.E. Henley, regard themselves as 'masters of their fate and captains of their soul' and those who regard their lives as being controlled by external forces. Rotter labelled the former group 'internals' and the latter group 'externals'. Subsequent findings demonstrated that, compared to externals, internals:

☐ Are more self-controlled
☐ Ask more questions
☐ Prefer activities dependent on skill rather than chance
☐ Accept more responsibility for their own behaviour
☐ Are less anxious.

Additional research revealed that internals are more willing and competent helpers. The lesson appears to be that the more empowered people feel, the less selfish and the more trusting they are likely to be.

The creation of relationships built on trust

Although Shakespeare wondered why 'men dare trust themselves with men', people who are empowered tend to be trusting and trustworthy. Although trust and vulnerability are related, Golembiewski and McConkie concluded that 'trusting environments allow individuals to unfold and flourish'. (Golembiewski and McConkie, 1975). Relationships built on trust and consistency encourage individual honesty and confidence; there is no need to doubt the quality of information received or to search for a hidden agenda. People who trust others are likely to demonstrate through their own behaviour that they can equally be trusted. Managers who have the goal of creating an elite team have to create environments and opportunities for the development of trusting relationships (see Chapter 4).

Activity 3.11 Use this activity to evaluate yourself and/or the organisation you belong to.
On each line give yourself a score which best reflects your current attitude or behaviour.

1 2 3 4 5 6 7 8 9 10

Welcome change -- Resistant to change

1 2 3 4 5 6 7 8 9 10

Sees alternatives -- Tunnel-vision

1 2 3 4 5 6 7 8 9 10

Likes self -- Dislikes self

1 2 3 4 5 6 7 8 9 10

Learns from mistakes -- Devastated by mistakes

1 2 3 4 5 6 7 8 9 10

Focuses on the present -- Focuses on the past/future

1 2 3 4 5 6 7 8 9 10

Assertive -- Non-assertive or aggressive

1 2 3 4 5 6 7 8 9 10

Balanced lifestyle -- Exclusive focus

1 2 3 4 5 6 7 8 9 10

Proactive -- Reactive

1 2 3 4 5 6 7 8 9 10

Accepts responsibility -- Blames others

1 2 3 4 5 6 7 8 9 10

Addresses -- Avoids

Total your score. The lower the mark, the more empowered the behaviour and attitudes.

Empowerment: key points!

☐ Empowerment is seen by many as an essential personal and organisational goal.

☐ People are empowered when they have the knowledge and skills to make and take meaningful decisions, ideally within a supportive, 'no-blame' culture, in which risk taking is encouraged.

☐ Empowerment is developed through the timely provision of:

  ☐ Training

  ☐ Resources

  ☐ Rewards

  ☐ Information

  ☐ Authority.

☐ While managers have a responsibility to be inspirational role models, everyone has the opportunity to develop his/her personal value system and his/her professional competencies, including the ability to model others.

Activities and goals that are regarded as meaningful both encourage and reflect empowerment, as do relationships built on trust.

☐ Delegation

Delegation is an important part of the empowerment process. Effective delegation enables the manager to concentrate on the tasks that only he/she can do, and develops the self-esteem and professional competencies of those delegated to. Ineffective delegation damages relationships, impairs results and creates negative stress. As Sondhi's DOPE model for time management (see Chapter 1) shows, managers need to prioritise tasks while having the self-discipline to focus on those activities that are uniquely theirs. The first question managers should ask themselves, then, is: 'Is it essential that *I* do this task?' If the answer is 'No', then delegate.

Activity 3.12 Consider the following:

☐ A manager of a private leisure centre
☐ A restaurateur
☐ Richard Branson.

List the essential jobs each should do.

To be an effective delegator requires a variety of personal qualities and interpersonal skills, the first of which is faith. Not in a religious sense of course, although the line in the Book of James that reads 'Faith without works is dead' (James 2:17) is as good as any in this context. For managers to 'let go of the reins', they have to have faith in the ability of others and in their own decision-making skills.

Relationships built on trust are an essential ingredient in the delegation process, but there are others of equal importance. The five key factors to be understood and managed are:

1. The quality of the result.
2. The ability of the individual.
3. The nature of the relationship.
4. Control.
5. Time.

1. The quality of the result

Managers need to be clear about the standard required. Does the result have to be of the very highest professional standard, or will something less suffice? The answer to this question will help identify the person to whom the work should be delegated, and the time allowed. The higher the required standard, the more capable the colleague needs to be. Delegated work should represent a meaningful, stimulating challenge, not a threat that induces a negative Code Orange state (see Chapter 1).

2. The ability of the individual

As indicated above, the ability of the individual needs to match the requirement of the task, which does not automatically mean that the individual has to have performed the task before. Indeed, as one of the purposes of delegation is to empower others, there are occasions when it is necessary to delegate a task and/or demand a standard that is new. Other points to bear in mind when considering the ability of the individual are:

☐ Experienced staff should need less supervision
☐ Committed lifelong learners will probably learn quickly and on their own.

3. The nature of the relationship

Personal communication skills combine with the organisational culture, reflected through the selected structure and systems, to determine the nature and efficacy of all professional relationships. Inadequacies in any of these can hinder the delegation process. Questions that managers need to answer include:

☐ Am I a good coach or a good performer – or both?
☐ What is my image and reputation – how will it impact on the person to whom I am delegating this task?
☐ Will my presence be viewed as threatening or comforting?

Answers to these questions will, again, help the manager decide to whom to delegate, and the nature of the control they exercise.

4. Control

This begins with what can be regarded as the 'delegation interview', during which the manager meets with the person he/she views as most appropriate for the task. The aim of this interview is to create a sense of willing acceptance. This is achieved by the manager highlighting the value of the task both to the organisation and the individual, and making clear his/her conviction that the person is equal to the challenge. The goals of the interview are to establish a shared understanding of the task through a definition that identifies the nature and quality of the required outcomes, available resources, the preferred style and method, and the method of control. The latter raises an additional two questions for the manager:

☐ What degree of discretion will I allow?
☐ What form of control will I employ?

The degree of discretion will be determined by an evaluation of the other key factors, not least the required quality of the outcome and the manager's understanding of how best to motivate and encourage the person delegated to. Some people would welcome the fact that they have to conform to certain agreed rules. Others would feel an urge to rebel. Some individuals would respond best to working within limits that have been formally agreed, while others would thrive on informality.

The form of control can be regular or by exception. It can be before or after the event. The latter gives great discretion to the subordinates, as it means they are monitored only by their performance against the required outcomes. When a secretary hands in a letter to his/her boss, it is an example of regular control before the event.

Activity 3.13 Consider the three people identified in Activity 3.12. Give an example of a task each should delegate. How might he/she keep control?

---

5. Time

In all probability, the person delegated to will already be engaged in a variety of tasks. The manager, therefore, has to make clear the level of priority to be given to the new work. Managers who delegate without helping their subordinates prioritise their workload are in danger of contributing to a feeling of disempowerment. The quality of the required outcome and the time available are useful guides for determining the level of priority to be given to the work delegated.

Activity 3.14 Do the people identified in Activities 3.12 and 3.13 have equal scope for delegation? Consider how the leisure centre manager could create the ideal conditions for empowering delegation.

Work overload and role underload

Work overload is most likely to occur when managers continually delegate tasks without regard for their subordinates' existing work load(s) and/or without establishing new priorities. Role underload is, according to Charles Handy, the result of managers delegating and subsequently feeling stripped of value and responsibility:

> *Delegation often, when first practised, creates a feeling of underload. The delegating manager feels naked and unneeded. Role underload is the form of role conflict which perhaps most seriously threatens an individual's self-concept. ... It is the most insidious, but most ignored, perverter of organizational efficiency.*

(Handy, 1993: 67–8)

This can be avoided if the managers have:

- ☐ A positive personal belief system, fuelling their self-confidence
- ☐ A clear awareness of the essential tasks only they can perform
- ☐ An understanding of delegation as a core management skill, and as a crucial measure of their ability as a manager
- ☐ Effective, trusting relationships with colleagues
- ☐ The support of an empowering organisational culture.

Effective delegation creates neither work overload nor role underload.

Upward delegation

Upward delegation occurs when a subordinate attempts to return the responsibility for a task they have been given back to the manager who delegated it. Upward delegation normally occurs when the subordinate experiences difficulties and is struggling to find a solution. In this situation should the manager be available in a supporting role? Of course. But the key word here is 'supporting'. If, upon being made aware of the problem, the manager offers to 'think about it and get back to you tomorrow with some ideas', roles have suddenly reversed; the manager is now reporting to their subordinate, and the task has been delegated upwards. Upwards delegation is to be avoided at all costs. Managers who are concerned with empowering others will encourage subordinates to use their initiative to create their own solutions. The time to discuss and agree this approach is during the initial delegation interview.

Delegation: key points!

☐ Managers should do only those essential tasks that are uniquely theirs.
☐ Delegation:
   ☐ Enables managers to focus on their essential tasks
   ☐ Develops the self-esteem and the professional competencies of those delegated to.
☐ To delegate effectively, managers need to have faith in:
   ☐ Their own decision-making skills
   ☐ The abilities of others.
☐ When delegating, managers need to be clear about:
   ☐ The required quality of the result
   ☐ The ability of the individual they are delegating to
   ☐ The nature of their relationship
   ☐ The best method of control
   ☐ The timescale
   ☐ The need to avoid upward delegation.

☐ Training

> *Learning organisations are possible because, deep down, we are all learners. No one has to teach an infant to learn. In fact, no one has to teach infants anything. They are intrinsically inquisitive, masterful learners who learn to walk, speak, and pretty much run their households all on their own. Learning organisations are possible because not only is it our nature to learn but we love to learn.*

(Peter Senge, 1993: 4)

Senge's confidence in humanity's natural thirst for learning is not always reflected in people's behaviour and attitudes. Is his confidence misplaced, or is it that, without encouragement and opportunity, many of us allow our learning instinct to be dulled by the ongoing demands of our personal and professional lives? The answer is most probably the latter, which is precisely why the philosophy of this book is to see those demands as the *reason for* pursuing learning with a child-like zeal.

Training is a core element of the empowerment process and can take many forms. The responsibility for ensuring the provision of appropriate training lies with:

1. Managers.
2. The organisation.
3. The individual.

1. Managers

Managers should know the developmental needs of their subordinates. They should be aware of the knowledge and skills they can develop on the job and those that will require attendance on specific training programmes or courses.

2. The organisation

The organisation depends for its success on well-trained people. There is, then, an organisational need to provide sufficient resources to demonstrate a commitment to training and to ensure that staff are engaged in work that makes the best use of their skills and knowledge.

3. The individual

Empowered lifelong learners take responsibility for their own development, planning their own progress, seeking out learning opportunities, making employers aware of their goals and needs. The effects of the best training programmes in the world are minimised if the people on them do not take at least some responsibility for their own learning. On a broader level it could be argued that professional associations and governments also have a responsibility to provide and promote opportunities for lifelong learning.

The training gap

This is the difference between people's current level of knowledge and skill and the level they need to achieve to be most effective in their professional role (see Figure 3.6). Managers should constantly monitor the extent of this gap for each of their subordinates, using this to determine training needs.

Figure 3.6
The training gap

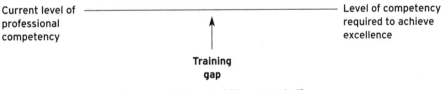

Current level of professional competency

Level of competency required to achieve excellence

Training gap

What knowledge and skills are needed?
In what order?

Formal and Informal training

Training can be broken down into two categories:

☐ On-the-job training
☐ Off-the-job training.

Formal on-the-job training is any form of supervised, structured training in the workplace. Informal on-the-job training includes *ad hoc* methods of learning, often involving impromptu demonstrations or question-and-answer sessions. Off-the-job training formally includes professionally-run courses and workshops and computer-based learning programmes. Informally it includes such activities as personal reading.

Activity 3.15   Identify the advantages and disadvantages of both formal and informal on-the-job and off-the-job training.

Training Needs Analysis

For professional training to be successful, it needs to satisfy three different, but overlapping, sets of needs. These are the needs of:

1. *The organisation.* The organisation benefits from training that improves its overall efficiency and effectiveness and is cost effective. Training therefore needs to be directed towards those people within the organisation who will make the most significant difference.
2. *The different professional roles within the organisation.* These benefit from job-specific training, with clear measures of improvement included. Managers have an important role to play in this process.
3. *Each individual.* Individuals benefit from training that is enjoyable and stimulating, satisfying their needs for personal growth and development. At this level, it is important that the skills developed in training are clearly transferable to the work environment.

A Training Needs Analysis is designed to identify and prioritise those needs, and provide the basis for determining training methods and outcomes. The value of particular training can be evaluated by answering a single question: To what extent has the training improved the combined performance of individuals and/or teams within our organisation?

The manager as trainer

A manager's responsibility is three-fold:

1. Guiding the training effort.
2. Ensuring implementation.
3. Training and/or tutoring.

1. Guiding the training effort

Managers can encourage and guide the training and learning process by:

☐ Drawing the attention of staff to all available resources
☐ Planning and/or booking staff on courses
☐ Offering personal encouragement
☐ Ensuring that individuals have clearly defined learning goals
☐ Playing the part of role model.

2. Ensuring implementation

Off-the-job training that is not implemented soon after its completion is usually wasted. Knowledge is forgotten if not applied, and skills that are not practised soon become inadequate. The manager therefore has to ensure not only that people apply their training, but that they share it with colleagues.

3. Training and/or tutoring

There are several ways in which managers can fulfil this function. First, managers can be responsible for providing on-the-job training. This may be done by assigning junior colleagues to more senior ones, enabling them to observe and then practise certain tasks. This approach needs to be thoughtfully planned and implemented. The ability to perform well is no guarantee of good coaching ability, so the senior colleagues need to be selected with care. Also, the process needs to be framed by an awareness of the learning cycle, with scope for feedback and review. On occasion, managers may also find themselves leading a more formal training session. If required to do so, key points to bear in mind are:

☐ Goals.
☐ The environment
☐ Behaviour and language
☐ Timing
☐ Structure.

Goals
Goals need to be:

☐ Challenging
☐ Specific
☐ Measurable
☐ Achievable
☐ Realistic
☐ Time-scaled.

Goals need to be made clear to the participants in advance or, at the very least, at the start of the training session. As a general principle, avoid the temptation of trying to achieve too much in one session. The more goals that are set, the greater the risk of confusion and muddle.

The environment

This needs to be stimulating for everyone involved, and free from distraction. An environment that stimulates different senses at different times, using, for example, visual aids and music or providing opportunities for movement and touch, will do much to keep everyone's attention high.

Behaviour and language

If operating as a trainer, it is important that you behave in a way that is consistent with the messages you are giving. Managers who have well-developed image management skills will automatically address this issue. Also, if demonstrating a practical skill, show only how it should be done. There is nothing to be gained by demonstrating the wrong method, and there is always the risk that a participant who is not paying full attention could mistake what you are doing for the correct way.

Use positive language that incorporates the three primary representation systems. For example, do not tell the trainees 'not to worry about how some of your colleagues might respond to this new approach'. That will serve only to start people worrying. As with behaviour, give instructions that detail only what you want to happen. The following activity reinforces this point.

Activity 3.16 Don't think of a green horse.

Timing

People learn best at the beginning and the end of a training session. To increase the likelihood of certain facts being remembered, include them at these times. Also, schedule short training sessions for the morning rather than the afternoon, as energy levels are much higher then.

Structure

Training sessions need a good beginning, clear and simple progression throughout and an excellent conclusion. A simple, but highly effective formula is:

☐ Tell the participants what they are going to do.
☐ Do it.
☐ Remind them what they have done.

This formula also applies to 'Persuasive presentations' (see Chapter 6).

The manager as mentor

In this role, the manager acts as personal tutor, role model and counsellor. It should be noted that only managers who have developed trusting relationships and who are temporarily able to 'step outside' the hierarchy of the organisation will be willingly accepted in this function. The term 'mentor' can be traced back to the ancient Greeks, when Ulysees entrusted Mentor to be a counsellor and helper to his son, Telemachus. In more recent times, Chapell and Watson defined a mentor as 'an experienced and trusted advisor and guide' (Chapell and Watson, 1994).

Mentoring is not a recent addition to the workplace. The purpose of the process – perhaps more positively and accurately viewed as a developmental relationship – is, according to Conway, to enable the mentee to '"stand outside the square", gain perspective and re-examine, reflect on and reprioritise their position' (Conway, 1998). Mentoring can occur in a formal and informal manner. When approached formally, it is organisation led – mentors and mentees are chosen, timetables are set, a training budget is allocated, and so on. The informal approach is a more natural process, built on a relationship that combines both professional and personal elements. Whatever way mentoring occurs, business leaders such as Sir John Harvey Jones see it as an essential requirement for personal and professional development.

The benefits of being a mentor

Organisations and mentees are not the only benefactors of the mentoring process. Effective mentors benefit through:

☐ The development of their job-specific, communication and people-management skills
☐ Gaining a wider perspective of the business function
☐ Recognition from peers and superiors
☐ Personal satisfaction.

The roles and skills of an effective mentor

Managers who are mentors, like managers who are leaders (see Chapter 4), need the ability to play a variety of roles. These include, but are not limited to:

☐ Teacher
☐ Friend
☐ Role model
☐ Counsellor
☐ Expert
☐ Stimulator.

Although some people demonstrate an intuitive understanding of the learning and mentoring process, the roles and skills required to be an effective mentor can be learnt, practised and developed by anyone with the desire, or need, to fulfil this function. Critical mentoring skills are:

☐ The ability to create trust
☐ The ability to develop the mentees' capabilities
☐ Listening
☐ The ability to provide constructive feedback.

Once developed, these skills need to be applied in the most appropriate way, at the most appropriate time.

Activity 3.17 Imagine you are in a mentoring role. How will you establish trust with the mentee? Consider not only the actions you will take, but also the attitudes you will show and the things you would *never* do.

Training: key points!

☐ People's natural desire to learn can be stimulated through a mixture of formal and informal training, creative environments and cultures.
☐ The responsibility for providing training lies with:
  ☐ Organisations
  ☐ Managers
  ☐ Individuals.
☐ The training gap is the difference between existing and desired knowledge and skills.
☐ Training can be both on-the-job and off-the-job.
☐ A Training Needs Analysis identifies the needs of:
  ☐ The organisation
  ☐ Specific jobs
  ☐ Individuals.
☐ It provides the basis for structuring effective training.
☐ Managers have a responsibility to:
  ☐ Guide the training
  ☐ Ensure implementation
  ☐ Act as trainer, role model, mentor and tutor.

☐ Appraisal

Managers are invariably involved in some form of appraisal system. Appraisal, like delegation, is a necessary management skill which, if done badly, does more harm than good. At its worst, Neil Glass describes it as: 'A fairly unsatisfactory process in which the unprepared (managers) evaluate the unwilling (subordinates) against the unmeasurable (loosely expressed targets)' (Glass, 1996: 175–6).

Traditionally, appraisal systems judge the effectiveness of an individual's past performance over a period of anything from three months to one year and use that to set new targets. For appraisal to be seen as a positive experience it needs to be regarded as a vital part of the training and learning process, with a clear focus on developing people rather than judging past efforts (see Figures 3.7(a) and 3.7(b)). The issue of financial reward, although central to appraisal, also needs to be addressed. A strong emphasis on the link between the two increases pressure on all parties involved and encourages vigorous, often emotional disputes if the results of the appraisal are not to the appraisee's liking. For appraisal to become a cornerstone of the training and learning process organisations need to find ways to break, or at least weaken, the perception that the only benefit of a successful appraisal is monetary reward.

Figure 3.7(a)
Past performance

Figure 3.7(b)
Training and development

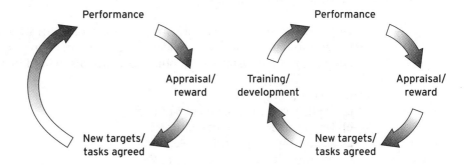

The appraisal system

This can be divided into six stages:

1. Agreeing job purpose and accountabilities.
2. Agreeing key objectives.
3. Determining key behavioural criteria.
4. Monitoring and reviewing performance.
5. Performance appraisal interview.
6. Agreeing developmental plans.

1. Job purpose and accountabilities

The job purpose is made clear through a statement that summarises the main reasons why the job exists and what it contributes to the organisation. A statement of accountabilities identifies the areas of responsibility associated with the job.

2. Objectives

These are agreed by the manager and the subordinate and need to reflect the purpose and accountabilities of the job, areas of priority and the overall business plan. The objectives will cover all main aspects of work and provide scope for the creation of new objectives as the year progresses and changes occur. Once agreed, objectives are recorded showing:

- ☐ The title of the objective
- ☐ What *action* will occur, by what *date*, and for what *reason*
- ☐ Interim stages and dates
- ☐ The way(s) in which the objective will be achieved
- ☐ Specific roles and responsibilities
- ☐ Measures of assessment
- ☐ Formal review dates.

Objectives can be measured using a variety of quantitative, qualitative or behavioural criteria. The measures selected need to be observable and absolute, not comparative. An objectives checklist would include:

- ☐ Were the objectives agreed?
- ☐ Do they cover the main areas of work?
- ☐ Do they reflect accountabilities?
- ☐ Are the objectives measurable?
- ☐ Are they challenging, not oppressive?
- ☐ Do they include personal development objectives?
- ☐ What assumptions underlie the objective?
- ☐ Does the individual have the resources and authority to achieve the objectives?
- ☐ Are the objectives written down?
- ☐ Is there provision for feedback, to enable changes to be made if necessary?

3. Behavioural criteria

These are the personal characteristics that are needed to ensure effective performance. A limited number of key behaviours and appropriate measures are agreed between the manager and the appraisee. As with objectives, these can be changed to meet new or unexpected demands.

Activity 3.18   Select a particular job you are, or have been, involved in that is/was not formally appraised. Write a statement identifying both job purpose and accountabilities. Record the key objectives using the guidelines above. Identify two or more measures from each of the categories: quantitative; qualitative; and behaviour.

Define success by completing these statements:

I was/we were succeeding if ...
I was/we were failing if ...

4. Monitoring and reviewing performance

Monitoring can occur formally and informally. Informal, ongoing monitoring often produces the most valuable insights. The purpose of monitoring is to:

- ☐ Identify success
- ☐ Identify failure
- ☐ Provide timely support
- ☐ Ensure the ongoing relevancy of the agreed objectives.

The three steps in this process are:

- ☐ Collecting evidence
- ☐ Giving feedback
- ☐ Agreeing action.

Collecting evidence
Acting as a monitor, the manager needs to collect evidence from a variety of carefully selected sources. This is recorded. It indicates the level of performance by showing:

- ☐ What has been attempted and how
- ☐ What has been said and how
- ☐ The results.

Activity 3.19   List at least five sources from which you would gather evidence if you were to monitor performance in the role/job identified in Activity 3.18.

Giving feedback and agreeing action
The reasons for giving feedback are to celebrate success and/or enable behavioural change. Feedback therefore needs to be specific, balanced whenever possible between positive and negative comments, and delivered in private. Subsequent action and follow-up meetings should always be planned.

5. The appraisal interview

An integral part of the appraisal process, appraisal interviews can have different purposes. These are:

- ☐ Performance review
- ☐ Problem-solving
- ☐ A combination of the above.

Performance review

There are two approaches and both are evaluative in nature: (i) the manager shares their evaluation and then persuades their colleague to follow specific recommendations; and (ii) the manager shares their evaluation and then encourages reaction, responding to their colleague's views in a non-judgemental way.

Problem-solving

The focus here is on the professional development of the appraisee. The manager does not present an evaluation but encourages their colleague to identify and discuss his/her areas of weakness. A plan of action is then agreed.

In combination

This incorporates both the evaluative and the developmental approaches. The interview begins with the problem-solving approach and then moves on to include the manager's evaluation the appraisee. Whatever the purpose and approach of the appraisal interview, managers can do much to ensure their effectiveness by:

☐ Understanding the other person and the relationship shared with him/her (Chapter 2)
☐ Having good communication skills (Chapter 2)
☐ Setting clear, shared objectives
☐ Timing the interview appropriately
☐ Preparing thoroughly.

Objectives

The objectives of a formal appraisal interview can be any of the following:

☐ To review performance against agreed criteria
☐ To identify and celebrate positive performance
☐ To agree areas of developmental need
☐ To agree a developmental plan
☐ To agree future objectives.

Timing

Traditionally, appraisal interviews are held on a quarterly and/or yearly basis. As the appraiser, the manager needs to ensure that these dates are agreed well in advance. Time needs to be available for:

☐ The appraiser to gather feedback on performance
☐ The appraisee to assess his/her own needs.

Preparation

The appraiser needs to be fully conversant with the appraisee's job purpose, behavioural criteria, existing development plans and review documents. All evidence of performance needs to be collected and evaluated, and the key topics for discussion identified. The meeting should be planned for a quiet environment, free from distractions. Finally, the appraiser should use his/her understanding of the appraisee and the relationship they share to determine the communication style and manner that will be best received, and to prepare for any possible disagreements.

6. Development plans

These record the actions jointly agreed to enable the appraisee to:

- ☐ Build on their strengths
- ☐ Transform their weaknesses
- ☐ Gain experience
- ☐ Gain knowledge.

The methods used to create this change will depend on what the appraisee needs to learn, their preferred learning style, the agreed timescale and the resources available. Development plans also need clear objectives and to be monitored throughout, enabling the manager to provide feedback.

Activity 3.20 List the methods of development and learning that would be/have been most appropriate for your role in the job under consideration in Activities 3.18 and 3.19.

Appraisal: key points!

- ☐ Appraisal is a key management responsibility.
- ☐ Done well, it is a valuable part of an individual's personal and professional development, and contributes to overall organisational effectiveness and efficiency.
- ☐ Done badly, it demotivates and damages relationships and self-esteem.
- ☐ Appraisal can combine both formal and informal methods.
- ☐ The appraisal system has six stages. These are:
    - ☐ Agreeing job purpose and accountabilities
    - ☐ Agreeing key objectives
    - ☐ Determining key behavioural criteria
    - ☐ Monitoring and reviewing performance
    - ☐ Performance appraisal interview
    - ☐ Agreeing developmental plans.

Summary: developing others

- ☐ The successful development of others is founded upon:
  - ☐ An understanding of the learning process
  - ☐ An appreciation of the value of generative learning
  - ☐ Recognition of potential barriers to learning and of the enormous human potential for learning
  - ☐ The creation of learning cultures and environments
  - ☐ A shared commitment to and agreed understanding of empowerment
  - ☐ Trusting relationships
  - ☐ An evaluation of training needs
  - ☐ Agreed, meaningful goals.
- ☐ The core skills are those associated with:
  - ☐ Managing self and self-image
  - ☐ Managing one-to-one relationships
  - ☐ Modelling
  - ☐ Delegation
  - ☐ Training
  - ☐ Mentoring
  - ☐ Appraisal and assessment.
- ☐ The aim is to: create environments, relationships and opportunities that encourage and enable never-ending individual and organisational development and growth.

A final thought

There is a story, perhaps apocryphal, of one of the world's greatest martial artists and most humble of men who, as head of a world-wide organisation, found that students he had worked hard to develop would occasionally turn their backs on him in the most hurtful of ways. As a caring teacher and mentor, these occasional experiences saddened him greatly, so he shared his pain with his mother. Her response serves as a great reminder to all teachers, trainers and coaches that the learning process, and the relationship(s) associated with it, will occasionally fail to produce the desired results and that while no one has the right to 100 per cent success, great people developers never give up. She said:

> Son, I know you're hurting, but the Good Lord Jesus had only twelve disciples and one of those betrayed him. You've got thousands of students around the world – and Jesus you're not!

References

Block, P. 1987. *The Empowered Manager: Positive Political Skills at Work*. San Francisco, CA: Jossey-Bass.

Chapell, J. and Watson, C. 1994. *Mentor Guide: The Trainer Development Programme*. London: Pergamon Open Learning.

Conway, C. 1998. *Strategies for Mentoring*. Chichester: John Wiley & Sons.

Dearlove, D. 1998. *Key Management Decisions*. London: Financial Times/Pitman Publishing.

Glass, N. 1996. *Management Masterclass*. London: Nicholas Brealey.

Goleman, D. 1996. *Emotional Intelligence*. London: Bloomsbury.

Golembiewski, R.T. and McConkie, M. 1975. 'The centrality of trust in group processes', in C. Cooper (ed.), *Theories of Group Processes*. New York: Wiley.

Handy, C. 1993. *Understanding Organizations*. Harmondsworth: Penguin Books.

Honey, P. and Mumford, A. 1992. *The Learning Styles Questionnaire* (3rd edn). Maidenhead: Peter Honey Publications.

Knight, S. 1999. *NLP Solutions*. London: Nicholas Brealey.

Ornstein, R. 1977. *The Psychology of Consciousness*. New York: Harcourt Brace Jovanovich.

Rotter, J.B. 1966. 'Generalized expectancies for internal versus external control of reinforcement', *Psychological Monographs*, 80: 1–28.

Senge, P. 1993. *The Fifth Discipline*. London: Century Business.

Sperry, R.W. 1968. 'Hemispheric deconnection and unity in conscious awareness', *Scientific America*, 23: 723–33.

Zaidel, E. 1983. 'A response to Gazzaniga: language in the right hemisphere: convergent perspectives', *American Psychologist*, 38(5): 542–6.

Further reading

Knight, S. 1999. *NLP Solutions*. London: Nicholas Brealey.

Glass, N. 1996. *Management Masterclass*. London: Nicholas Brealey.

O'Connor, J. and Seymour, J. 1994. *Training with NLP*. London: Thorsons.

Leading and working in groups and teams (1)

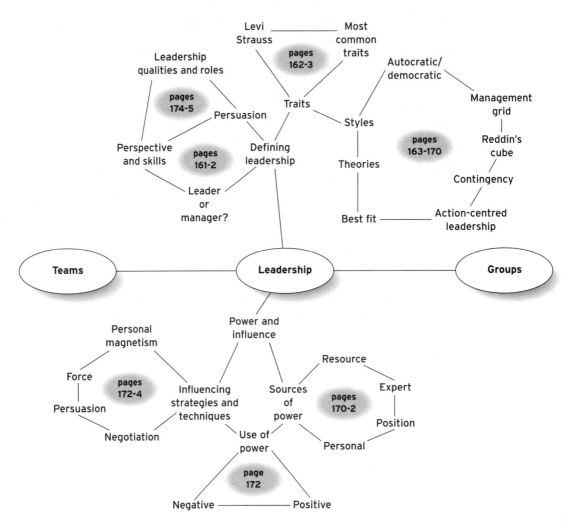

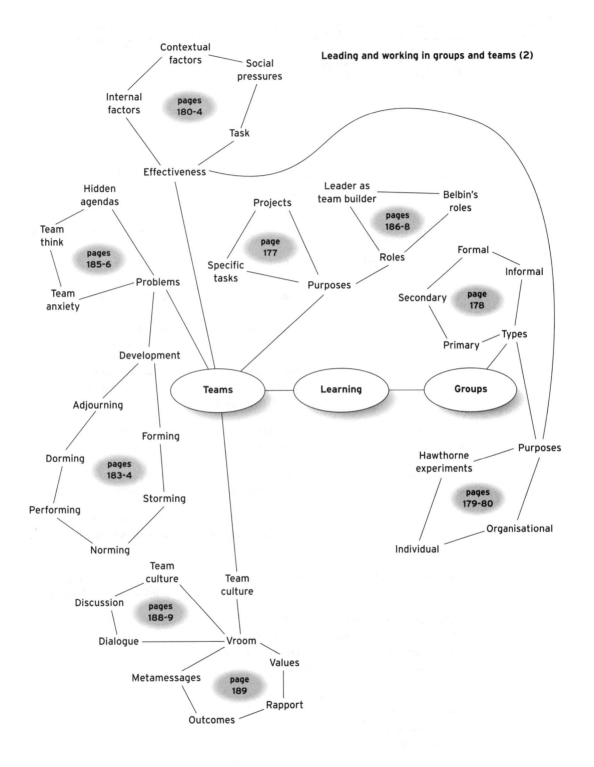

Leading and working in groups and teams (2)

Leading and working in groups and teams

Leadership appears to be the art of getting others to want to do something you are convinced should be done.

(Vance Packard, *The Hidden Persuaders*)

This chapter will develop your:

Awareness of:	Knowledge of:	Capability to:
The concept of leadership.	Leadership theories.	Distinguish between leaders and managers.
Factors influencing leadership.	The relationship between the leader, the led, the task and the environment.	Adopt approaches that reflect and control these factors.
The qualities of a successful leader.	Leadership responsibilities, roles and skills.	Assume the role of leader.
The concepts of power and influence.	Different power sources and ways of influencing.	Recognise and use power and to influence appropriately.
The differences between, and purposes of, groups and teams.	The Hawthorne studies. The leader as a team builder.	Differentiate between between groups and teams.
Team development.	The stages teams go through.	Recognise and manage each stage of team development.
Factors influencing team effectiveness. The concept of team learning. The concept of team impression management.	Team roles. Team communication. Blockages to team effectiveness.	Create effective teams.
The relationship between these topics and the skills in Chapters 1 and 2.		

☐ Leadership

Great leaders tend to attract a great deal of attention. They appear as men and women with outstanding physical and mental fortitude, a wealth of experience, a deep understanding of others, the ability to establish a shared vision and motivate those around them to the highest level, the courage to confront conflict, the skill and determination to triumph, and the wisdom to create resolution. The skills covered in the first two chapters of this book are essential leadership skills. As Warren Bennis writes:

> *People skills deserve more attention than they often receive in discussions of leadership ... Ultimately, a leader's ability to galvanize his co-workers resides both in his understanding of himself and in his understanding of his co-workers' needs and wants...*
>
> **(Bennis, 1998: 155-6, 163)**

Perhaps great leaders attract so much attention because they are rare, gifted individuals who have little in common with the rest of us? Perhaps, like Nelson Mandela and Indira Gandhi, they are also the product of their time, individuals who rise to the fore in response to unique situations and needs? Or perhaps leadership is first and foremost a manner of behaving that can be learned, a combination of skills and attitudes that can be practised and developed, a variety of roles we can all learn to play?

Beliefs about leadership have influenced all forms of organisations and institutions – even educational and political systems. Yet the definitive answers to the essential questions remain undiscovered. Different responses appear to contain different elements of truth, and different cultures expect different behaviours from their leaders. Is there anything of which we can be certain? Perhaps only one thing: being a leader is rarely easy!

Activity 4.1   What is a leader's role(s) and purpose? Identify both for each of the following leaders:

☐ The captain of an ocean-going liner
☐ The manager of a football club
☐ The political leader of a country.

Defining leadership

Defining leadership includes, in part, differentiating the role of leader from that of manager.

Activity 4.2   Write six words you associate with the role of leader and that of manager. What are the differences?

Through their book, *Leaders: the Strategies for Taking Charge* (1985), Warren Bennis and Bert Nanus concluded that leaders could be differentiated from managers because 'Managers are people who do things right and leaders are people who do the right things' (Bennis and Nanus, 1985). This difference in skill and perspective was emphasised by Sondhi, who wrote:

> *The key differences between a leader manager and a typical manager are that leaders:*
>
> ☐ *Think in the longer term.*
> ☐ *Create relevant links with elements of the external environment.*
> ☐ *Influence beyond their immediate boundaries through their social and political skills.*
> ☐ *Emphasise the importance, through application, of vision, values and motivation.*
> ☐ *Challenge the current process and situation, adapting where necessary.*
>
> **(Sondhi, 1999: 92-3)**

Daniel Goleman, writing about 'managing with heart', suggests what leadership is *not*: 'Leadership is not domination, but the art of persuading people to work towards a common goal' (Goleman, 1996: 149). In essence, managers who are leaders have a wide-ranging, long-term perspective, a combination of professional, personal and political skills, the ability to create and share a meaningful vision, and to motivate and persuade others, while constantly looking for ways of improving existing systems. In short, whatever individual strengths they might have, all leaders influence people and therefore eventual outcomes.

Activity 4.3   Think of a person you regard as a great leader. List the qualities you feel made/makes him/her great.

Ask a friend or colleague to do the same for a leader of their choice. Do not show them your list. Compare the results. How do you explain the differences?

The differences in the results of Activity 4.3 can be explained in a variety of ways. First, no two leaders are the same: they demonstrate different traits. Secondly, personal perception filters will have led you both to value – and therefore highlight – different aspects and styles of leadership. Finally, leadership style is influenced by a number of variables. The qualities needed to be an effective leader therefore vary from one situation to another.

Leadership traits

Trait theories stem from the assumption that the individual skills and attitudes of a leader are more important than the situation and associated variables. Levi Strauss identify six attributes it expects in its corporate leaders:

☐ Strategic opportunism
☐ Capability for managing highly decentralised organisations
☐ Global awareness
☐ Sensitivity to diversity
☐ Interpersonal competence
☐ Community building.

The question remains, however, 'Do all great leaders share common traits?' Theorists argued that if common leadership traits could be identified through research, they could be the focus of subsequent leadership training and development. Unfortunately, researchers have found it impossible to produce an agreed, detailed list. The diversity of traits identified may, in part, reflect the bias of the different researchers, and certainly suggests that great leaders come from different backgrounds and are great because their particular traits match the demands of the situation. For example, great wartime leaders, like Winston Churchill, are not always so effective in times of peace.

Although trait theories did not produce the anticipated definitive results, most studies did highlight such traits as:

☐ Intelligence
☐ Initiative
☐ Self-confidence
☐ Persistence
☐ Ability to manage uncertainty and stress.

The problem remains, however, that no leader has possessed *all* the traits identified, and if the list is reduced to the common minimum it becomes a basic checklist of essential qualities rather than an essential descriptor of that which guarantees greatness.

Leadership styles

Style theories reflect the different ways in which leaders exercise power. They stem from the assumption that leadership style directly determines the effectiveness and productivity of subordinates. The two styles usually compared are autocratic (structuring) and democratic (supporting). Using this model (see Figure 4.1), leadership style can be identified by answering the following questions:

☐ To what extent do leaders *tell* staff of their decisions?
☐ To what extent do leaders *sell* their decisions to staff?
☐ To what extent do leaders enable staff to *participate* in decision-making?
☐ To what extent do leaders *delegate* decision-making to staff?

Figure 4.1
Tannebaum and
Schmidt's (1973)
model of leadership
style (adapted from
Certo, 1994)

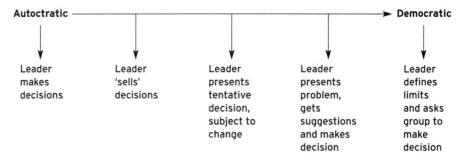

Autoctratic ─────────────────────────────────→ Democratic

| Leader makes decisions | Leader 'sells' decisions | Leader presents tentative decision, subject to change | Leader presents problem, gets suggestions and makes decision | Leader defines limits and asks group to make decision |

Activity 4.4   Review the behaviour of three different leaders. How would you define their style? How appropriate is/was it?

Blake and Mouton (1964) defined the leader-manager's style by the extent to which his/her concern was for production or people (see Figure 4.2). This enables us to add a fifth question to those listed above:

☐ To what extent does the leader emphasise production over people?

Figure 4.2
The management
grid

Concern for People	9	**Country Club Management** Production is secondary to lack of conflict and good relationships	**Team Management** Production is the result of combining people and task requirements
	8		
	7		
	6	**Middle of the road** Production is the focus, but not exclusively so – 'Fair but firm'	
	5		
	4		
	3	**Impoverished Management** Effective production is impossible because of the indifferent, lazy attitude of those involved; conflict is inevitable	**Task Management** Managers' responsibility is to plan, direct and control subordinates' work; people are practical resources, like machinery
	2		
	1		

         1   2   3   4   5   6   7   8   9 **Concern for production**

Activity 4.5   Using Figure 4.2, is the 'Middle-of-the-road' approach always the most suitable?
     Identify a situation and environment in which the 'Country Club Management' style would be most effective.
     Do the same for 'Team Management' and 'Task Management'.

This issue of effectiveness was addressed by W.J. Reddin (1970), who transformed the grid into a cube which featured names representing different types of leader-manager (see Figure 4.3). A 'Missionary' manager, according to Reddin, cares highly for people, has low regard for production and is ineffective. A bureaucrat, on the other hand, is highly effective if a job requires conformity to certain rules, but cares little for either people or production.

Figure 4.3
Reddin's cube
(1970)

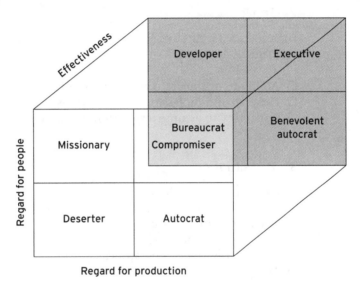

While evidence suggests that a supportive style of leadership does decrease internal conflicts and staff turnover, the notion that it ensures significant increased productivity cannot be fully proven. In work of a highly repetitive nature, a structured leadership style tends to increase productivity in the short term, but can also lead to a lowering of morale which may, in the longer term, impact negatively on productivity.

Contingency theories

Research by Tannebaum and Schmidt (1973) identified three key variables. These are:

1. The leader.
2. The led.
3. The situation.

1. The leader

As previously discussed, all leaders possess a mixture of natural traits, learned skills and personal beliefs and assumptions that influence their style. In *The Leadership Factor* (1988), J.P. Kotter argued that in dynamic and complex environments effective leaders create an agenda for change and build a strong implementation network. This is achieved by creating a shared vision of what can be achieved, a vision that motivates and encourages teamwork by taking into account the long-term interests and needs of all involved. As Max de Pree wrote: 'The first responsibility of a leader, is defining reality' (De Pree, 1989:11). It can also be achieved by building meaningful relationships with appropriate sources of power.

2. The led

For leaders to be effective, their style has to be influenced by, and reflect, their subordinates':

☐ Ability to operate effectively as part of a team
☐ Personal and professional expectations and developmental needs
☐ Capability to assume responsibility and manage ambiguity and change.

3. The situation

Situational factors include:

☐ The type of organisation
☐ The organisation's size
☐ The organisation's geographical spread
☐ The problems facing the organisation
☐ The organisation's stage in its lifecycle.

Figure 4.4
Lifecycle and
leadership style

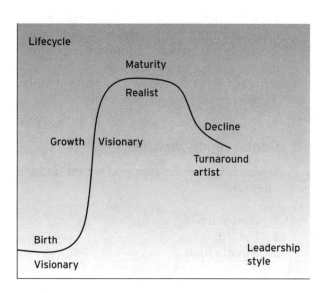

The problems organisations face change as they move through their lifecycles. As shown in Figure 4.4, to be most effective, leadership style needs to change accordingly.

Birth

In the early days, a visionary leader, who can communicate a vision of the future and influence those within and outside the organisation, is required. The leader must also be able to recognise and take opportunities for growth, and have the strength to protect the fledgling organisation from competitors.

Growth

As the organisation grows, the visionary leader becomes an information manager. He/she must also be able to balance the demands and challenges of growth and to act as a figurehead.

Maturity

When the organisation reaches maturity, the visionary needs to be replaced with a realist: an experienced leader who is both analytical and creative.

Decline

In decline, the organisation needs a leader who is a tough, results-focused fighter, capable of communicating new messages and turning the situation around.

The above highlights the point that in different situations, different types of leader are needed. Given that leadership style is influenced by, and needs to reflect, a variety of internal and external factors, the conclusion seems to be that:

☐ There is no one best leadership style
☐ Style alone is not the determining factor of great leadership.

Perhaps this is why some researchers have focused on what leaders actually do, rather than the style in which they do it?

Action-centred leadership

Management theorist John Adair suggested that leaders have to manage three sets of interrelated needs (Adair and Thomas, 1998). These are:

1. Task needs.
2. Team needs.
3. Individual needs.

As Figure 4.5 indicates, if the leader fails to satisfy one set of needs, there will be a negative impact on the other two sets.

Figure 4.5
Adair's model of
needs

1. Task needs

Essentially, for a team to have a meaningful existence it needs to have goals, and the resources to enable it to perform tasks well. The leader's responsibility is to provide the conditions which best meet the demands of the task. To satisfy task needs, leaders can:

☐ Define and share objectives and targets
☐ Define, divide and allocate tasks
☐ Identify then secure all necessary resources
☐ Use the most appropriate methods of control
☐ Identify influences that can affect the progress of the task; monitor them if they occur; communicate them to others.

Activity 4.6   Identify three other ways leaders can satisfy task needs.

---

2. Team needs

The setting of appropriate goals and the provision of sufficient resources do not alone guarantee cohesive team-working. Leaders have a responsibility to praise and direct, and to create situations and experiences which foster team spirit and morale. To satisfy team needs, leaders can:

☐ Ensure the team understands the significance of the task
☐ Agree with the team the standards of behaviour required, and set a personal example
☐ Offer private constructive criticism
☐ Offer public praise
☐ Recognise and resolve conflicts speedily.

Activity 4.7   Identify three other ways leaders can satisfy team needs.

---

3. Individual needs

People who function as part of a team also have individual needs beyond those relating to the task and the team. The leader's responsibility is to identify those needs and ways of satisfying them (see Chapter 3). To satisfy individual needs, leaders can:

☐ Motivate appropriately (Chapter 1)
☐ Delegate appropriately (Chapter 2)
☐ Provide formal and informal opportunities for personal and professional development (Chapter 3)
☐ Consult, acknowledge and implement good ideas (Chapter 5)
☐ Ensure that individuals feel physically and emotionally safe.

Activity 4.8   Identify three other ways leaders can satisfy individual needs.

From this perspective, the effectiveness of leaders is not measured by the manner in which they make decisions, or their particular people/production focus, but by the observable actions they take to identify and then satisfy these three sets of needs.

Activity 4.9   Think of a leader you have observed for a period of time. List the actions he/she took to satisfy each set of needs. Add additional actions you feel he/she could have taken under the following headings: task needs; team needs; and individual needs.

The 'best fit' approach

The bottom line is that leaders cannot exist without followers. A team that prefers a supportive leader, for example, whilst working on a task that is loosely defined with no rigid deadline, would probably not respond well to a leader who adopts a structured approach. In this situation the team and the task 'fit', but the leader is isolated. To ensure the best possible fit between the leader, subordinates and task, leaders have to be able to play a variety of roles, and to change their approach and emphasis according to the situation they are in. In his excellent book, *The 6 Dimensions of Leadership* (2000), Andrew Brown discusses the leader as:

☐ Hero
☐ Actor
☐ Immortalist

☐ Power-Broker
☐ Ambassador
☐ Victim.

However, Peter Senge (1993) defines the leader of a learning organisation as a combination of:

☐ Designer
☐ Teacher
☐ Steward.

What is clear from these descriptors is a shift away from the leader as a technical expert. Great leaders, according to Brown and Senge, have great personal and interpersonal skills. They are powerful, flexible, sometimes selfless communicators, capable of influencing, inspiring, protecting, representing and developing others. Senge argues that leaders generate a creative tension within their organisations because of their ability to define a new reality that has to be achieved. Brown concludes that the best leaders are multi-dimensional:

> *Being a constantly successful leader requires excellence in most, if not all, of the six dimensions of leadership. Ideally, leaders should be believable heroes, fine actors, high self-esteem immortalists, astute power-brokers, sensitive ambassadors and, on occasions, calculating victims. If this sounds difficult and demanding, then that is because being an effective leader in our contemporary world is a challenging business.*
>
> (Brown, 2000: 182)

One element that ties all of Brown's and Senge's roles together is power. Leaders generate and express their power through the roles they choose to play.

Power and Influence

If leaders cannot exist without followers, they cannot survive without power. Power is contextual, based on a mixture of beliefs and facts, and is never one-sided. Leaders use their power to influence others. Success is determined by:

☐ The degree of power they are able to exert
☐ The manner in which they exert it
☐ The timing.

As discussed in Chapter 2, power can be formal, informal and even imagined. The degree of power leaders hold will determine the options open to them. The application of limited power can have great influence, but only if the placement, timing and method of delivery are perfect. There are various types of power, particularly:

1. Resource power
2. Expert power

3. Position power
4. Personal power

1. Resource power

Sometimes referred to as reward power, this is the power derived from the possession of valuable resources and, as Handy observes, 'it is implicit in most calculative contracts' (Handy, 1993: 127). The resources themselves can take myriad forms, from the ability to grant status to the provision of training. Of course, resource power is only a reality when other people value the resources at the leader's disposal. However, when that is the case, it needs to be administered with sensitivity and care. Leaders who flaunt their power to reward are often unpopular. Most people do not like to be reminded of the fact that they can, effectively, be bought.

2. Expert power

Unlike resource power, expert power tends to be more willingly acknowledged and admired. For most people, the easiest influence to accept is that coming from an expert. One possible reason for this is that, in one sense, the power of the expert is given by those who are influenced. Although it is possible to be an unknown expert in a particular field, it is not possible to wield influence until that expertise is recognised by others. The expert, therefore, is relatively powerless, in terms of his/her ability to influence, until he/she is rewarded with public recognition.

How are experts identified? Experts are recognised in different ways and at different levels because expertise is comparative. In its most simple form, people with a greater knowledge of an important topic than anyone else in their environment are acknowledged as the experts. If everyone recognises this difference, these people are given a degree of power. However, should other individuals arrive on the scene with even more knowledge, the mantle will be transferred and the power balance will shift.

3. Position power

This is the power that comes automatically with a particular title or position. It is power that belongs to a role rather than an individual. When the current CEO moves on, his/her replacement will assume the power commensurate with the position. While position power is dependent on resource power and other forms of organisational support and recognition, it does bring with it control over a number of important assets such as:

☐ Information
☐ Access to various networks
☐ The right to organise systems, environments, communication channels, etc.

Leaders who make the most of position power invariably do so through their ability to control these less obvious power sources.

4. Personal power

This is the unmistakable, but undefinable, charisma that some people possess. It is a power unique to certain individuals, although it can be enhanced by expert status or the holding of a particular position or role. As with expert power, personal power exists only when it is recognised by others and so it brings with it a degree of fragility, a dependence on those who are being influenced.

As discussed at the beginning of this book, a different form of personal power is that which comes from a lifelong commitment to learning, a willingness to garner new experiences, develop new skills and challenge existing mindsets. Not everyone can possess the charisma demonstrated by some great leaders. Indeed, not everyone can become a leader – but the personal power that comes from striving to achieve one's potential is available to all.

The use of power

All forms of power can be used positively or negatively. Each type of power has an agreed purpose, or legitimacy, and agreed physical, psychological and sociological boundaries within which to operate. If applied beyond those boundaries, or if used to damage, distort or delay legitimate processes, it becomes negative power.

Everyone in an organisation has a degree of power. It follows, therefore, that everyone has the capability to exercise that power negatively. This occurs most often during times of low morale, uncertainty or disenchantment. Leaders aiming to limit displays of negative power by their subordinates can do so by creating successful organisations that incorporate effective systems of communication, valued reward structures and clear opportunities for personal and professional growth.

Activity 4.10   Identify leaders who have great: resource power; expert power; position power; and personal power.

Think of a leader you have observed at first hand. What power sources did he/she have? How did he/she demonstrate that power?

Influence

Power of any kind enables one person to influence another. The manner in which this is done and the reasons for doing so determine whether that power is being used positively or negatively. 'Push' strategies are those which influence people through the imposition, or threatened imposition, of costs. 'Pull' strategies are those which offer rewards. More specifically, people with power can influence others by:

☐ Negotiation
☐ Persuasion

☐ Force
☐ Personal magnetism.

They can create changes to:

☐ The environment
☐ Rules and procedures
☐ Goals and targets.

The type of power a person holds determines the ways they exert influence. For example, only people with great physical power or skills and/or substantial resources have the capability to apply force.

Activity 4.11   Which power sources support the following?

☐ Negotiation
☐ Persuasion
☐ Environmental changes
☐ Changes to rules and procedures.

Negotiation
This will be examined more fully in Chapter 7. Negotiation, or bargaining, depends upon the parties involved having resources that are valued by the other parties. The process can be either formal or informal, and centres upon the notion of rewards and costs.

Persuasion
Persuasion is rarely a matter of logic and factual argument. Expert, position and resource power, along with an emotional appeal, can all play a part in enabling one person to persuade another. Even leaders who make a genuine attempt to persuade purely by the validity of their argument risk compliance because of their position and associated power.

Personal magnetism
Charisma can be an influencing factor but people are more often influenced by someone they trust and respect. Individuals who establish trusting relationships and demonstrate, and create, empathy (see Chapter 2) are more likely to influence others than a purely charismatic figure.

The environment
Organisations are made up of three interrelated environments:

☐ Physical
☐ Psychological
☐ Sociological.

These environments affect, and are in turn affected by, everyone within them. Leaders can influence these environments by:

☐ Ensuring physical safety
☐ Providing a variety of stimuli and reducing monotony
☐ Minimising isolation
☐ Setting stimulating, challenging but achievable targets
☐ Encouraging a sense of ownership.

Activity 4.12   Under the following headings, identify three other ways leaders can positively influence each environment: physical; psychological; sociological.

The size and geographical spread of an organisation increases the challenges and issues facing a leader wanting to influence environments. Indeed, attitudes towards the environment, people's relationship with it and ability to influence, or be influenced by, it vary markedly from culture to culture (see Chapter 8).

Leadership qualities

We began this chapter by considering trait theories and the difficulties associated with them. However, the work of Goleman (1996) and Dulewicz and Higgs (1999) on emotional intelligence provides a new and useful approach to defining and developing leadership qualities. Consider, for example, the seven elements of Emotional Intelligence:

☐ Self-awareness
☐ Emotional resilience
☐ Motivation
☐ Interpersonal sensitivity
☐ Influence
☐ Decisiveness
☐ Conscientiousness and integrity.

How effective would leaders be if they lacked expertise in these areas? Andrew Brown writes: 'The true multi-dimensional leader does not merely understand the different leadership roles, but accommodates them with maturity, wisdom, integrity and courage' (Brown, 2000: 190).

Maturity

This is not, according to Brown, biological maturity, although in some cultures seniority does come with age. Rather, it describes an intellectual and emotional state of being that enables one to view one's own accomplishments and abilities dispassionately, to avoid bias, prejudice or stereotyping, to have interpersonal sensitivity that is not influenced negatively by personal ego needs.

Wisdom

Wisdom could be recognised as the ability to make the most appropriate decisions based on the information available. It certainly requires an intuitive grasp of the situation. Leaders who are most likely to be regarded as wise are those who combine the maturity described above with curiosity, a willingness to learn, and the ability to see the big picture.

Integrity

One significant challenge facing leaders today is maintaining personal and organisational integrity in the face of ever-increasing competition and demands. As discussed in Chapters 1 and 2, people who have created a sense of rapport by aligning their beliefs, values, behaviours and environments, who are empathetic and demonstrate a high level of emotional intelligence, are most likely to maintain high levels of personal integrity. On an organisational level, integrity also requires synergy between the shared vision and corporate action. To misquote Trollope, leaders demonstrate integrity through their wisdom, maturity, resolution and determination to resist the 'temptation of power'.

Courage

Courage can be regarded as the glue that holds the other qualities together. Without the courage to act, to accept responsibility, to face up to challenges and critics, to speak the truth, to change and yet remain true to one's sense of personal identity, all else remains a theoretical exercise. Without courage, integrity wilts. Whatever their technical expertise and/or levels of interpersonal and strategic skills, leaders have to have a degree of courage that is at least commensurate with their role. Interestingly, courage is also a vital part of the '5I Creativity' model (see Chapter 5), and the relationship between leadership and creativity is highlighted by Warren Bennis in his work *On Becoming a Leader*: 'A leader is, by definition, an innovator. He does things other people haven't done or don't do. He does things in advance of other people. He makes new things. He makes old things new' (Bennis, 1998: 143).

Leadership : key points!

☐ Managers are not automatically leaders. Leaders demonstrate different skills and perspectives. For example, leaders:

☐ Think in the long term

☐ Create a shared vision

☐ Establish important links and networks

☐ Challenge the norm.

☐ Trait theories focus on identifying and understanding leadership qualities and skills. They can never be wholly accurate because no two leaders are identical.

☐ No single leadership style is best suited for every situation.

☐ Leaders with a flexible approach focus on managing three key variables:

☐ Themselves

☐ Their subordinates

☐ The situation

☐ and on meeting the needs of:

☐ The task

☐ The team

☐ The individuals involved.

☐ They achieve this, in part, by assuming appropriate roles and through the application of:

☐ Resource power

☐ Expert power

☐ Position power

☐ Personal power.

☐ Their purpose is to influence environments and people in pursuit of a common goal.

☐ Leaders need:

☐ Strategic and interpersonal skills

☐ The maturity and wisdom to make appropriate decisions

☐ Integrity to operate within agreed ethical boundaries

☐ The courage to act.

☐ Groups and teams

Talent wins games, but teamwork and intelligence win championships.

(Michael Jordan, 1994: 20)

Groups and teams are not necessarily the same. Edgar Schein defined a group as: 'A number of people who interact with one another, are psychologically aware of one another, and perceive themselves to be a group' (Schein, 1988). However, this does not make clear how often people need to meet together, or how many people there need to be, before a group is formed.

Activity 4.13   Using Schein's definition, what is the largest group you belong to? What is the smallest?
Identify exactly how people in these groups:

☐ Interact with each other
☐ Are psychologically aware of each other
☐ Regard themselves as a group.

Teams can be thought of as a special type of group. Teams are formed to undertake specific tasks and projects. Teams share:

☐ A common goal
☐ Collaboration
☐ Coordination of activities
☐ Regular interactions.

Teams are made up of a predetermined number of people – the right number for the task at hand. The relationships between the team members is built on trust and an awareness of, and respect for, each other's abilities. These abilities dovetail, and members recognise this. There is, as the cliché reminds us, no 'I' in team, and team members demonstrate this by putting the team's needs ahead of personal requirements.

Activity 4.14   What is the largest team you belong to? What is the smallest?
Identify the specific tasks each team performs. Identify the common goal(s).

The nature of organisational groups and teams

It is almost impossible to work in an organisation and not belong to a number of groups and/or teams. To put it another way:

☐ Personal and professional development is helped or hindered by one's ability to operate as a group/team member and the group/team's ability to maximise potential and performance.
☐ Organisational effectiveness and efficiency is directly linked to the effectiveness and efficiency of the groups and teams within it.

Before we examine the different nature and purposes of groups and teams, one point needs to be made clear: *teams can fail!* They can fail to achieve agreed objectives. They can fail to meet deadlines. They can fail to meet individual as well as corporate needs. Not only can they fail, but through their failure they can create negative stress, damage relationships and set back career prospects.

Peter Senge asks the question: 'How can a team of committed managers with individual IQs above 120 have a collective IQ of 63?' (Senge, 1993: 9). The simple answer is because they can! Not surprisingly, therefore, teams under pressure can, and often do, fail spectacularly. Chris Argyris states: 'Most management teams break down under pressure. ...The team may function quite well with routine issues. But when they confront complex issues that may be embarrassing or threatening, the "teamness" goes to pot' (quoted in Senge, 1993: 24–5)

In the following pages we will explore not only what groups and teams do, how they are created, and what can make them effective, but also the blockages to success and learning.

Group classification

Groups can be divided into the following classifications:

☐ Primary
☐ Secondary
☐ Formal
☐ Informal.

Primary and Secondary groups

Primary groups are relatively small groups that meet and work together on a regular basis. The people involved share a clear group identity, often inventing a name or nickname for the group. Secondary groups are those that meet less regularly (a quarterly board meeting, for example) and comprise people who do not interact constantly.

Formal and Informal groups

Formal groups are deliberately created by organisations to meet expressed corporate goals or needs. Formal groups are therefore purpose-driven and are made up of individuals with specific titles, roles and responsibilities. Informal groups tend to form by themselves and reflect people's need to meet together and socialise. They can incorporate people who also meet together formally, but in the informal setting roles change and, consequently, individuals instinctively feel a member of one group more than the other. Informal groups can have as much influence within organisations as their formal counterparts. Managers need to understand the norms that exist within them, their methods of communication and their leaders.

Activity 4.15   Identify one informal group within an organisation with which you are/have been associated. How does the informal group meet, communicate and behave? What is its level of influence within the organisation? How is this manifested?

Whether groups are primary or secondary, formal or informal, they always influence the ways individuals behave.

The Hawthorne experiments

These experiments, conducted in the 1920s by a team of researchers led by Elton Mayo, were responsible for much subsequent interest in group dynamics. Two main experiments were carried out.

In the first experiment a group of six women were taken from their factory-line in a Relay Assembly Test Room and asked to work around a table. The initial purpose of the experiment was to discover if changes in lighting would affect their productivity. Consequently, as the women worked, the intensity of the light was progressively increased. With each increase, the women were asked how they felt about the new level. They reacted positively at each stage and their productivity increased. However, when the level of lighting was reduced back to the original factory level, the women continued to improve their productivity.

A new experiment was carried out, in which the women were given more breaks and a lunchtime meal. They were also given a group bonus and varied start and finish times. After each change, the women were again consulted and again their productivity rose. When the conditions were eventually returned to the way they had been prior to the experiment, the women continued to break productivity records.

Analysis revealed that the primary reasons for the increase in productivity were not the changes made during the experiment, but the fact that the women:

☐ Felt part of a special group
☐ Felt special and important
☐ Formed good relationships with each other and with the researchers/supervisors.

In order to test the hypothesis that motivation, productivity levels and quality of work were influenced by relationships among group members, and between workers and their manager/boss, a new group was selected and observed in a second experiment. This consisted of 14 men in the Bank Wiring Room who had divided themselves into two separate groups. The group that worked at the front of the room thought themselves to be of a higher status than the group at the back. It was observed that the men had established their own group norms and rules, which did not always tie in with those of the company. Individuals who ignored these boundaries were ostracised, and so a uniformity of behaviour and results was encouraged. Individual productivity, it was discovered, was influenced more by social membership of a group than by innate ability.

The conclusion

The Hawthorne experiments have been criticised and the results are open to various interpretations. However, they were successful in generating debate about the importance of groups, leaders and motivation within the workplace. Two important lessons have been drawn from the experiments:

1. Informal, as well as formal, groups not only influence individual behaviour, but the quality and nature of the relationships and social interaction

among group members impacts significantly on personal and whole-group performance.

2. Groups are made up of individuals who have their own purposes for belonging. These include:

☐ Social needs
☐ Establishing an identity
☐ Gaining help and support
☐ Sharing a common activity.

The purposes of teams

As we have already discussed, teams serve organisational and personal purposes. Organisational purposes include:

☐ Distribution and management of work
☐ Problem-solving
☐ Decision-making
☐ Coordination and liaison
☐ Information processing
☐ Conflict resolution
☐ Increasing commitment and involvement.

Although some of these activities can be combined, for teams to satisfy organisational needs they need to focus on specific functions. Teams operate differently, and need to be managed differently, according to their function, which is why significant problems can arise when a team is required to perform two different functions. This is not to say that the same people cannot belong to different teams; they simply need to ensure that the different groups have different titles, methods of operating, environments, etc.

Activity 4.16 What are the organisational purposes of a formal group you belong to? How successful is the group in achieving its purpose? How is success measured? What is your individual purpose for belonging to the group?

Team effectiveness

Teams operate at two levels: task and social processes. An effective team is one that operates well on both levels. The factors that influence the effectiveness of teams are:

1. Contextual.
2. Internal.

1. Contextual factors

The three contextual factors we will consider are:

- ☐ Team size and composition
- ☐ The task
- ☐ The environment.

Team size and composition

Team size is influenced by the nature of the task the team has to perform. Theoretically, the larger the team, the more skills, knowledge and experience are contained within it. However, large teams limit personal opportunities and, when the team exceeds ten people, sub-groups tend to form.

Managers who are creating a new team, or who are evaluating the effectiveness of an existing team, need to consider not only the best size, but also the best composition. Essentially, teams can be either homogeneous or heterogeneous. Homogeneous teams are characterised by:

- ☐ Shared beliefs and values
- ☐ Minimal conflict
- ☐ High personal satisfaction
- ☐ A need for conformity
- ☐ Limited creativity.

Heterogeneous teams exhibit:

- ☐ A wide range of views
- ☐ Greater conflict
- ☐ Increased creativity.

When determining the make-up of a team, managers need to answer two questions: What is the purpose of the team? And which team type is more likely to make decisions that will be accepted throughout the organisation? The answers may not always match. For example, a heterogeneous team would be the obvious choice if the purpose was creative problem-solving. However, the same team might face great difficulties 'selling' their solution to an organisation that values traditional approaches and limited risk-taking. Teams which do not represent the culture of the organisation can be isolated and find the results of their work challenged, while homogeneous teams can lack the necessary variety and group dynamics that are required for certain tasks.

The task

The principles for setting a team task are essentially no different from those discussed in Chapter 3. The task needs:

- ☐ To be well defined
- ☐ To be realistic

☐ To be acknowledged as important
☐ To present the right degree of challenge
☐ To be time-scaled appropriately.

The environment

Teams that are made up of the right mix of individuals and are given appropriate tasks invariably struggle if the environmental conditions are not supportive. For teams to be effective, managers need to ensure they have:

☐ Adequate and easy access to necessary resources
☐ Wide recognition
☐ Status
☐ Knowledge that their decisions will be acted upon.

2. Internal factors

The primary internal factors that influence team effectiveness are:

☐ Leadership style
☐ Motivation
☐ Group development
☐ Social functions
☐ Interaction.

For information regarding leadership style and motivation, review the first part of this chapter and Chapter 1 respectively.

Team development

Once formed, teams go through an evolutionary process that transforms them from a collection of individuals into a single, efficient unit with a shared and valued identity. The behaviour of the people within the team, the issues and problems they face, and the team's overall effectiveness, are determined to a great extent by the team's stage in this developmental process. The ability to recognise and understand these stages enables both managers and team members to limit conflict within the team by acknowledging the natural inevitability of their situation, and to create situations and apply strategies to speed up the team's transition. Barry Tuckman identified and labelled four stages of team development:

1. Forming.
2. Storming.
3. Norming.
4. Performing.

1. Forming

When the team first meets, members focus on finding out about each other's experiences, characteristics, skills, attitudes and expectations. At this stage preliminary hierarchies are established and tested, initial roles are tried out, and tentative relationships formed. The first individual tasks are also assigned, and rewards and privileges are agreed. In the forming stage, people tend to come together with a mixture of optimism and caution.

2. Storming

After the formation of the team, the results of the initial structures, relationships and tasks become clear. Individual performances do not always meet expectations, weaknesses begin to show, and disagreements can arise. This 'storm' necessitates adjustments to the original agreements and procedures; the hierarchy and methods of control may be altered and relationships reviewed.

Storming is a natural, though not inevitable, part of team development. Teams can become extremely effective without ever experiencing these difficulties, but those that do need to accept them as a common part of the process.

3. Norming

Teams that experience a 'storm' of conflict either quickly develop strategies for overcoming it or are motivated to do so by a rapidly approaching deadline. When the storming phase is passed, the team decides upon the rules and norms most suited to its organisational and individual purposes and needs. Relationships within the team are now developing, and people share a commitment to an agreed way of working together. Outsiders would see an obvious level of cooperation between team members.

4. Performing

This is the final stage, in which the team is operating as an efficient unit. Roles, relationships, procedures, style and privileges are agreed and understood by all. The focus is now only on achieving the set objectives.

Two other stages have also been suggested. These are:

☐ Dorming
☐ Adjourning.

Dorming

Dorming occurs when a team feels pressured to conform. Such pressure, applied by any source with more power than the team, forces the team to suppress its dissent or feign agreement.

Adjourning

Teams that meet only to accomplish a specific task – a project management team, for example – are required to adjourn once that task is accomplished. If the team is brought back together at some point in the future, the original stages of development may be experienced anew.

Activity 4.17   Think of a newly formed team you were a part of. How did the team demonstrate each of the stages described above? What happened to enable the preliminary stages to be worked through?

Make a list of comments and behaviours you would associate with each stage. List tactics and strategies you would employ as a leader to enable a team's safe and speedy transition through each stage.

Social processes

The extent to which a team successfully manages a variety of social processes, sometimes referred to as maintenance functions, also influences its overall effectiveness. The most obvious social processes are:

- ☐ Involving and controlling
- ☐ Supporting and responding
- ☐ Managing conflict
- ☐ Providing positive feedback
- ☐ Acknowledging feelings
- ☐ Creating a safe, supportive, inspiring physical environment.

As this list suggests, to be an effective team member means not only having an appropriate level of professional and technical expertise, but also well developed personal and interpersonal skills.

Interaction

Teams that do not communicate effectively are unlikely to perform effectively, although in teams that constantly perform to a high standard, members often need minimal communication because they already know what needs to be done, how best to do it, and what the others in the team are doing. Communication is perhaps the most important element in team-working. As a general rule, the responsibility for ensuring effective patterns of communication within the team lies with the leader, who needs to take into consideration such factors as team size, time scale, the nature of the task and individuals' attitudes and levels of expertise.

Team problems

As previously stated, teams do not always perform well. Indeed, the assertion that 'a camel is a horse designed by a committee' reflects a widely-held view about the inherent pitfalls in creating specific teams. The most common problems teams face are:

1. Team anxiety
2. Team-think
3. Hidden agendas.

1. Team anxiety

Effective teams perform at levels greater than the sum total of their parts. On these occasions individuals do more than simply pool their skills – they inspire each other. However, teams are potential breeding grounds for more than just inspiration. Anxiety and doubt can also spread throughout a team, damaging communication, cohesiveness and performance. While, in theory, individuals working alone would appear more vulnerable to feelings of anxiety, people in close-knit teams are often easily influenced by the concerns and doubts of other team members. In such situations, the ability to pace and lead (see Chapter 2) provides a useful means of defusing, rather than accentuating, the problem.

Activity 4.18   Imagine you are the manager of a successful sports team. As the result of rumours about possibly damaging legal action between current and ex-members of the board, the players are distracted and lose two games in a row. Team anxiety is apparent. Some players begin to wonder if they are about to go through a 'bad spell'. Others are heard to say that this 'might not be their season'. What strategies would you employ to minimise and then end this outbreak of team anxiety?

---

2. Team-think

Team-think describes the potential for teams to misread a situation and agree to a decision that is wholly inappropriate, without realising their mistake. It is most likely to occur when loyalty to the team takes precedence over individual conscience, when conflict and open expression of disagreement are strongly discouraged in favour of harmony and apparent high morale. Teams suffering from team-think tend to look at few options, are blind to risks inherent in their preferred response, and are slow to change even when the signs are that their strategy is not working. Irving Janis (1972) identified eight symptoms of team-think:

☐ A sense of invulnerability
☐ Quick rationalisations to explain evidence contrary to the group view
☐ A lack of moral and ethical awareness
☐ A willingness to stereotype those outside the group, particularly those who oppose the group's decisions
☐ The application of swift, if subtle, pressure on anyone who voices doubt
☐ A refusal to discuss personal feelings or concerns with anyone outside the group

☐ A refusal to consider alternate views once a decision has been made

☐ A keenness to apply the rule of collective responsibility to subdue dissenters.

To this list could be added one further symptom that is often demonstrated by senior and middle management teams:

☐ A desire to keep information 'within our group'.

Activity 4.19 As an external consultant brought in to help revitalise the flagging fortunes of a small textiles company, you realise that the six members of the board, who have all been in post for many years, are suffering from team-think. How would you resolve this? What recommendations would you make?

---

3. Hidden agendas

To be effective, teams have to satisfy individual purposes and needs. For this to happen, individual goals and aspirations have to be shared. Whatever communication pattern operates within a group, the communication itself needs to be congruent; messages need to reflect accurately what the messenger is thinking and/or feeling. If a mismatch occurs, if, for example, a person lacks the skills to be congruent or, on a more sinister note, if personal interests take over from team loyalty and a hidden agenda comes into play, the value of communication is undermined and team performance can suffer. Hidden agendas can cause gradual, long-term damage and, when revealed, can result in the breakdown of relationships or, in the worst-case scenario, team anxiety as people begin secretly to question the motives of everyone around them.

The leader as team builder

First, leaders need to understand the demands of the task or project. This enables them to focus on bringing together people with the right mixture of technical and interpersonal skills and experience. As a general principle, it is useful to ensure that there is one person in the group with a clear task orientation balanced by one more focused on social maintenance processes.

Activity 4.20 As a team leader how can you ensure that individuals are not following a hidden agenda? Complete the list below by identifying other behaviours that can impact negatively on group performance.
1. Restricting information.
2. Lying.
3. Conflicts within the team.
4.
5.
6.

The research carried out by Meredith Belbin (1986) and colleagues at Henley Management College enables leaders to move beyond a general principle and be far more specific in their selection of people to play particular team roles (see Table 4.1).

Table 4.1 Belbin's team roles.

Type	Typical features	Positive qualities	Allowable weaknesses
Implementer	Conservative, predictable	Organising abilities, hard-working, self-discipline	Inflexibility, unresponsive to new ideas
Coordinator	Calm, self-confident, controlled	Objectives driven, treats and welcomes all contributors without prejudice	Average intellect and creativity
Shaper	Highly strung, outgoing, dynamic	Challenges inertia, ineffectiveness or complacency	Provocative, impatient
Plant	Individualistic, serious-minded, unorthodox	Genius, imaginative, knowledgeable, intellectual	Disregards practical details or protocol
Resource investigator	Extrovert, curious, enthusiastic, communicative	Contacting people, exploring new possibilities, responsive to challenges	Low attention span
Monitor–Evaluator	Sober, unemotional, prudent	Discretion, judgement, hard-headed	Lacks inspiration, or the ability to motivate others
Team worker	Socially orientated, sensitive, mild	Promotes team spirit, responds responds well to people	Indecisive in a crisis
Completer–Finisher	Conscientious, orderly, anxious	Perfectionism	Reluctance to 'let go', worry
Specialist	Single-minded	Dedicated, supplies important knowledge and/or skills	Narrow focus, ignores the bigger picture

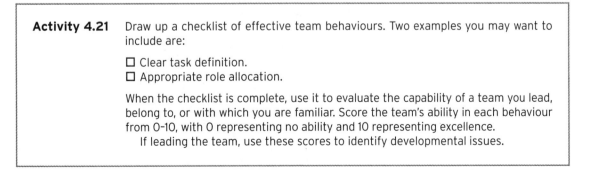

Activity 4.21 Draw up a checklist of effective team behaviours. Two examples you may want to include are:

☐ Clear task definition.
☐ Appropriate role allocation.

When the checklist is complete, use it to evaluate the capability of a team you lead, belong to, or with which you are familiar. Score the team's ability in each behaviour from 0–10, with 0 representing no ability and 10 representing excellence.

If leading the team, use these scores to identify developmental issues.

Secondly, leaders need to have a clear idea of how an effective team interacts and performs. With a checklist of behaviours drawn up, the leader has a focus for team development and for monitoring and measuring performance.

Thirdly, leaders have to develop trust within the team and between the team and leader. Two ways of achieving this are to:

☐ Encourage and ensure open communication
☐ Give team members discretion.

Open communication starts with the leader. In effect, the leader has to set the example. For a leader to expect openness from team members he/she first has to be open with the team. This means, to some extent, sharing potentially sensitive information and trusting the team to handle it appropriately. Giving team members a high level of discretion calls for a good deal of courage and awareness on the part of the leader. Once trust has been established, it is then possible to involve the team in identifying its own developmental issues and in determining the distribution of work.

Fourthly, leaders have to be alert to potential conflicts within the team, to understand and recognise the difference between conflict and creative tension, and have the skills and strategies for managing this (see Chapter 3).

Fifthly, leaders have to be able to manage those unexpected problems and crises which originate outside the team. To do this, leaders may need any or all of the following:

☐ Emotional stability
☐ An extensive, support network
☐ Access to additional resources
☐ The ability to motivate the team to face new challenges
☐ The ability to create learning situations out of crises.

The concept of team learning is addressed by Peter Senge in *The Fifth Discipline* (1993), in which he distinguishes between 'discussion' and 'dialogue'. Senge writes:

> the word 'discussion' has the same root as percussion and concussion. It suggests something like a 'Ping-Pong game where we are hitting the ball back and forth between us'. ... Clearly, this can be useful, but the purpose of a game is normally 'to win' and in this case winning means to have one's views accepted by the group.
>
> By contrast with discussion, the word 'dialogue' comes from the Greek dialogos. ... Bohm suggests that the original meaning of dialogue was the 'meaning passing or moving through ... a free flow of meaning between people, in the sense of a stream that flows between two banks.'
>
> **(Senge, 1993: 240))**

To achieve this sharing of meaning in the search for a greater understanding, teams need to:

☐ Suspend individual and/or shared assumptions (Chapter 9)
☐ Regard each other as colleagues
☐ Make use of a facilitator to maintain the context of the discussion.

Finally, and perhaps most important of all, leaders need to understand that *elite teams have elite cultures*. These are built upon:

☐ Positive and powerful shared beliefs and values
☐ A strong sense of team identity
☐ A strong sense of belonging and purpose
☐ Shared vision
☐ Clearly established group norms
☐ The use of symbols
☐ The sharing of stories about past or present team members and team successes
☐ A sense of elitism: a determination to be the best, reflected in rigorous entrance requirements and tests, and ongoing, demanding training.

One way leaders can lay the foundation for an elite team is by using the VROOM approach, in which team members are encouraged to focus on five essential factors:

1. *Values.* The team explores and understands what each member needs from his/her membership, the values it holds and how these can be met.
2. *Rapport.* People learn about each other's individual styles and skills.
3. *Outcomes.* The team clarifies and agrees key result areas.
4. *Outcomes.* The team then determines the most appropriate ways of measuring performance.
5. *Metamessages.* The team explores and agrees the key beliefs held regarding its purpose and the ways in which it will, and will not, behave.

Finally, elite teams present a carefully managed team image. Impression management, as discussed in Chapter 1, is as important for teams as it is for individuals.

Activity 4.22 Identify five ways in which teams can present a cohesive team image.

Groups and teams: key points!

- ☐ Groups are made up of people who:
  - ☐ Interact formally or informally
  - ☐ Are psychologically aware of each other
  - ☐ Regard themselves as a group.
- ☐ Teams are special groups.
- ☐ Teams serve organisational and individual purposes.
- ☐ Organisational purposes include:
  - ☐ Distribution of work
  - ☐ Problem-solving
  - ☐ Decision-making.
- ☐ Individual purposes include:
  - ☐ Social needs
  - ☐ Help and support
  - ☐ Establishing an identity.
- ☐ For teams to be effective, they have to operate well at two levels:
  - ☐ Task
  - ☐ Social processes.
- ☐ The factors that influence team effectiveness are:
  - ☐ Group size and composition
  - ☐ The task
  - ☐ The environment.
- ☐ Homogeneous groups and teams are characterised by:
  - ☐ Shared beliefs
  - ☐ Minimal conflict
  - ☐ Limited creativity.
- ☐ Heterogeneous groups and teams exhibit:
  - ☐ A wide range of views
  - ☐ Greater conflict
  - ☐ Increased creativity.
- ☐ Team development encompasses four stages:
  - ☐ Forming
  - ☐ Storming
  - ☐ Norming
  - ☐ Performing.
- ☐ The most common problems teams face are:
  - ☐ Team anxiety
  - ☐ Team-think
  - ☐ Hidden agendas.
- ☐ Leaders play a significant role in creating elite teams.

☐ Leaders must ensure that the team:
  ☐ Understands the task
  ☐ Is made up of the 'best' people in their 'best' roles
  ☐ Has appropriate resources
  ☐ Uses the most appropriate communication pattern, and gets the balance right between discussion and dialogue
  ☐ Has trust
  ☐ Can learn from all experiences
  ☐ Has a powerful culture.
☐ Creating effective groups and/or elite teams is a significant leadership challenge.
☐ Teams can fail!

Summary: leading and working in groups and teams

☐ Successful leadership and teamwork is founded upon:
  ☐ An understanding of the differences between leaders and managers
  ☐ The recognition and appropriate use of different leadership roles, styles and associated power
  ☐ An understanding of the differences between groups and teams
  ☐ A knowledge of appropriate team composition
  ☐ The creation of an elite culture and a shared vision.
☐ The core skills are those associated with:
  ☐ Management of self and self-image
  ☐ Managing one-to-one relationships
  ☐ Developing others
  ☐ Interpersonal sensitivity
  ☐ The management of power
  ☐ Communication and role-playing.
☐ The aim is to create and/or lead the most effective teams.

A final thought

Actually, three final thoughts. We'll begin with our perception that leaders, like artists, are ultimately measured by their ability to influence others. For that reason, leadership can be regarded as: 'Inspiration in action'.

Now we'll stand gratefully on the shoulders of two giants. First, Warren Bennis who wrote: 'To an extent, leadership is like beauty; it's hard to define, but you know it when you see it' (Bennis, 1998: 1). The very final thought, however, belongs to the incomparable Michael Jordan, who summarises the challenge, excitement and potential loneliness of leadership when he says, quite simply: 'A leader can't make excuses. There has to be quality in everything you do' (Jordan, 1994: 34).

References

Adair, J. and Thomas, N. 1998. *The John Adair Handbook of Management and Leadership*. London: Thorogood.

Belbin, M. 1986. *Management Teams*. London: Heinemann.

Bennis, W. 1998. *On Becoming a Leader*. London: Arrow Books.

Bennis, W. and Nanus, B. 1985. *Leaders: the Strategies for Taking Charge*. New York: Harper & Row.

Blake, R.R. and Mouton, J.S. 1964. *The Managerial Grid III*. London: Gulf Publishing Company.

Brown, A. 2000. *The 6 Dimensions of Leadership*. London: Random House.

Certo, S.C. 1994. *Modern Management*. Boston: Allyn and Bacon.

De Pree, M. 1989. *Leadership is an Art*. London: Arrow Books.

Dulewicz, V. and Higgs, M. 1999. 'Can Emotional Intelligence be measured and developed?', *Leadership and Organisational Journal*, 20(5).

Goleman, D. 1996. *Emotional Intelligence*. London: Bloomsbury.

Handy, C. 1993. *Understanding Organizations*. Harmondsworth: Penguin Books.

Janis, I.L. 1972. *Victims of Groupthink*. Boston: Houghton Mifflin.

Jordan, M. 1994. *I Can't Accept Not Trying*. New York: HarperCollins.

Kotter, J.P. 1988. *The Leadership Factor*. New York: Free Press.

Packard, V. 1957. *The Hidden Persuaders*. Montreal: Pocket Books of Canada.

Reddin, W.J. 1970. *Managerial Effectiveness*. New York: McGraw-Hill.

Schein, E. 1988. *Organizational Psychology* (3rd edn). Englewood Cliffs, NJ: Prentice-Hall.

Senge, P. 1993. *The Fifth Discipline*. London: Century Business.

Sondhi, R. 1999. *Total Strategy*. Bury, Lancashire: Airworthy Publications.

Tannebaum, R. and Schmidt, W.H. 1973. 'How to choose a leadership pattern', *Harvard Business Review*, May/June.

Further reading

Brown, A. 2000. *The 6 Dimensions of Leadership*. London: Random House.

De Pree, M. 1989. *Leadership is an Art*. London: Arrow Books.

Bennis, W. and Nanus, B. 1985. *Leaders: the Strategies for Taking Charge*. New York: Harper & Row.

Bennis, W. 1998. *On Becoming a Leader*. London: Arrow Books.

Senge, P. 1993. *The Fifth Discipline*. London: Century Business.

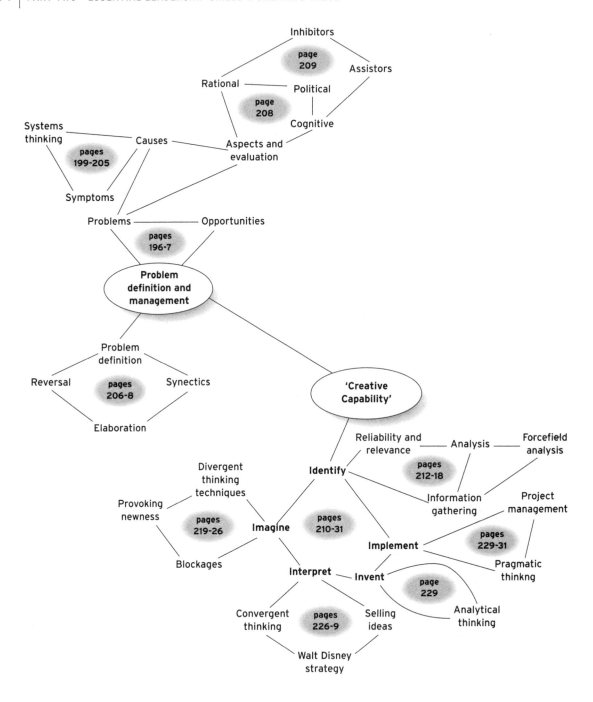

Creative Problem-Solving

A wise man will make more opportunities than he finds.

(Francis Bacon)

This chapter will develop your:

Awareness of:	Knowledge of:	Capability to:
The concept of helicopter vision.	The relationship between perception filters and problem definition.	Identify the root causes of problems.
The value of systemic thinking.	The relationship between problems and opportunities.	Identify the rational, cognitive and political dimensions of business problems. Identify problem assistors and inhibitors.
The concept of 'Creative Capability'.	The stages of the 'Creative Capability' process: ☐ Identify ☐ Imagine ☐ Interpret ☐ Invent ☐ Implement.	Collect, analyse and apply appropriate information. Distinguish between and apply a variety of thinking styles: ☐ Convergent ☐ Divergent ☐ Analytical ☐ Pragmatic. Create and 'sell' valuable new realities.
The relationship between creativity, learning and change.	The qualities of the creative individual, team and organisation.	Build and manage creative teams. Encourage and manage organisational change.

☐ Managing problems

Several groups of third-year Sports Science students recently gave presentations to a local entrepreneur. Their task was to recommend one way he could improve his business in the coming year. The students had worked hard, researched thoroughly and practised their presentation skills. The businessman was impressed by their effort and commitment. His only criticism, which he repeated several times, was, 'They are not thinking outside the box.' His observation was both accurate and important. Although some groups had been quite creative in the nature of their recommendation, none had fully explored all the weaknesses *and benefits* of their proposal. Overall, their work showed an understanding of much relevant theory, but little in the way of original thought and application.

In a rapidly changing world, managers who are leaders:

☐ Examine situations and problems from myriad perspectives
☐ Create and evaluate a multitude of possible options for growth
☐ Justify, recommend and sell the chosen idea to key stakeholders
☐ Ensure the implementation of that idea to agreed criteria.

The creative manager has a good understanding of him/herself and others and is a skilled communicator, capable of gaining trust, motivating his/her teams and presenting new ideas in a persuasive and compelling manner. Aware of the relationship between creativity, learning and personal and organisational change, he/she ensures the personal and professional development of colleagues, and the growth of a culture which thrives on uncertainty and is founded on a quest for continual improvement. The creative manager is at once a dreamer and a realist, who shares with Ralph Waldo Emerson the certainty that 'Imagination is not a talent of some, but is the health of all'. He/she is also aware that business and management problems need not automatically be viewed in a negative light. A problem may actually be positive in that it presents an opportunity that can be exploited. Secondly, problems do not reveal themselves. They are identified, interpreted and usually addressed by people within an organisation. How they are viewed is determined initially by the perception filters of those involved (see Chapter 2). These filters may include:

☐ Professional experience
☐ Beliefs about the organisation's ability to respond to the problem successfully
☐ Limited availability of information
☐ Organisational culture.

Once a situation is viewed purely as a problem, a negative mindset is likely to set in. At least some energy and time will then be spent on deciding whose fault the problem is, followed often by recrimination, denial and blame. As problems occur within an organisation, internal politics and the desire for self-preservation combine as individuals and/or teams struggle to avoid being blamed. This vicious circle plays no part in problem-solving and reflects a culture that fails to accept mistakes as part of the learning process (see Chapter 3). It is one reason why managers choose to deny, minimise or ignore problems.

By contrast, opportunities exist to be exploited. They create a more positive energy which managers can harness. Individuals and/or teams are usually keen to be acknowledged as the ones who identified, or created, a valuable opportunity. Other people within an organisation usually welcome the chance to become involved in taking advantage of it. In short:

☐ Problems constrain
☐ Opportunities motivate.

It is important, however, that managers who focus on opportunities rather than problems are seen to be realistic. A positive approach that fails to acknowledge certain key facts is unlikely to inspire optimism and support. Telling a man dying of thirst that the glass of water you are offering is half full, rather than half empty, is unlikely to change his perception or improve his plight.

Activity 5.1   Make a commitment to reframe the way you view problems. Approach them by using (and completing) the sentence: 'In this situation, the opportunities that are open to me, or that I can create, are ...'

Later in this chapter, the technique known as 'mind mapping' will be discussed. You can use this technique as one way of identifying these opportunities. Before that, however, consider the following situation:

In Nottinghamshire, the number of private health clubs increased by 50 per cent in a ten-year period. During the same time many other leisure facilities, including cinemas, restaurants, bowling alleys and an ice rink, were also built or improved. The problem for the owner of an established health club is a dramatic increase in direct and indirect competition, and a consequent increase in buyer and supplier power.

What opportunities exist?

Causes and symptoms

Managers need to distinguish the root cause of the problem they experience from the myriad symptoms that surround and reflect it. A manager wanting to benchmark a professional highly skilled at identifying the root cause of a problem should observe a good osteopath at work. Consider the following conversation recorded as an osteopath, Marianne, plied her trade:

Marianne: Tell me, Peter, what seems to be the problem?
Peter: I've injured my leg. I'm suffering from pains all the way down it and pins and needles in my foot.
Marianne: When did you first notice the problem?
Peter: At the weekend I did some heavy gardening. I noticed a bit of stiffness in my lower back after a couple of hours digging. That actually got worse over the next few days.
Marianne: Did you do anything to solve the problem?

Peter: I just rested. It did the trick. Although as my back got better, the pain started in my leg. Now my back's fine, but I'm in agony with my leg!
Marianne: I see. Time, I think, for me to take a look at it...

The subsequent examination led Marianne away from Peter's leg to his lower back. As an experienced healer, Marianne knew that, although most patients identify the point of their pain as the source of their problem, it is rarely the case. The body is a complex system. Damage that may go unnoticed to one part of the system can, over a period of time, manifest itself through referred pain and malfunction elsewhere. So it was with Peter. When digging in the garden, he had actually caused damage to his fifth lumbar vertebra. Although the pain had gone from his back, the problem had not. The swelling around his damaged disc was putting pressure on a nerve which, in turn, was causing the pain in his leg and foot. By correcting the injury to his spine, Marianne balanced Peter's structure and ended his pain.

This analogy applies directly to the manager's role within an organisation. Managers need to be business osteopaths. Organisations, like bodies, are complex systems made up of interrelating functions. Organisational problems are revealed through a variety of symptoms, for example:

☐ A drop in sales
☐ A failure to meet deadlines
☐ An inability to change rapidly to meet market needs.

To address these symptoms by increasing the sales team or offering additional incentives to complete on time or employing a new Human Resources manager is akin to placing an ice pack on a swollen knee when the cause of the problem is actually a displaced vertebra. Such responses may provide a short-term fix, but the effects of the problem, if left untreated, will worsen and spread until the system eventually breaks down completely. Managers, then, need to develop the ability to:

☐ See their organisation as a systemic whole
☐ Differentiate between cause and effects
☐ Simplify complexity
☐ Think and talk in terms of influencing factors and relationships
☐ Create and maintain a fully functioning, balanced system
☐ Create maximum effect with minimum effort.

In addition to the skills and attitudes detailed in the previous chapters, managers also need to demonstrate helicopter vision and systemic thinking.

Helicopter vision

This is the ability to establish a detached overview of a situation. Helicopter vision, also referred to later in this chapter as 'hawk' vision, enables a manager to observe dispassionately the interaction between the different elements of a system, and so to identify the causes of problems, areas of possible improvement and/or opportunities for growth. Helicopter vision is one example of the many paradoxes that challenge the creative manager who, in this case, has to switch from being passionate and involved to being dispassionate and detached. The ability to do this is discussed more fully later in this chapter under the heading 'Creative Capability' (see pp. 210–32).

Systems thinking

Peter Senge describes systems thinking and its relationship with complexity and change thus:

> Systems thinking is a discipline for seeing wholes. It is a framework for seeing interrelationships rather than things, for seeing patterns of change rather than static 'snapshots'. ... Today, systems thinking is needed more than ever because we are becoming overwhelmed by complexity. ... All around us are examples of 'systemic breakdowns' ... - problems that have no local cause. ... Complexity can easily undermine confidence and responsibility. ... Systems thinking is the antidote to this sense of helplessness. ... [It] is a discipline for seeing the 'structures' that underlie complex situations, and for discerning high from low leverage change. That is, by seeing wholes we learn how to foster health. To do so, systems thinking offers a language that begins by restructuring how we think.
>
> (Senge, 1993: 68-9)

The cornerstone of systems thinking, of understanding complexity and connectedness, is the application of *feedback loops*. Rather than attempting to break down complex systems into their component parts, the systemic thinker represents the system as a series of interrelated feedback loops, identifying the relationships that exist between the various elements and the direction and levels of influence.

The comic and singer, Mike Harding, once said, 'No man is an island, apart from Fred Madagascar.' The systemic equivalent is: 'Every part of a system influences every other, either directly or indirectly.' To ignore the systemic nature of organisations, in terms of both the organisations' internal functions and their interaction with external environments and influences, is to risk:

- ☐ Continual short-termism
- ☐ Costly, ineffective solutions
- ☐ Encouraging the language of blame
- ☐ Missing opportunities
- ☐ Organisational breakdown.

Systems thinking and language

The ways we structure our language influence the ways we think, which in turn influence the ways in which we perceive the world. The English language, with its linear structure, is used primarily by peoples who believe in and talk about:

☐ Direct, obvious and often close relationships between cause and effect (read newspaper headlines or listen to politicians' sound bites)
☐ Spiritual beliefs that traditionally focus on a linear transition from earthly existence to life on a spiritual plane (from Earth to heaven or hell, with perhaps a stop-off at purgatory *en route*)
☐ The linear progression of time (hence the urgency to 'be on time' and an acceptance of the principle that 'time is money')
☐ Individual ability to influence events, others and environments directly (consider the American dream).

Of course, this is not to imply value judgements about western media, politicians, religion or ideals.

By contrast, an Asian language (for example, Sanskrit), which is more circular in structure, was created by people who believed in and talked about:

☐ Indirect, subtle and often distant relationships between cause and effect (consider the belief in the law of karma, which states that the effects of one's actions may not be experienced until a following lifetime)
☐ Spiritual beliefs that focus on a circular relationship between physical and spiritual existence (reincarnation is a belief in the cycle of life, death and rebirth until one perfect life has been lived)
☐ A cyclic perception of time that lacks the urgency of immediateness generally felt in the West (see the above, or try persuading an Indian businessman in Delhi that your meeting absolutely has to begin at 10am as agreed!)
☐ A strong sense of society, and a need to co-exist within nature rather than trying to control it (compare the Asian extended family concept to the western nuclear version).

The point here is that linear language structures encourage linear thought processes and a belief that cause and effect are often closely linked in both time and space, while more circular structures encourage systemic thought and a more willing acceptance of possible distance between cause and effect.

As an example of how linear thinking influences behaviour, consider the following statements made by two neighbours in dispute:

Mr Smith:
I am antagonistic towards Mr Jones because he plays his music far too loud. When I ask him to turn it down, he does the opposite. He is an uncaring anti-social neighbour, which is why I've reported him. He is responsible for the problem between us.

Mr Jones:
Mr Smith is a bully. He came banging on my door, shouting about the volume of my music, threatening me with all sorts if I didn't turn it down. I don't give in to bullies, so I turned my music up even louder. Mr Smith has caused this problem through his aggressive attitude.

Who is responsible for the situation? Both. Neither. It depends on your perspective. A systemic thinker would represent the situation using a feedback loop, taking away the language of blame in the process. (See Figure 5.1). Now

Figure 5.1
A feedback loop

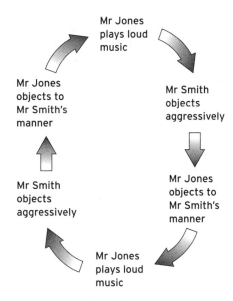

there is seen to be neither first cause nor final effect, but rather a series of interrelated elements each influencing the other, creating a self-perpetuating system. Once the situation is represented as a system, it becomes clear that each element is at once both cause *and* effect. A feedback loop can therefore be created by continually asking the questions:

☐ What is this element influenced by (directly and indirectly)?
☐ What does this element influence (directly and indirectly)?
☐ What is the significance of this element?
☐ Can these elements be combined or simplified?

This, in its most simple form, is the language of systems thinking.

Feedback loops show circles of influence and are continuous. Linear systems have a beginning and end. Feedback loops acknowledge the complexity of situations and environments, and help identify points of maximum leverage. Linear systems attempt to simplify complexity by identifying the supposed definite cause and rushing towards the most obvious answer.

Activity 5.2   Think of any event you have experienced in the last two days. Can you say with absolute certainty what the single cause of it was? Use a feedback loop to draw the system that the event was actually one part of. How does that change the way you view and feel about the event?

Reinforcing and balancing feedback systems

Reinforcing feedback systems are those that promote growth, in which the system generates a momentum in a given direction. Reinforcing systems often demonstrate how a small change, which may otherwise go unnoticed, can build on itself until it becomes an obvious, often powerful, force. Reinforcing systems can also reflect a pattern of decline. They can be virtuous or vicious cycles. Imagine a schoolteacher consistently offering praise to a pupil who is rarely complimented or encouraged (see Figure 5.2), or a snowball rolling down a mountain, gradually turning into a destructive avalanche.

Figure 5.2
A reinforcing loop

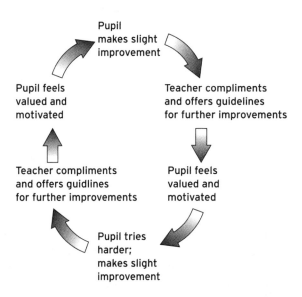

Activity 5.3   Draw a reinforcing feedback loop.

Balancing feedback systems operate whenever there is a specific goal to be achieved. Their purpose is determined by the goal and the stability created by achieving it. As discussed in Chapter 1, balanced performance is the hallmark of longevity. Failure to establish balance brings with it a price that is often unacceptable, which is why balancing systems seek to reduce the gap between what exists and what is desired. Nature is replete with balancing systems. When the human body becomes too hot, it sweats; when we feel hungry, we eat.

Organisations have myriad balancing systems. The difficulty in recognising and managing them all is that many organisational goals are implicit. If, for example, there is an unstated belief in the importance of tradition, attempts to create organisational change will be blocked and thwarted at every turn. No amount of staff training or consultancy will overcome this. The goal of those who value tradition will be to stay as they are or, at least, slow down the rate of change. Consequently, they will seek to balance the demand for change through inertia and a focus on the past. Once the situation is recognised for what it is – a balancing system in operation – the key influencing elements and the opposing goals become clear, and a strategy for change that focuses on the actual source of the resistance can be implemented.

As a general principle, when managers find themselves in a situation in which nothing *seems* to be happening no matter what strategies and initiatives they employ, there is a balancing system in operation. Figure 5.3 shows a balancing system in which the goal is to achieve a desired cash balance.

Figure 5.3
A balancing loop

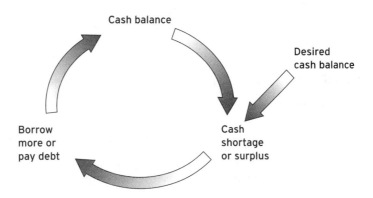

Cash balance

Desired cash balance

Borrow more or pay debt

Cash shortage or surplus

Activity 5.4   Draw a balancing feedback loop.

Delays

One of the highest leverage points for improving system performance is the minimalization of system delays.

(Ray Stata, quoted in Senge, 1993: 89)

Delays between actions and consequences are a natural part of most systems. Systemic thinkers identify all possible delays and minimise those they can. Misjudging the length and potential consequences of delays can be the cause of confusion and/or failure. Unrecognised delays can have devastating effects. When identifying systems, managers need to ask:

☐ Where do delays occur?
☐ What are their duration?

☐ What are they influenced by?
☐ Can they be avoided and/or minimised?
☐ What are the implications on the system of doing either of the above?
☐ What are the implications of doing *neither* of the above?

Figure 5.4 shows a balancing system with a delay, in which the goal is to achieve a desired bodyweight.

Figure 5.4
A balancing loop
with delay

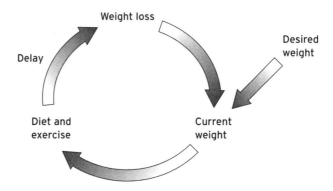

Activity 5.5   Draw a balancing or reinforcing feedback loop with a delay.

Systems thinking and elephants

Systems thinking encourages accurate and meaningful problem definition by enabling managers to see the whole picture. Consider the following story:

> *Three blind men grabbed hold of an elephant and gave their respective thoughts. 'It is a hollow pipe,' said the first, holding the trunk. 'No, it is a pillar,' said the second, feeling a leg. 'You are both wrong,' said the third. 'It is wide and rough, like a rug!'*

The moral for managers is: *You cannot understand the truth of a situation, the causes of a problem for example, unless you understand the system it is a part of.* This does not mean that every situation has to be studied within the complete organisational context. Sometimes understanding the systems that operate within a specific function is sufficient. The trick is knowing which systems to understand and resisting the urge to compartmentalise. After all, if you cut an elephant in half, you do not get two smaller elephants.

A slump in sales

Earlier in this chapter we referred to a drop in sales as one example of an organisational problem. Faced with this problem, a manager with linear thought processes may determine the cause thus:

Sales slump -- Inadequate sales team
   (Problem)   (Cause)

His/her solution would therefore probably be to replace, or add to, the existing sales team. A systemic thinker would approach the problem differently. In order to determine the system, he/she may begin by asking the question: 'What are the key drivers of sales?'

Activity 5.6   Answer this question, by listing the elements that influence sales.

The next step would be to determine the relative level of influence each element has upon the system.

Activity 5.7   Rank the elements you have identified, placing the most influential at the top of the list.

With that done, the systemic manager would review his/her list to see if any of the elements can be combined, simplified or even ignored, given the nature of the particular problem.

Activity 5.8   Review your list. First of all, ask: 'Can I ignore any elements without limiting my capability to resolve this problem?' Then see if you can combine or simplify any of the remaining elements. Now rewrite what is probably a shorter list.

The next step would be to draw the feedback loop, incorporating the elements still in the list.

Activity 5.9   Draw the feedback loop. Begin with 'Sales' and work backwards, identifying the element that is, in your opinion, most influential - the key driver of sales. Repeat this process until the loop is complete.

    Is it a reinforcing loop or a balancing loop? Are there any delays within the system?

With the 'Sales' feedback loop complete and the relationships between the key elements and their respective levels of influence identified, the manager is now well placed to determine the root cause of the sales slump, and from there to define the problem in an accurate and useful way.

Problem definition

Problem definition is the next crucial step in creative problem-solving. For reasons discussed in other chapters – the role of perception filters, organisational culture, etc. – there is a tendency for people to define problems in ways with which they are comfortable and, often, experienced. Also, problems that are seen as new are far more challenging and potentially more stressful than those which bear some semblance to problems previously encountered and managed. Equally, problems that remain undefined often remain unresolved. The key for managers facing problems with which they are unfamiliar is to find ways of making them appear familiar and accessible. There are three techniques for doing this:

☐ Synectics
☐ Definition elaboration
☐ Definition reversal.

Synectics

Synectics is a popular creative problem-solving technique which has at its root the principle of applying what is known to that which is less known, or vice versa, with the aim of creating new insights. The process is as follows:

1. Define the problem (known).
2. Distort the definition using analogies or metaphors (unknown).
3. Analyse the distortion.
4. Apply the results of the analysis to the original problem.
5. Explore the new insights created.

Once the problem has been defined, the metaphor or analogy can be developed by asking questions such as:

☐ What does this problem/situation remind me of?
☐ How does it make me feel?
☐ What is it similar to?

The value of creating analogies or metaphors is that by analysing them managers are often able to identify aspects of the problem they might otherwise have missed. The most useful analogies include action/movement, are easy to visualise, are based on familiar events/situations, and compare things that are not obviously similar. Analogies can also be:

☐ Personal – people imagine themselves as the problem
☐ Direct – people apply facts and technology directly to the problem
☐ Symbolic – people represent the problem using symbols/images
☐ Fantasy – people begin by identifying their perfect solution.

After an inauspicious beginning, a newly formed international business team met for a two-day workshop to define and resolve the problem they faced.

The problem was defined as 'an inability to function effectively as a team'. One team member described the situation as 'trying to make square pegs fit into round holes'. This led to the development of a jigsaw metaphor, which led, in turn, to the issues associated with cross-cultural team-building being identified and explored through a consideration of how to make a perfect jigsaw. Using this metaphor as their focus, individuals began to acknowledge the professional and emotional difficulties they faced when trying to accept and adapt to the working styles and behaviours of team members from other countries. As one man said, 'I feel like I am being shaped to fit into the team, and I don't like the shape I'm being forced into.' The workshop was a success. The team took significant steps towards resolving their problem. Two interconnecting pieces of a jigsaw became their unofficial symbol.

Activity 5.10   Define a problem you currently face. Use the synectics approach to gain new insights into it.

Definition elaboration and reversal

Editors are excellent at seeing text from a number of perspectives other than the one presented by the writer. If a paragraph is not quite right, a good editor may ask:

☐ How will this work if it is reversed?
☐ How can this be stated differently?
☐ Is there anything else to say, or is there too much detail?

Depending on the problem with the text, any of the above can lead to a solution. Sometimes sentences do need simply reversing to make them effective. Sometimes the passage needs to be completely rewritten. Sometimes it is overwritten and needs to be streamlined.

These same questions can be applied to problem definitions to gain new perspectives and insights. There is often more than one perspective from which to view a problem. This means that there is often more than one appropriate definition of a problem. And this means that there is often more than one appropriate response/answer. Managers, of course, do not have to rely solely on their own ability to elaborate on problem definition. Different perspectives can often be gathered simply by asking colleagues how they see the problem, or by identifying and exploring any similar past experiences.

The ability to see two different perspectives simultaneously is referred to as Janusian thinking, after the two-headed Roman god Janus. As a general rule, the more adept an individual is at Janusian thinking, the more likely he/she is to:

☐ Identify and examine opposing viewpoints
☐ Engage in an original perspective

☐ Be inspired to explore beyond the generally accepted boundaries of a problem.

Einstein's realisation that apparently opposite states (motion and rest) can be present at the same time led to the development of his theory of relativity. We may not all develop solutions, theories or systems that change the world, but we can, within the context of our own personal and professional lives, create valuable new realities.

In summary, the first stage in the creative process is problem definition, because it guides and directs the creative journey. Given that, we aim to conclude this stage with a definition that begins with the words 'How to ...' By doing this, the definition shifts from a summary of the key issues to an explicit consideration of what needs to be done. Consider, for example, how the following simple definition would help focus and direct the manager and/or team responsible for it: '*How to* increase sales without changing, or adding to, any of our staff.'

Activity 5.11 Develop your understanding of the problem you defined in Activity 5.10 further by asking the questions:

☐ Is the reverse true?
☐ How do other people define it?
☐ Can it be stated differently?
☐ Is it similar to any past experience? If so, what can I learn from that?
☐ Do I have enough detail? Or is there too little or too much?

Now redefine the problem as a 'How to ...' statement.

Problem evaluation

Business problems have three aspects which need to be identified, understood and acted upon. These are:

1. *Rational.* The problem is viewed in a logical way, the focus being on a clinical evaluation of the economic effects of the problem and the organisation's capability to resolve it and exploit any opportunities it presents.
2. *Political.* The problem has to be understood and addressed within the context of the organisation as a whole, the focus being on understanding different internal perspectives, capabilities, relationships and agendas.
3. *Cognitive.* As discussed previously, every problem is viewed and translated through individuals' mental processes. A manager's cognitive style determines how he/she perceives each problem and the importance he/she subsequently places on it.

There is, of course, a degree of overlap between these three aspects, with both the rational and the political aspects being underpinned by the cognitive.

To further their understanding of a particular problem, managers need to be clear about:

☐ The organisation's current situation
☐ The organisation's goals
☐ The external and internal assistors
☐ The external and internal inhibitors.

This requires a strategic capability. In essence, an organisation's current position is determined by the extent to which it is matching its resources and capabilities to the demands of the environment – the degree of synergy between the industry's key success factors and the organisation's distinctive competencies. This is perhaps best summarised in a SWOT analysis, which is a summary of a detailed internal analysis of the organisation and a detailed external analysis of the industry and social environments.

Assistors are those factors that help the organisation to achieve its goals. Inhibitors are those factors that limit progress. As indicated, assistors and inhibitors exist within both the organisation and its environment. With assistors and inhibitors identified, managers need to determine:

☐ How the organisation can maximise internal assistors
☐ How the organisation can capitalise on external assistors
☐ Who is responsible for addressing internal inhibitors – and what should be done
☐ Appropriate organisational strategies for minimising or avoiding the effects of external inhibitors.

Activity 5.12   Consider an organisation you have some experience of. Using the following headings, identify key assistors and inhibitors.

	Internal	External
Assistors		
Inhibitors		

Techniques, models and issues associated with information gathering and analysis, and the creation and implementation of new ideas and solutions, will be explored in the next section of this chapter – 'Creative Capability'.

Managing problems: key points!

☐ Business and management problems can often be viewed as positive and lead to opportunities that can be exploited:
  ☐ Problems constrain
  ☐ Opportunities motivate.
☐ Problems cannot be resolved until their root cause is identified. Core skills are:
  ☐ Systems thinking
  ☐ Helicopter vision.
☐ Systemic thinkers focus on:
  ☐ Circles of causality
  ☐ The degrees and directions of influence exerted by the different aspects of the system.
☐ These are depicted through feedback loops. Basic feedback loops:
  ☐ Are reinforcing in nature
  ☐ Are balancing in nature
  ☐ Include delays.
☐ The key to defining and managing problems is to make the unfamiliar seem familiar and accessible. Techniques for doing this include:
  ☐ Synectics
  ☐ Problem elaboration
  ☐ Problem reversal.
☐ The three facets of a problem that need to be addressed are:
  ☐ Rational
  ☐ Political
  ☐ Cognitive.
☐ Problem assistors and inhibitors exist both with the organisation and its environment.

☐ Creative Capability

Creativity Capability refers to the process, and associated skills and attitudes, through which managers create valuable new realities. But valuable to whom? New products, processes or systems need to be of value to clients and stakeholders. The 5I Creativity wheel developed by Parker (see Figure 5.5) comprises five key elements:

☐ Identify
☐ Imagine
☐ Interpret
☐ Invent
☐ Implement.

Figure 5.5
The 5I Creativity
wheel

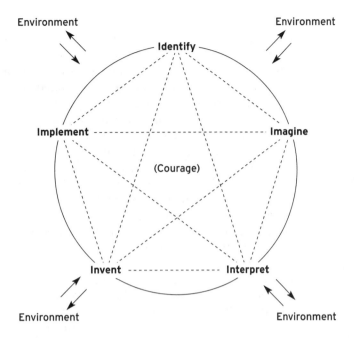

These are represented in the form of a loop to show that the process which we have termed 'Creative Capability' is continual, and circular and interactive. This loop is placed within an environment 'box' because forces operating within social and professional environments:

☐ Provide the stimuli that encourage creative processes
☐ Determine the direction those processes take and, to some extent, the boundaries within which they function
☐ Provide a mixture of inhibitors and assistors.

The environment 'box' also highlights the fact that, for an idea to become a valuable new reality, it has to be accepted by sufficient or significant members of an environment, and then has to influence or change attitudes or behaviours within that environment.

Creative Capability is not purely a response to identified problems, but is also the framework for continual personal and professional growth and improvement. Each element can be understood through a consideration of its:

1. Purpose.
2. Required skills/processes/techniques.
3. Most appropriate attitudes.
4. Metaphor.

Because it is circular in nature, Creative Capability can be examined by beginning at *any point* in the process. If, for example, a potential new reality has been invented and 'sold', the initial focus will be on implementation.

Once that is achieved, it is necessary to identify its degree of success and the implications for the rest of the organisation/environment. When that is clear, the task is to imagine how the situation can once again be improved, and so on. Because it is interactive, the different elements of the Creative Capability process can – *should* – be applied at different stages. For example, any weaknesses in the process of implementation have to be *identified* before improvements can be *imagined* and applied.

All creative endeavours take place within specific environments. Indeed, such endeavours are often inspired, and are always influenced, by particular problems, opportunities, theories or behaviours existing within that environment. Once complete, the results of these endeavours are then evaluated by significant individuals or groups, or a wide spectrum of the populace, and, if accepted, a valuable new reality is born. In this way the creative process influences or changes some aspect of the environment that inspired it. The process is dependent throughout on:

- ☐ An understanding of the environment within which one is operating
- ☐ The ability to identify and define meaningful problems, issues or opportunities within that environment
- ☐ The ability to determine the right time to move from stage to stage
- ☐ Knowing how much time to allocate to each stage
- ☐ Courage.

While the first four are self-explanatory, the last – the individual and organisational courage to draw from the past, squeeze the present and so create the future – will be addressed later.

We will begin our consideration of the key elements of the Creative Capability process with 'identifying' the problem.

Identify

1 Purpose

To draw the current picture.

2 Skills/processes/techniques

- ☐ Systems thinking
- ☐ Information-gathering
- ☐ Information analysis
- ☐ Problem definition
- ☐ Time management.

As systems thinking and problem definition have already been discussed in this chapter and time management was discussed in Chapter 1, the focus here will be on information-gathering and analysis.

Information gathering

Information, like problems, rarely reveals itself. It has to be searched for, recognised, selected and understood. For a consideration of information-gathering interviews and questioning techniques and principles, refer back to Chapter 2.

Faced with a problem to be solved, managers need to ask themselves the following questions:

☐ How much time can I allocate to information collection?
☐ What are the potential sources of information?
☐ How can I determine the reliability and relevance of information?
☐ What information do I need before I can make a decision?

Given that there can be limitless sources of information available, managers need a clear approach to information-gathering and problem-solving. Without this, they risk wandering for an undefined period of time through what is potentially an information minefield. We will consider: (i) heuristics; and (ii) information types.

Heuristics

The term 'heuristic' has a Greek origin, meaning 'serving to find out or discover'. In essence, an heuristic is a method of investigation and discovery that is used to help simplify complexity and so ensure completeness of research, analysis and conclusion. There are different types of heuristics. Some, for example the availability heuristic, which evaluates the frequency of a happening based on how easily people can bring it to mind, can be the causes of irrational behaviour and/or inaccurate conclusions.

One analytical method that is of use to managers is to investigate a given situation by asking what are the:

☐ Affects
☐ Attitudes
☐ Causes
☐ Circumstances
☐ Characteristics
☐ Effects
☐ Form
☐ Functions
☐ Method
☐ Materials
☐ Organisation
☐ Purpose
☐ Relationships
☐ Values.

Although not every topic will be relevant to every situation, by working through this list managers will identify all the key elements involved.

There is much research to suggest that heuristics are essential for good higher-order thinking. By finding a set of rules, or adopting a procedure that enables the development of satisfactory solutions, managers will not only save time but increase their effectiveness. Good thinkers do not simply think longer, harder or more clearly than others; rather, they think in specific directions using the methods that are most likely to be productive.

Information types
Journalists break information down into three categories:

☐ Essential
☐ Useful
☐ Interesting, but irrelevant.

Of course, the problem of how to categorise each piece of information accurately still remains. The way managers think about and view the problem will determine the importance they place on the information received. This is why clear problem definition and a specific method of investigation and discovery are so important.

Activity 5.13   Read several newspaper articles about the same event. Divide the information contained in each into:

☐ Essential
☐ Useful
☐ Interesting, but irrelevant.

Notice how information selection and analysis differ from one newspaper to another. What are the lessons for managers?

Information analysis
Once the appropriate information has been gathered, or the time limit has expired, the focus turns to analysis. The purpose of information analysis is to identify relationships and/or patterns that exist within the information gathered. Competent analysts order and structure information in such a way that it directs decision-making. Methods of analysis include:

1. Classification.
2. Categorisation.
3. Numerical.
4. Association.
5. Correlation.
6. Causation.

1. Classification

This is the process by which information is grouped according to predetermined external criteria. McKinsey's 7S model, for example, provides the following groupings for managers analysing an organisation's internal environment:

- ☐ Strategy
- ☐ Systems
- ☐ Skills
- ☐ Style
- ☐ Staff
- ☐ Structure
- ☐ Shared values.

2. Categorisation

Information is again divided into groups. This time the groups are determined by the common features of the information itself. For example, in a SWOT analysis all features regarded as strengths are grouped together.

3. Numerical

This defines any method of analysis in which numbers are combined to provide an understanding of how they relate to each other. Financial analysis, using various ratios to determine organisational success, is an obvious example.

4. Association

This refers to the recognising of relationships between various data. Associations can become apparent through the use of other methods of analysis and/or through the application of systems thinking.

5. Correlation

A development of association, correlation identifies the extent to which one factor changes in step with another. An example would be the way in which increased market share often leads to increased profitability.

6. Causation

A development of correlation, causation explains the cause-and-effect link between the factors involved. The dangers of assuming simple and immediate linear structures of cause and effect were discussed earlier. Again, systems thinking is a core skill.

Activity 5.14   Look again at the newspaper articles you selected for Activity 5.13. Which of the above methods of analysis were used, or implied? How accurately have causes and effects been identified?

Depicting information

As discussed in Chapter 2, people favour different representation systems when they communicate. Using visual stimuli to depict information can aid analysis, enabling people to see patterns and relationships they might otherwise have missed. The other side of the coin is that some visual representations – graphs being the most obvious example – enable the manipulation of information, emphasising a bias or trend that supports a particular point of view.

The types of visual aid managers may use include:

☐ Diagrams
☐ Flow charts
☐ Graphs
☐ Matrices.

In essence, their purpose can be any one, or any combination, of the following:

☐ To simplify complexity
☐ To identify trends
☐ To show relationships between variables
☐ To identify the stages in a process
☐ To support a point of view.

Forcefield analysis

A forcefield analysis enables a manager to identify and analyse a different type of information: the assumptions held by stakeholders about the industry and/or other forces that will impact upon a new idea. This provides an insight into the degrees of resistance and support a new initiative is likely to receive. This knowledge is useful not only in the 'Identify' stage of the Creative Capability process, but also in the 'Interpret' stage when proposals have to be presented and 'sold' to stakeholders.

A forcefield analysis comprises three steps. First:

☐ Identify each stakeholder's assumptions
☐ Determine whether they are supportive or resistant
☐ Assess the importance of the assumption (use a 0–10 scale)
☐ Assess the degree of certainty attached to the assumption (use a 0–10 scale) (see Figure 5.6(a)).

The second step is to plot these assumptions or forces on a graph. This can be used to determine the key factors to be addressed (see Figure 5.6(b)).

With these assumptions clearly identified and defined, the forcefield analysis can now be carried out (see Figure 5.7).

The question the manager needs to address is 'How can I best use the assumptions or forces that are supportive to overcome those that are resistant?'

Figure 5.6(a)
Forcefield analysis
step 1: stakeholder
assumptions

Stakeholders	Major assumptions	Importance	Certainty
A	Supportive: Resistant:		
B			
C			

Figure 5.6(b)
Forcefield analysis
step 2: stakeholder
analysis

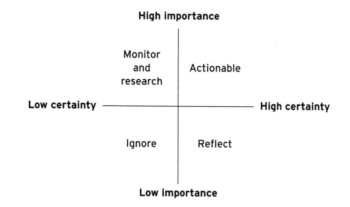

Figure 5.7
A forcefield
analysis

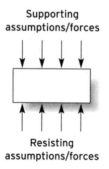

Activity 5.15 Think of a change you have been involved in, or have observed, within an organisation. Carry out the three steps of the stakeholder/forcefield analysis in relation to that event. How did the supportive and resistant assumptions reveal themselves? How were they managed? What impact did they have on the outcome?

Information reliability and relevance
Information reliability and relevance are determined by:

- ☐ The source
- ☐ The timing
- ☐ The manager's own bias and perceptions
- ☐ The manager's and organisation's goals.

Sources of information can be external or internal to an organisation. In order to determine reliability and relevance of information presented by either source, managers need to know:

- ☐ Why the source is providing the information – their agenda
- ☐ How and when they collected the information
- ☐ Whether they have made any intentional or unintentional changes to the original information (for example, have figures been rounded up or down?)
- ☐ If the information is complete.

Crucial information that is presented too late may be reliable but is of no relevance. Conversely, information that is produced hurriedly after only minimal research may be incomplete. It can therefore be seen as relevant but unreliable.

In terms of managing their own bias, managers need to be aware of the dangers of automatically favouring information simply because it:

- ☐ Is readily available
- ☐ Supports their existing beliefs and expectations
- ☐ Limits possible conflict
- ☐ Relates to topics with which they are already familiar
- ☐ Is interesting
- ☐ Is the first information received on a given topic.

For managers faced with the task of 'drawing the current picture', the skills outlined above need to be supported by the most appropriate attitude.

3. Most appropriate attitudes

The primary attitude required at this stage of the Creative Capability process is 'disassociation'. This does not imply that managers should not care about the problem. Far from it. The creative thinker is capable, among other things, of balancing the many paradoxes contained within the creative process. One of these can be expressed thus: *The creative manager needs to be passionate and committed, but also able to disassociate him/herself from the situation when necessary.* Without the ability to take a dispassionate overview, systems cannot be seen in their entirety, complexity cannot be simplified, relationships cannot be identified, and root causes cannot be uncovered. The 'business osteopath' has to know when to take a hands-on approach, when to try something new and when to step back a pace and simply watch the system in action.

Other examples of creative paradoxes include:

☐ Memory is essential for learning from the past, but habit is the antithesis of creativity
☐ Creative managers need to be passionate, but shifting perception requires objectivity
☐ Elite teams share powerful beliefs and values, but powerful beliefs and values create their own bias that blinds.

4. Metaphor

The metaphor for the manager's role during this stage of the creative process is: The Hawk.

Moving clockwise around the Creative Capability wheel, the next key element is 'imagine'.

Imagine

1. Purpose

To imagine possible improvements or solutions to the current problem or issue.

2. Skills/processes/techniques

☐ Divergent thinking
☐ Provoking newness
☐ Teamwork.

As team skills were discussed in Chapter 4, the focus here will be on divergent thinking and techniques for provoking newness.

Divergent thinking

Divergent thinking is the ability to create myriad options without falling into the trap of trying to evaluate them at the same time. Good divergent thinkers use their knowledge of a problem or situation as a springboard from which they enjoy and explore as many different perspectives as time allows. Divergent thinkers understand that, at this stage of the creative process, it is essential to *play* with possibilities, without fear of where that may lead and with disregard for real or imagined boundaries. One reason why children are so creative is because they are experts at *play*. However, children rarely, if ever, create realities which change some aspect of a professional or social environment. So, although children cannot be creative in the ways that managers can, managers still need to employ a childlike quality whenever they are required to create possible solutions or options for growth. And this leads us to another creative paradox: *Creative managers have to take their work and role seriously, but need to appreciate and apply the creative power of play.*

Before considering techniques that can be used to provoke new perspectives and ideas, let us take a moment to identify potential blockages to the creative process.

Blockages
These include:

☐ Habitual thought patterns and/or behaviours
☐ Bias
☐ The mistaken belief that the first idea is always the best one
☐ The mistaken belief that the identical problem/challenge presented itself in the past and the very best solution is known
☐ Misinformation – including too much or too little
☐ Organisational/functional culture
☐ Lack of persistency
☐ Lack of passion
☐ Unwillingness, or inability, to play
☐ Fear of failure
☐ Fear of success
☐ Fear of the unknown
☐ Imagining boundaries – physical, financial, staffing etc. – that do not exist
☐ Inability to turn an idea into a reality
☐ Inadequate communication skills
☐ Lack of Emotional Intelligence
☐ Inability to use different thinking styles.

Creative managers do not have to possess *all* the skills and attitudes required to overcome the above, but they do need to know which aspects of the creative process to delegate to which staff. Some people will be excellent at information-gathering, analysis and problem definition, for example, while others will more naturally be divergent thinkers, inventors or project managers.

Activity 5.16 Evaluate your ability and/or desire to excel at the following creative skills. For those skills you do not have significant experience of, use your instinct; if it has a strong appeal, score it highly.

Research
(Information-gathering, analysis and problem definition)

1 -- 10
No skill/No interest   Highly skilled/Very interested

Divergent thinking/Imagining
(Creating new ideas and perspectives; imagining possibilities)

1 -- 10
No skill/No interest   Highly skilled/Very interested

Convergent thinking/Interpreting
(Evaluating ideas, selecting, justifying and 'selling' the preferred option/solution)

1 -- 10
No skill/No interest   Highly skilled/Very interested

Inventing
(Turning an idea into a reality to agreed specifications and deadlines)

1 -- 10
No skill/No interest   Highly skilled/Very interested

Implementing
(Project management skills)

1 -- 10
No skill/No interest   Highly skilled / Very interested

Provoking newness

In the film, *Dead Poet's Society* (1989), there is a scene in which the school-teacher, played by Robin Williams, has his pupils stand on their chairs to gain a new perspective of their classroom and himself. There are many techniques other than physical movement that can be used to shock the mind into identifying new perspectives. We will consider:

☐ Blue sky thinking
☐ Brainstorming
☐ Distortion
☐ Negation
☐ Word association
☐ Mind mapping
☐ Bisociation.

Blue sky thinking

Using this technique, people are asked to imagine the perfect solution without regard for possible barriers or realistic limitations. Blue sky thinkers simply dream the perfect dream and, once that is clearly drawn, they work backwards, from perfection to reality, identifying which parts of the dream can be created and which cannot. The key during this part of the blue sky thinking process is to approach each aspect of the dream with a determination to make it happen, rather than searching for the reasons why it cannot happen. The question to focus on is therefore 'What do we have to do to turn this part of our dream into reality?' Blue sky thinking encourages people to challenge existing, or imagined, boundaries rather than simply accept them.

One way to involve as many people as possible in this process is to provide a suitably large, visible and easily accessible space in which thoughts and ideas can be recorded as and when they occur. Sometimes referred to as 'brown paper processing' (because you can simply fasten a roll of paper on an office or corridor wall), this approach ensures that the topic under consideration maintains a high profile and encourages people to be inspired by the thoughts and ideas of others.

Activity 5.17   Think of a situation you are involved in that could be improved. Spend some time blue sky thinking. Decide how the situation would be if it was perfect. Determine what you would have to do to turn each part of your dream into reality. What barriers exist? Which of these are really insurmountable?

Brainstorming

A team brainstorming session would go as follows:

1. Select a team leader or facilitator.
2. Ensure that the problem/issue is defined appropriately.
3. Spend some time at the start of the session ensuring that everyone is relaxed, excited and energised – that they are in the mood for divergent thinking. Too often teams meet for a creative problem-solving session – sometimes at the end of the day when energy levels are low – and launch straight into a technique like brainstorming. Not surprisingly, the results are often poor. Creative thinkers, like athletes, need to warm up the 'muscles' they are about to exercise before applying any techniques. How this is done needs to be agreed within the team. It might, for example, involve joke-telling, lively conversation or even singing a song! Whatever the technique used, the team should not move on to brainstorming, or any other divergent thinking strategy, until energy levels are high and the atmosphere within the room is vibrant. If this cannot be achieved, rearrange the meeting.

Activity 5.18   This exercise is one that can be used to warm people up for creative thinking. Try it for yourself.

Start at the top left and follow the alphabet through to 'Y' and back again. Say each letter out loud and do the following actions at the same time:

L = raise your left arm and right foot.
R = raise your right arm and left foot.
T = raise both arms and stand on tip-toe.

A L B R C L D T E L

F R G R H T I L J T

K R L L M L N L O T

P L Q R R L S R T L

U R V R W L X L Y L

This exercise is reproduced from David Molden (1996) *Managing with the Power of NLP* (London: Pitman Publishing)

4. Sit the team at a round or U-shaped table.
5. Agree a time limit for the creation and sharing of ideas.
6. Ask each team member for an idea or solution. Give limited thinking time, and create and maintain a fast pace.
7. If an individual does not answer quickly, let him/her 'pass' and move on to the next person.
8. Record *all* answers on a flipchart for all to see.
9. If several members are struggling to offer ideas, the facilitator can change the format and encourage anyone/everyone to call out ideas.
10. Stop when the time runs out or the team as a whole starts flagging.

When brainstorming, *do not*:

☐ Allow idea generation to begin until the right mood is clearly established
☐ Allow any evaluation of ideas until after all ideas are recorded or the time has run out. Idea generation needs to be done in an energetic, playful manner. Evaluation requires convergent, not divergent, thinking and is addressed in the next stage of the Creative Capability process
☐ Allow the team to run out of ideas. The facilitator must always close a brainstorming session leaving the team wanting more time for ideas, rather than knowing that it has exhausted its capability.

Distortion and negation
As with the synectic techniques discussed previously, distortion and negation encourage new perspectives and insights through imagining changes to something that is well known. The technique works as follows:

1. Define the problem/situation appropriately.
2. Set the mood for creative 'play'.

3. List all the known elements and aspects of the subject.
4. Select any one element and brainstorm ways in which it can be distorted. It can be bigger, smaller, reversed, increased in importance, made insignificant, etc.
5. Repeat this for as many elements as you wish.

Evaluating the potential relevance of any of these distortions is, again, the next stage of the process and will be discussed under the heading 'Interpret'.

Negation is one particular distortion that can be especially useful. It involves simply denying the existence of key elements and asking the questions:

☐ What would (have to) happen if this did not exist?
☐ What would replace it?
☐ How would the system have to change?
☐ Is this an essential element?

Activity 5.19 Select a household item. Determine a way of improving it by using distortion and/or negation.

Word association

Most people are aware of the game of word association, linking unexpected words with immediate responses, making connections without logical thought. This technique is a variation on this game. The procedure is:

1. Define the problem/situation appropriately.
2. Set the mood for creative 'play'.
3. Select a totally unrelated topic and involve everyone in the team in a round or two of word association, using the new topic as the starting word. For example, your team might be meeting to identify possible solutions to a marketing problem, but the basis for its word association might be 'lion'. The first person might then offer the word 'pride'. Responding to that, the second person might say 'fashion', the third person 'image', and so on.
4. With the word association list complete, take time to scan through it, combining words if appropriate, to see which words help spark ideas for the problem.
5. Record all initial thoughts and ideas, even if they do not seem immediately useful. When you evaluate your results, aspects from two seemingly meaningless ideas may combine to create a winning solution.

Word association is a useful technique for forcing people to distance themselves from the immediate problem, and so approach it from an unusual and unexpected perspective.

Mind mapping

Developed in the mid-1970's by Tony Buzan, Peter Russell and Mark Brown, 'mind mapping' is a technique that is widely used by managers for note-taking and note-making, but it can also be applied as a creative problem-solving device. The process is:

1. Place a sheet of paper, no smaller than A4 size, horizontally in front of you.
2. In the centre of the page define the problem.
3. Draw 'trunks' (thick lines) emanating from this central title.
4. Put your main ideas on these 'trunks' – one on each.
5. Connect sub-ideas or related points to each trunk.
6. Use a different colour for each main idea and its associated connections.
7. Use pictures or diagrams to represent your thoughts – the more of your senses you can engage, the more appealing your mind map will be, the easier it will be to look at and the more attention you will pay to it.
8. Show connections between different ideas by using dotted lines from one element to another.

Mind mapping can be used individually or as a group. Teams can use this technique either by creating one large mind map between them, or by each person drawing his/her own personal mind map, which is then passed on to the next person in the team who adds his/her own ideas, before passing it on again. In this way everyone contributes to every mind map. Figure 5.8 gives an example.

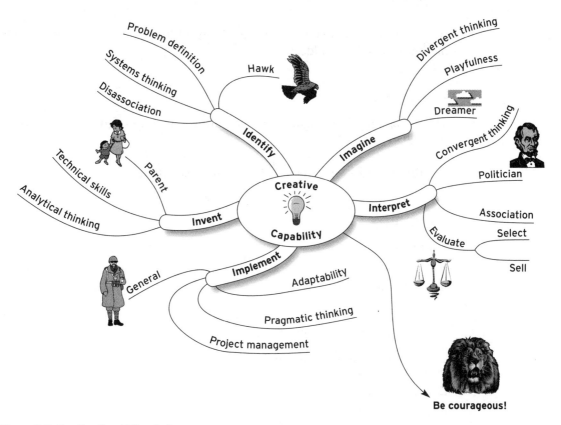

Figure 5.8 Creative Capability mind map

Activity 5.20   Study the Creative Capability mind map in Figure 5.8. Now create your own mind map summarising any chapter in this book.

Bisociation

An essential aspect of the creative process, bisociation is the ability to combine two aspects of a situation or object, or two ideas or thoughts, to create something valuable and new. The principle of bisociation often comes to the fore in the latter stages of the techniques outlined above, when a variety of ideas and thoughts have been created and recorded, enabling connections to be made.

3. Most appropriate attitudes

The primary attitudes required at this stage of the creative process are:

☐ Playfulness
☐ Passion.

A sense of hypomania, or 'flow', as discussed in Chapter 1, is invaluable in aiding the free flow of ideas.

4. Metaphor

The metaphor for the manager's role during this stage of the creative process is: The Dreamer.

Continuing clockwise, the next key element is 'interpret'.

Interpret

1. Purpose

To evaluate the options identified; to select, recommend and 'sell' the preferred choice.

2. Skills/processes/techniques

☐ Convergent and evaluative thinking
☐ The Walt Disney Strategy
☐ Selling ideas
☐ Presentation skills.

As persuasive campaigning, selling ideas and presentation skills will be discussed in Chapter 6, the focus here will be on convergent thinking and the Walt Disney Strategy.

Convergent thinking

Convergent thinking is needed because:

☐ Divergent thinking ensures the creation of many ideas
☐ Not all ideas can be good ones
☐ Not all ideas can be recommended
☐ A selection therefore has to be made.

The successful evaluation of ideas is dependent to a great extent on accurate problem definition and associated parameters. Ideas can only be evaluated against agreed criteria and using agreed methods. The most effective evaluation includes the most appropriate mix of information, opinion and insight. This mix needs to be set against an understanding of organisational goals, culture, resources, capabilities, time constraints, etc. Questions that can be asked include:

☐ What are the tangible benefits of this idea?
☐ What problems would its implementation create?
☐ What would have to be managed to turn this idea into an acceptable reality?
☐ What emotional responses does/would it create – and why?
☐ What are the costs associated with this idea?
☐ Do we need any additional information?

Creative problem-solving teams can choose to approach questions such as these in one of two ways: (i) to divide the questions between the members, asking people to focus only on one specific question, with the aim of presenting their findings on a given date; and (ii) to address each question as a team, with every member offering his/her opinions and insights collectively. Either way, the facilitator needs to be capable of accurately summarising the key points and moving the evaluation and selection process forward.

In one sense, convergent thinking is at the very heart of the Creative Capability process. The ability to recognise the very best ideas and to dismiss the others is one skill that separates the most creative individuals and teams from the rest of us. One technique that combines both divergent and convergent thinking is the Walt Disney Strategy.

The Walt Disney Strategy

Although this is the creative process that Walt Disney used when working alone, it lends itself to a team approach. Few individuals are as competent at all aspects of the creative process as Disney! The three phases of the Strategy, each depicted by characters, are:

1. Dreamer.
2. Realist.
3. Critic.

1. The Dreamer

This is the imaginative, divergent thinking phase, during which the Dreamer visualises the perfect solution. It is Disney's version of the blue sky thinking technique. Once it is complete and 'drawn', it is passed on to the Realist.

2. The Realist

In this phase, the focus is on how to make the dream a reality. The Realist makes no attempt to evaluate the Dreamer's vision, being concerned only with different ways of making it happen. Once these are agreed and detailed, they are passed on to the Critic.

3. The Critic

This is the phase in which consequences are identified and examined. The Critic constantly poses the question 'What if ...?' in order to ensure that the Realist's plans are logical, practical and have taken into account all relevant factors. This is not a negative, cynical phase. The Critic is as committed to a successful resolution as both Dreamer and Realist. This is why it is essential that each plays his/her part perfectly.

If the Critic identifies problems with the Realist's plan, he/she passes it back with a request for the issues to be addressed. With that done, the Realist returns it again. This continues until the Critic is satisfied or there is an acknowledgement that the plan is terminally flawed. In the latter case, the Dreamer is asked to create another vision.

Walt Disney played all three roles himself, using different settings to help him shift character and perspective. Creative problem-solving teams can apply his strategy by dividing themselves into three smaller teams, determined by individual skills and preferences. People who find it easy to imagine, for example, would form the Dreamers while others would choose to act as either Realists or Critics. The team leader or facilitator would observe the entire process, watching for any signs that the process is losing focus.

3. Most appropriate attitudes

The primary attitudes required at this stage of the creative process are:

☐ Association
☐ Adaptability
☐ Sensitivity.

People need to be able to:

☐ Make associations between options and likely consequences, benefits and costs
☐ Adapt to changes – being able to discard ideas, even if they are their own
☐ Be sensitive to the perceptions and feelings of others.

4. Metaphor

The metaphor for the manager's role during this stage of the creative process is: The Politician.

The next key element in the process is 'invent'.

Invent

1. Purpose

To create the new product, system, etc. to agreed specifications.

2. Skills/processes/techniques

☐ Analytical thinking
☐ Appropriate technical/professional skills.

Methods of analysing information were discussed earlier in this chapter. The skills needed to turn an agreed idea into a reality are, of course, determined by the nature and purpose of the organisation and the solution itself.

3. Most appropriate attitudes

The primary attitudes required at this stage of the creative process are:

☐ Attention to detail
☐ Love.

Metaphor

The metaphor for the manager's role during this stage of the creative process is: The Parent.

Continuing clockwise, the next key element is 'implement'.

Implement

1. Purpose

To manage the change process. To create a new, working organisational 'picture'.

2. Skills/processes/techniques

☐ Pragmatic thinking
☐ Project management skills.

The pragmatic manager is primarily concerned with practical consequences and results, rather than theory. A detailed consideration of project management skills would require another book. Suffice to say, that project management has the following three dimensions:

1. Objectives.
2. Management processes.
3. Levels.

1. Objectives
These are:

☐ Scope
☐ Organisation
☐ Quality
☐ Cost
☐ Time
☐ Risk.

2. Management processes
The ability to:

☐ Plan
☐ Organise
☐ Implement
☐ Control.

3. Levels
There are three:

☐ Integrative
☐ Strategic
☐ Tactical.

3. Most appropriate attitudes

The primary attitudes required at this stage of the creative process are:

☐ Balance
☐ Adaptability.

Project managers have to balance the varying objectives, levels and demands while adapting to changing circumstances.

4. Metaphor

The metaphor for the manager's role during this stage of the creative process is: The General.

Once the General's task is complete, the 'newness' will eventually become the organisational norm. Over time this valuable 'new' reality will lose some of its value in the light of changes/developments within its environment, and the process will begin again.

Courage

Courage is an attitude that needs to be prevalent throughout the entire Creative Capability process. To take a decision is to commit to a risk. To act upon that decision is to step into the unknown. Creative managers are explorers who are committed to pushing back the frontiers within which their organisation operates, and who are willing to explore new possibilities and places. Without courageous explorers organisations are forever trapped within boundaries of their own – and the environment's – making. Courage is not the absence of fear or uncertainty, but the willingness to act despite those feelings.

How can individuals and/or organisations ensure they have the courage required to explore the 'unknown'? The following list, based on attitudes and behaviours previously discussed, is not offered as a definitive guide, but as a stimulus for further thought:

1. Reward risk-taking.
2. Have a positive attitude towards mistakes.
3. Identify clearly the pain associated with *not* being courageous.
4. Identify clearly the benefits of *being* courageous.
5. Encourage curiosity and inquisitiveness.
6. Create and maintain a sense of 'play' and 'fun' rather than seriousness and work.
7. Value perseverance.
8. Understand the realities of the so-called 'flight, freeze or fight' syndrome.
9. Employ appropriate stress and pressure management techniques.
10. Explore further the fields of Neuro-Linguistic Programming (NLP) and Emotional Intelligence.

The purpose of analysis is to inform action. Sometimes the value of excellent analysis is undermined because people lack the courage to act appropriately. While courage is needed in every step of the Creative Capability process, it is best applied as the result of meaningful investigation and reflection.

Activity 5.21   Think of times in your life when you have been courageous. What prompted your behaviour? What were your reasons or intentions? What were the incentives? How could these be applied to other situations?

Creative Capability: key points!

☐ Creativity is influenced by and in turn influences the environments in which it occurs.

☐ Creative Capability is an ongoing process, comprising five key elements:
  ☐ Identify
  ☐ Imagine
  ☐ Interpret
  ☐ Invent
  ☐ Implement.

☐ The primary thinking styles that correspond to each of the five elements are:
  ☐ Systems thinking and analytical thinking
  ☐ Divergent thinking
  ☐ Convergent and evaluative thinking
  ☐ Analytical thinking
  ☐ Pragmatic thinking.

☐ The ability to create myriad ideas is only one, important, part of the process. Points to bear in mind are:
  ☐ Not all ideas are good ones
  ☐ Aspects from different ideas can often be combined
  ☐ Ideas have to be evaluated against agreed criteria
  ☐ Good ideas are of no value if they cannot be 'sold'
  ☐ Good ideas that have been 'sold' are of no value if they are not implemented appropriately.

☐ Valuable new realities cannot be created without the courage to act, the willingness to learn and the perseverance to continue.

Summary: creative problem-solving

☐ Successful creative problem-solving is founded upon:
  ☐ The ability to recognise and/or create opportunities rather than think in terms of problems that constrain
  ☐ The ability to view situations from a variety of perspectives
  ☐ Knowledge of the environment(s) within which one is operating
  ☐ Passion
  ☐ Persistence
  ☐ Playfulness
  ☐ Courage.
☐ The core skills are those associated with:
  ☐ Managing self and self-image
  ☐ Managing one-to-one relationships
  ☐ Developing others
  ☐ Leadership

☐ Teamwork
☐ Systems thinking
☐ Divergent thinking
☐ Convergent and evaluative thinking
☐ Information gathering and analytical thinking
☐ Project management and pragmatic thinking.
☐ The aim is to create valuable new realities.

A final thought

Creativity springs from a mind absorbed in the 'now', is shaped in hands skilled by the past, is seen through eyes that envision the future. There is a point in the creative process when the process itself must matter above all else – when thoughts of success or failure, reward or completion, are forgotten and when the creative act is the only thing. This is what we might call *Creative Zen*. This absolute commitment, the courage to seek out the point of 'no return', of complete absorption, is shared by creators and explorers alike. As André Gide wrote:

> *One does not discover new lands without consenting to lose sight of the shore for a very long time.*

(A. Gide)

References

Gide, A. 1927. *The Counterfeiters*. New York: Knopf.
Molden, D. 1996. *Managing with the Power of NLP*. London: Pitman Publishing.
Senge, P. 1993. *The Fifth Discipline*. London: Century Business.

Further reading

Sherwood, D. 1998. *Unlock Your Mind*. Aldershot: Gower.
Dearlove, D. 1998. *Key Management Decisions*. London: Financial Times/Pitman Publishing.
Buzan, T. 1995. *The Mind Map Book*. London: BBC Books.
O'Connor, J. and McDermott, I. 1997. *The Art Of Systems Thinking*. London: Thorsons.
Csikszentmihalyi, M. 1996. *Creativity: Flow and the Psychology of Discovery and Invention*. New York: HarperCollins.

Essential leadership skills 2: sharing value

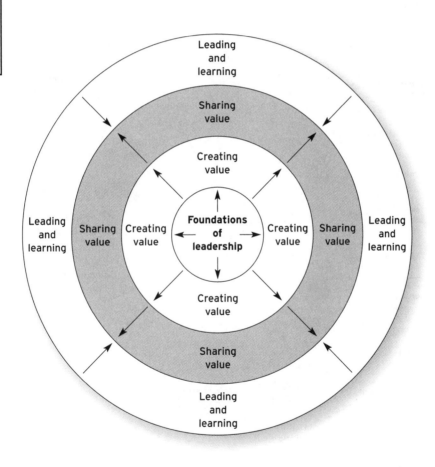

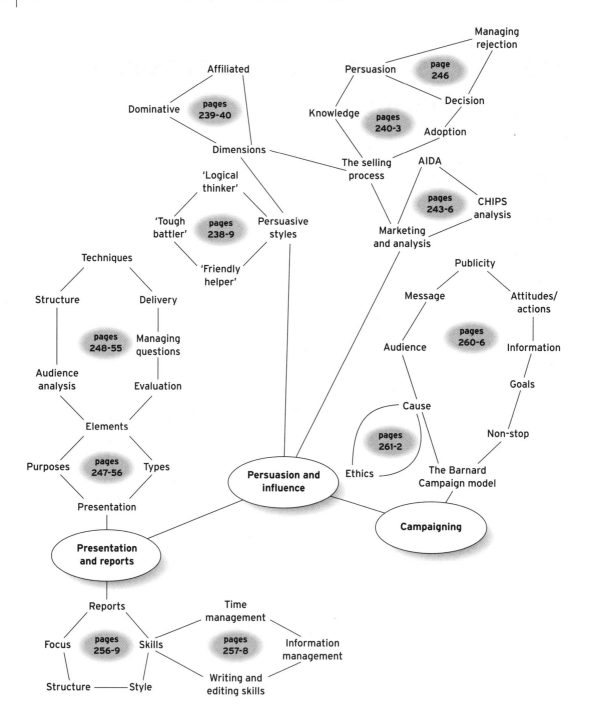

Part Three

Selling ideas and persuasive campaigning

Everyone lives by selling something.

(Robert Louis Stevenson)

This chapter will develop your:

Awareness of:	Knowledge of:	Capability to:
How to introduce new ideas.	The four stages of acceptance: ☐ Knowledge ☐ Persuasion ☐ Decision ☐ Adoption.	Introduce new ideas appropriately.
How to persuade and influence. How, and why, to switch styles. The concept of need satisfaction.	Persuasive styles: ☐ 'Friendly helper' ☐ 'Tough battler' ☐ 'Logical thinker'. 'CHIPS' analysis.	'Sell' new ideas.
Presentation principles.	Planning and delivering a presentation. Audience analysis. Presentation structure. Performance skills. Managing questions. Evaluating performance.	Prepare and deliver persuasive presentations.
Report-writing principles.	Planning and writing a report. Audience analysis. Purpose(s). Structure. Style.	Write influential reports.
Campaign principles.	The Barnard Campaign model: ☐ Cause ☐ Audience ☐ Message ☐ Publicity ☐ Attitudes/action ☐ Information ☐ Goals ☐ Non-stop campaigning ☐ Movement and momentum.	Plan and manage a persuasive campaign.

☐ Persuasion, influence and selling

Great ideas, great products and great talents are not always immediately recognised as such. Indeed, in the early stages of their development, they are often
resisted or dismissed. Consider this Western Union internal memo dated 1876:
'This "telephone" has too many shortcomings to be seriously considered as a
means of communication. The device is inherently of no value to us.' Or the
fact that Margaret Mitchell's *Gone with the Wind* was rejected by 38 publishers.
Or the fact that the great opera singer Enrico Caruso was told by his teacher
that 'he had no voice at all'. Or, wonderfully, the fact that Walt Disney was
once fired for 'lacking ideas'! In his book, *Management Consulting*, Philip A.
Wickham writes:

> *Businesses rarely recognise good ideas instantly and pursue them without
> question. ... In business, having good ideas is not enough. ... Ideas must be
> communicated in a way which convinces people that they are good and
> worth implementing.*

> (Wickham, 1999: 13, 15)

The mental flexibility needed to envisage ways of creating valuable new realities has to be matched by the flexibility, mental toughness and skills needed
to sell the idea, cope with and learn from rejection, and campaign persuasively. In the words of the anonymous writer: 'Blessed are the flexible, for they
shall not be bent out of shape.' Managers need that flexibility and a variety of
associated skills if they are to present, campaign for and 'sell' new ideas.

Persuasion and Influence

Much of what has been covered in previous chapters regarding understanding and managing oneself, communication skills and styles, how to create
rapport, understanding others and the use of power is relevant here. Many
human interactions centre around a need to create influence. Maureen
Guirdham (1995) analyses different persuasive styles by identifying them as:

☐ *The 'friendly helper'* 'Friendly helpers' influence by appealing to other
  people's emotions. They demonstrate friendliness, optimism and
  concern; they are encouraging and make clear their desire for compromise. 'Friendly helpers' can be gullible, and run the risk of being taken
  advantage of.
☐ *The 'tough battler'* 'Tough battlers' influence by taking the initiative and
  pushing forwards for results. They are often domineering, issuing orders
  and/or setting challenges. Willing to take risks, they can be viewed as
  arrogant or even threatening – a perception that can prevent 'tough battlers' from creating the influence they desire.
☐ *The 'logical thinker'* 'Logical thinkers' influence by placing the emphasis
  on facts, figures, rules and regulations. In short, they appeal to other
  people's logic. They are thorough in their research of a situation or idea,

and orderly and fair in their analysis and presentation of it. 'Logical thinkers' run the risk of winning the minds but not the hearts of those they wish to influence. They can be seen as nit-picking and too rigid in their approach.

The most persuasive style?

None of the above can be defined as the best. The greatest skill lies in having the flexibility to adapt one's style to match the demands of the situation. Managers with excellent influencing skills will use the style most likely to appeal to those they seek to influence. By contrast, inexperienced or single-style influencers may struggle to 'sell' a potentially life-saving idea because of their inability to frame it appropriately. If persuading 'logical thinkers', for example, the odds are stacked against you if you put your energy and focus into appealing to their emotions.

Activity 6.1	Identify three people you know who, in your opinion, naturally use each of these styles. To determine the accuracy of your evaluation, listen to and observe these people when they are being persuasive. Once you are certain about their preferred style(s), ensure you use it whenever you have to influence them.

In *The Psychology of Interpersonal Behaviour* (1967), Michael Argyle discusses a different, two-dimensional approach to identifying and analysing persuasive styles.

Dominative and affiliative dimensions.
In this approach, as shown in Figure 6.1, a dominative–dependent dimension combines with a high affiliative-low affiliative dimension to create four persuasive styles. Argyle suggests that the most effective style combines an acceptable level of domination with a supportive, engaging manner. This would be defined as a dominative–high affiliative approach. The least effective style, he argues, is a dependent–low affiliative style, which exhibits evasion or withdrawal and concession.

Although there is obvious value in this approach, the fact remains that the situation should be the key determinant of influencing style. Managers who depend on their ability to influence and persuade, rather than on the wielding of position power, need to be fluent in all the communication skills discussed in Chapters 1 and 2, as well as the technicalities and practicalities of their argument.

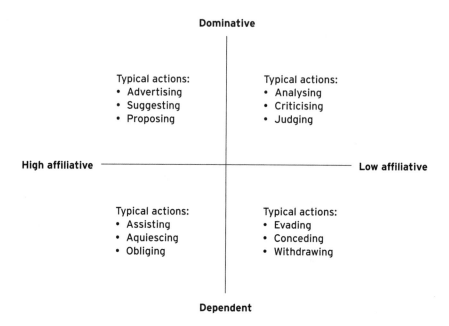

Figure 6.1
Dominative and affiliative persuasive styles

Selling

Great sales personnel all have one thing in common: the ability to make the buyer forget that the interaction is being managed with the sole purpose of ensuring that he/she parts with his/her money or agrees to a proposition! Although in this section we will be using the terms 'sellers' and 'buyers', we are not referring only to those people who sell products. Managers wishing to introduce a new idea, system or strategy, or to encourage an individual to change in some way, also need persuasive 'selling' skills.

The best sales men and women share the following characteristics and skills:

☐ They are personable, warm and engaging
☐ They create rapport quickly, matching their style and attitude to that of the potential buyer
☐ They identify a potential buyer's needs and self-image and match their messages to these
☐ They recognise and respond to any subtle shifts in the buyer's attitude
☐ They understand and highlight the benefits and value of what they are selling
☐ They manage their own image effectively, satisfying the buyer's expectations.

In short, effective communicators have an increased chance of being effective sellers. Creative geniuses who lack the ability to sell their work will fail to create the influence they seek.

The selling process can be broken down into four stages:

1. Knowledge.
2. Persuasion.
3. Decision.
4. Adoption.

Activity 6.2 Assess your current persuasiveness and style by responding to the following statements:

When trying to influence someone, I naturally appeal to his/her emotions.

Always ------------------------------- Never

When trying to influence someone, I naturally create logical arguments using facts and relevant data.

Always ------------------------------- Never

When trying to influence someone, I am naturally dominant - giving orders and pushing for the results I want.

Always ------------------------------- Never

When trying to influence someone, I naturally try to balance emotional compatibility with logic and toughness.

Always ------------------------------- Never

When trying to influence someone, I naturally base my style and approach on my understanding of the other person.

Always ------------------------------- Never

When trying to influence someone, I choose the setting with care and try to establish the most appropriate atmosphere and mood.

Always ------------------------------- Never

When trying to influence someone, I naturally try to balance dominance and support.

Always ------------------------------- Never

When trying to influence someone, I make more concessions than I would like.

Always ------------------------------- Never

When trying to influence someone, I achieve my goals.

Always ------------------------------- Never

Although we will consider each stage independently, they should be regarded as influencing elements in the 'selling system', rather than as stand-alone components. For example, the management of data not only increases the potential buyer's knowledge of the product, idea or choices on offer, but is part of the process of persuasion which in turn influences the buyer's eventual decision. As with all systems, it can be necessary for the purpose of study to isolate elements, but their relevance and worth can only be fully understood and judged as a functioning part of the system – through the relationships they share and degree of influence they wield on the other elements.

1. Knowledge

The seller's first task is to present the potential buyer with both the right information and the *right amount* of information to excite and maintain his/her interest. There are various ways this can be done prior to the face-to-face interaction, for example advertising, reports and the use of third-party intervention, but in each case the nature of the information, particularly the key areas of focus, and the manner in which it is presented, need to be determined by an understanding of the buyer's perspectives and needs. The sellers also need to be aware of the most likely questions raised by the information they present, and have appropriate responses prepared.

Another important point relating to the management of information is that *the order in which you present the information directly influences the conclusion(s) drawn*. Persuasive sellers structure and time the release of information for maximum effect, creating a progression that is intended to lead the potential buyer to the seller's desired conclusion.

2. Persuasion

Persuasive arguments combine the most meaningful information, appropriately sequenced and presented in the most persuasive style, with 'proof' of how the buyer's needs will be satisfied. Sellers who are skilled questioners are able to:

☐ Gather useful insights into the buyer's needs and perceived priorities
☐ Pose questions, the answers to which encourage the buyer towards a sale.

3. Decision

People tend to make decisions incrementally. Details, arguments and insights combine over time until a conclusion is reached. Sellers skilled in whole-body listening are able to recognise when, and how, they have made an incremental progression towards closure, and build on this success.

4. Adoption

People change their minds, which is why contracts provide 14 days for the buyer to cancel. There is no guarantee, therefore, that once a buyer has agreed to purchase a product, accept a new approach, change strategy, etc., he/she will take the final step and make that commitment. Successful sellers manage the transition from decision to adoption with as much care as any other part of the selling process, aware of the fact that it is not complete until adoption has been realised and maintained. The key factors for success at this stage are:

☐ Expect the buyer to doubt his/her decision
☐ Be prepared to respond to further questions and uncertainties
☐ Identify associated forces and factors that could influence the buyer's final decision
☐ Prepare your responses to those forces and factors
☐ Focus on the remaining issues; do not be distracted by thoughts of how close to closure you are
☐ Stay calm.

Once the product/proposal has been adopted, the seller's aim is two-fold:

☐ Ensure that the adoption has the most appropriate life-span
☐ Ensure that the relationship between buyer and seller is of the most appropriate duration.

In situations in which longevity of adoption and the relationship is essential, excellent ongoing customer care plays an important role (see Chapter 2).

Key elements of these four stages are evident in a variety of marketing practices, and in methods of analysis intended to aid the creative selling process. An example of each is included.

AIDA

AIDA is an an acronym for:

☐ Attention
☐ Interest
☐ Desire
☐ Action.

It forms the purpose and structure of all forms of advertising.

Attention

Creators of posters, billboards, fliers, etc. work on the principle that they have only one second in which to get a person's attention. In a face-to-face interaction, the seller obviously has longer than that – although not necessarily much longer! Remember that people trying to 'sell' themselves at interview have to make a good first impression and, when given the opportunity to pitch a new idea for a book or a film outline, writers are often asked to do so in one sentence or within ten seconds. If they cannot get the potential buyer's attention in that time, the opportunity is missed. The message, then, is simple: *Get the potential buyer's attention as quickly as possible.*

Interest

Once you have the buyer's attention, develop his/her interest in your proposal. Attention is the springboard to interest. To gain interest you have to understand your audience and how it perceives itself and its needs, then answer its, as yet, unasked question, 'What's in it for me?'

Desire

By highlighting the benefits of what you are offering, you create desire. This is achieved by:

☐ Understanding and addressing concerns the potential buyer(s) have
☐ Explaining the benefits of what is on offer
☐ Making it clear that the costs are acceptable.

Once the people you are appealing to want to buy into your offer, they are ready to be told what action they need to take.

Action

This needs to be simple, easy to understand and easy to accomplish. It also needs to be time-scaled, with the advantages of taking prompt action clearly identified.

Visual aids

Materials produced following the AIDA principles include any, or all, of the following:

Attention
☐ A photo and/or headline guaranteed to attract attention
☐ The headline will sell a benefit
☐ The headline will be brief
☐ The language used will be positive not negative
☐ The seller's unique selling proposition will be highlighted.

Interest
☐ The headline is not repeated
☐ The potential buyer will be told something he/she did not already know about what is on offer

☐ Some phrases will be in speech marks – they create and hold interest
☐ The reader will be addressed as 'you'
☐ Linking phrases will be used to ensure an easy transition from one section to the next
☐ Key phrases or words will be repeated
☐ Sentences will be short and simple.

Desire
☐ The text will shift from highlighting benefits to reassuring the reader that he/she can afford what is on offer
☐ The text will emphasise the value of what is offered
☐ The most likely concerns will be addressed.

Action
☐ The first action needed will be identified
☐ A reward may be offered for prompt action
☐ The action will be easy to remember and accomplish.

CHIPS analysis.

This method of analysis is designed to help the creative seller address the five factors that most significantly influence decision-makers. These are:

☐ Costs
☐ Help
☐ Innovation
☐ Prestige
☐ Security.

Costs
Dependent on the nature of what is on offer, costs can be financial, emotional or both. Sellers need to:

☐ Be able to estimate and time-scale the financial costs
☐ Understand any emotional costs and have strategies for managing them
☐ Highlight the benefits, making clear why the costs are justified.

Help
Emphasise how the offer will help the buyer to assist and/or support others.

Innovation
Emphasise the positive new aspects of what is on offer; show how it will contribute towards the development of a valuable new reality.

Prestige

Answer the question 'What's in it for me?' A sale is unlikely unless that question is answered satisfactorily.

Security

Ease concerns about the degree of risk involved by emphasising the safety and/or quality of what is on offer and by making clear why there is only limited risk. If it is a high-risk proposal explain why it is the best or the only option and outline the strategic 'safety net' that will be in place.

However, no matter how good the offer or how skilled the sales person, there are inevitably times when the proposal is rejected. This can be particularly difficult to manage for a person trying to sell his/her own product or idea. It is one reason why another creative paradox states: 'You have to be passionate to be creative, but don't stay in love with your own idea!'

Managing rejection

Rejection can create negativity, self-doubt, anger or even total surrender. The key to managing rejection lies in three, interrelated skills:

☐ Viewing every interaction as a learning experience, no matter what the outcome
☐ Reframing rejection
☐ Understanding the reality of an emotional response.

As discussed in Chapter 1, thinking in terms of outcomes rather than success or failure encourages a focus on learning and enables potentially negative experiences to be reframed. It can also help remove the fear of rejection which, in itself, can hinder performance.

The first step in managing the emotional response to rejection is to question the very nature of the response by asking such questions as:

☐ Am I feeling angry or hurt?
☐ Am I feeling rejected or disappointed?
☐ Am I feeling rejected or embarrassed?

The very act of posing such questions distances a person from his/her feelings and, consequently, begins to lessen them. Also, by clarifying the emotion, an accurate perspective is gained. Feeling disappointed or embarrassed, for example, is far less painful than rejection.

Activity 6.3   Think of an idea that would improve an organisation you are familiar with. Use the CHIPS analysis to identify what you would say to sell the idea.

Persuasion, influence and selling: key points!

☐ Ideas do not sell themselves.
☐ Persuasive styles can be defined as:
  ☐ 'Friendly helper'
  ☐ 'Tough battler'
  ☐ 'Logical thinker'.
☐ Or along dominative-affiliative dimensions.
☐ No single style is best.
☐ The most persuasive managers adopt the style that best meets the demands of the situation.
☐ Selling is dependent upon:
  ☐ Excellent communication skills
  ☐ An understanding of the needs, concerns and possible limitations of the potential buyer.
☐ The four stages of the selling process are:
  ☐ Knowledge
  ☐ Persuasion
  ☐ Decision
  ☐ Adoption.
☐ AIDA provides an additional focus and structure. It stands for:
  ☐ Attention
  ☐ Interest
  ☐ Desire
  ☐ Attention.
☐ A CHIPS analysis concentrates on:
  ☐ Costs
  ☐ Help
  ☐ Innovation
  ☐ Prestige
  ☐ Security.

☐ Persuasive presentations

The purpose of any presentation is two-fold:

☐ To deliver a predetermined message in an engaging manner
☐ To persuade your audience to do something it would not have done had you not made your presentation.

Effective presenters combine an understanding of their subject and their audience with high-level performance skills. A presentation is not a natural interaction. It is formally agreed, requires planning, has clear objectives (although the parties involved do not always share the same objectives), and its results can have significant consequences. The most persuasive presentations are logically and emotionally compelling. They are engaging in their simplicity and style. They question and answer, challenge and invite, introduce and lead. They are informative, affirmative and insightful in appropriate measure. They are far more than the words shared. They are, essentially, the manager's expression of performance art. Effective presentations combine the following elements:

☐ Audience analysis
☐ Structure
☐ Techniques
☐ Rehearsal and delivery
☐ Managing questions
☐ Evaluation.

Audience analysis

In a business presentation, as in any other, both audience and presenters have a part to play. The presenters attempt to engage, influence and persuade. The audience listens and observes, questions and evaluates. Prior to a presentation, it is essential for the presenters to answer the following questions:

☐ What is the make-up of the audience?
☐ How can I/we create value to my/our arguments and ideas for our audience?
☐ What is the degree of overlap – the common ground between what 'I' want to say and what the audience wants to hear?
☐ What structure, content and style will be most acceptable to my/our audience?

The importance of audience analysis cannot be overstated. The 'right' message delivered to the 'right' audience in the 'wrong' way will often be rejected.

Structure

Presentations can be divided into six main elements:

1. Pre-introduction
2. Introduction
3. Main body of the presentation
4. Pre-ending
5. Conclusion
6. Questions.

The nature and content of these elements is determined in advance depending on audience analysis and the desired outcomes.The preparation of a presentation can be divided into two steps. The first step focuses on identifying the most natural order of progression and creating the most natural structure. This can be achieved by:

☐ Listing every possible topic that could be included
☐ Identifying topics that overlap and combining them
☐ Deleting anything that is not directly relevant
☐ Grouping points into appropriate sections
☐ Deciding on the most logical order.

This ensures an easy-to-follow structure which, ideally, appears so simple and obvious it belies the thought and care taken to create it. As a basic principle: *If the audience is impressed by the complexity of the structure, it has been distracted from your message.*

The second step focuses on how best to engage the audience and maintain its interest and involvement throughout. This includes:

☐ Structuring creatively, but simply
☐ Finding interesting ways of getting your message across (ways that are interesting to *this* particular audience)
☐ Selecting anecdotes and appropriate examples
☐ Selecting visual aids.

Anecdotes and examples must be suitably brief and obviously relevant. As with all communication, the more senses you stimulate and the more representation systems you use, the greater the chance of engaging all audience members. Given that, bear in mind that visual aids include objects. Physical symbols of key points can be powerful reminders, acting as influential metaphors for your message.

If writing notes to refer to during the presentation:

☐ Use card or stiff paper
☐ Use large writing or type
☐ Use lower case print only
☐ Use wide margins (this allows for extra notes)
☐ Use a new card for each new topic
☐ Use simple headings and phrases.

1. Pre-introduction

Making a presentation is a lot like going fishing. Just because the audience is there does not mean it is automatically going to 'bite'. Fish do not leap out of the water into a fisherman's net. Audiences do not accept proposals until they are convinced – and audiences have to be engaged and encouraged before they become convinced (they have to be interested in the bait on offer, drawn towards it, hooked and reeled in). Just like a fish, an audience can be lost at any time in the proceedings. Just like fishermen, presenters have to understand that simply turning up and going through the motions is no guarantee of success. It does not matter how long you stand in the 'presentation water', if you have not done your preparation, and if you do not have the right skills, it is unlikely that you will be successful. And unsuccessful presenters, just like fishermen, blame anyone but themselves for the 'ones that got away'.

The purpose of the pre-introduction is to settle the audience, ensure its attention and establish the mood that best suits your needs and the audience's expectations. Be creative in the way you achieve this. You may, for example, use:

☐ A quotation
☐ A question

☐ An anecdote
☐ A rhetorical device
☐ Humour.

If asking a question, or using any other device that requires thought on the part of the audience members, have the confidence to pause for a suitable period of time. Only the most confident and experienced presenters are comfortable with silence. Also, if possible, use the pre-introduction to make eye contact with all members of your audience, and present the image that most meets its needs and expectations. Remember the importance of body language and the tone, clarity and pace of the voice in face-to-face communication. Therefore use the pre-introduction to demonstrate relaxed, expansive movement; the larger the arena, the more exaggerated your gestures need to be. As a general rule, the body's extremities reveal nervousness – hands and fingers fidgeting, or unnecessary foot movement – so pay particular attention to controlling them. Being still, when it is appropriate to be so, can be as difficult under pressure as maintaining a silence.

If using an anecdote or question, make sure it relates clearly to the audience's experience and/or world view. It will relax the audience and be a useful starting point in creating rapport.

The pre-introduction is important because although the audience is present, it does not always follow that it is listening or paying attention. Presenters who begin suddenly with their introduction risk having the first, crucial, part of their message ignored. The pre-introduction, when done well, acts as bait to a fish. It is impossible to ignore.

Finally, an engaging, interest-grabbing pre-introduction sets the tone for what is to follow. As performance art, presentations share much in common with films, plays or even books. If they do not start well, the audience quickly loses interest.

Activity 6.4   Think of a topic – a hobby perhaps – on which you can deliver a 15-minute presentation. Imagine an audience you can present it to. What style and approach would your audience appreciate most? Plan your pre-introduction.

---

2. Introduction: hooks, fish and benefits

The purpose of the introduction is to hook the audience by outlining your eventual conclusion, and making clear the benefits on offer to audience members if they accept your proposal. Once this is achieved, outline what is to follow and begin to reel them in.

To use the analogy of a journey, a presentation should not be a 'mystery tour', with the audience unsure of the route or the final destination. By making clear the purpose and overall structure of the presentation, presenters enable the audience to relax and focus on the message. It knows where it is going and can concentrate solely on how well it is being taken there. A simple but effective formula for ensuring clarity of structure is as follows:

☐ Tell the audience what you are going to do
☐ Do it
☐ Remind them of what you have just done (the key points).

3. Main body of the presentation

This needs to focus on the key questions or topics and be divided into clear sections and sub-sections, with natural connections linking one section to the next. Bearing in mind that the audience has not heard the presentation before, the pace needs to be fast enough to enthuse and interest, but not so fast that key points are missed or misunderstood. Use reminders to clarify complexity and show the relevance of each point to the main purpose of the presentation.

4. Pre-ending

The pre-ending serves two important purposes. It is used to indicate the fact that the presentation is almost over (audiences are often shocked by sudden, unexpected endings) and to summarise the key points.

5. Conclusion

This is at least as important as any previous part of the presentation. Use it to highlight key conclusions and provide an unforgettable ending. This is essentially the end of your journey. It needs to have been worth the 'trip'. A great performance without an equally great ending is always a disappointment to an audience.

6. Questions.

Refer to the section on 'Managing questions' (see page 254) below.

Activity 6.5   Plan the ending you would use for the presentation identified in Activity 6.4. How, and why, would it make a lasting impression on your audience?

Presentation techniques

Common and effective presentation techniques are:

☐ The use of rhetorical devices
☐ Imagery
☐ Body language
☐ Voice variety
☐ Visual aids.

Rhetorical devices

There are various techniques, all of which aim to engage, intrigue or inspire the audience. Examples include two-part contrasts, puzzle-solution formats, lists of three, combined formats and position takers.

Two-part contrasts

Some of the best-remembered quotes in history are remembered because of the way they create a contrast. Consider this famous phrase: 'Ask not what your country can do for you. Ask what you can do for your country.'

Puzzle-solution formats

Presenting the audience with a puzzle is an excellent way of engaging its attention. The most common form of puzzle is a rhetorical question. For example, the first line of the presentation might be: 'I'd like to begin by asking you a question ...' Or, at a later stage in the presentation, you might pose the question: 'Where do we go from here?' When using a rhetorical question, always:

☐ Ensure it cannot be misunderstood
☐ Ensure its relevance is clear
☐ Create an appropriate silence to allow the audience to consider its answer(s)
☐ Return to it, and answer it.

Lists of three

The politician's favourite! Lists of three can involve three words, phrases, or sentences, for example Tony Blair's 'Education! Education! Education!'

Combined formats

Combined formats are created, quite simply, by combining any of the above.

Position takers

This is a two-stage process in which the presenters describes a situation about which they are expected to take a position and then state, and justify, their position. This technique is useful because it meets audience expectation and adds to the simplicity of the overall structure.

Imagery

As mentioned earlier, physical objects can become powerful symbols and reminders of the main points of a presentation. Imagery, however, can also include the use of metaphors and descriptions of a possible future. As with the use of rhetorical questions, it is essential to ensure the relevance of all imagery that is used.

Body language

Presenters should be aware of the relationship between body language and the use of the space within which they are presenting. A willingness to move throughout the space indicates confidence and control. Also, it enables presenters to use specific areas for specific purposes. For example, if the presentation contains several humorous anecdotes, they could all be delivered from the same place. The most important messages would then be delivered from a different spot. Audiences learn very quickly how to interpret behaviour. So, when presenters begin to move to the 'humour place', audiences will be mentally ready and willing to laugh. When the presenters return to the spot from which they deliver their most important points, again the audiences' mood will change accordingly. The benefits of using space in this way, are that it increases the presenters' control of the audience and the audience understands what is happening and is therefore also confident and relaxed.

Voice variety

The pace, volume and clarity of the speaker's voice quite literally sets the tone for the presentation. In a small, intimate arena presenters can draw the audience in by lowering the tone of their voice and pausing slightly as they ask an important question or deliver a crucial message. They can show their own enthusiasm and commitment for an idea by talking more loudly and at a faster pace. Presentations that are well structured include appropriate techniques and are based on detailed audience analysis. They can lose much of their persuasiveness if the presenters do not know how to play the instrument that is their voice.

Visual aids

Visual aids are important because they engage the audience and because 'a picture paints a thousand words'. Irrespective of the type of visual aids used, they need to be:

- ☐ Simple
- ☐ Clear
- ☐ Uncluttered
- ☐ Stimulating
- ☐ Informative
- ☐ Shown long enough for the audience to study and understand them, but removed once the subject has changed.

Hand-outs should be offered at the end of the presentation. If given out at the beginning, there is a risk that the audience will be distracted from the presentation.

Rehearsal

Selecting appropriate techniques and combining them well is at the heart of great delivery. However, presentations, like all other forms of performance art, need to be physically rehearsed, eventually in front of critical friends and in an environment that resembles the venue as closely as possible. Rehearsals should be staged throughout the preparation process to enable alterations to be made to content, structure and style.

Also, whenever possible, check out the venue prior to the day of the presentation. Ensure that it is appropriately lit and well ventilated, and that the technical equipment you require is available. The size of the venue, and the size of your audience, will influence presentation style. If presenting to a panel of five, for example, the situation is likely to become far more interactive than if presenting to an audience of one thousand. Finally, ensure you have back-up equipment available in case of any breakdown.

The principles and techniques outlined in Chapter 1 are of value in managing any nervousness associated with delivering a presentation.

Managing questions

This is the most challenging part of the presentation, when, to a degree, control is handed over to the audience and presenters can only respond to whatever is asked of them. When planning for and managing questions, the key points to bear in mind are:

☐ In a team presentation, agree beforehand which topics people will answer questions on
☐ Share the responsibility equally
☐ Use your audience analysis to identify the most likely areas of questioning
☐ Use the main body of your presentation to lead the audience into asking questions for which you are prepared
☐ Avoid showing nervousness, fear or annoyance, no matter what the question or criticism
☐ If the question is not clear, or if the questioner poses several questions together, ask for clarification and direction
☐ Never respond to an apparently critical or threatening question with the words, 'Yes, but ...' The word 'but' in this context simply means 'You are wrong ...' and can provoke argument and an entrenchment of views. Presenters need to be seen to work with their audiences/questioners, not against them.

Evaluation

Presentation performance needs to be evaluated by both the presenters and the audience, and feedback should be given. The most obvious measure of success is whether or not the idea, service or product was 'sold'. However, even if that is accomplished, it is likely that there were areas that could have been improved. Do not ignore any instinctive interpretation felt immediately after the presentation,

Table 6.1 Types of presentation

Sales presentation	To superiors	A seminar	To inspire	Research findings
Choose the team with care	Focus on the essential facts, not the detail(s)	Prepare well in advance	Highlight audience achievements	Focus on key findings, not meaningless data
Allow two-thirds of the time for questions and answers	Provide insight along with information	Check out the venue	Challenge and entertain	Highlight those results most likely to inspire the audience to action
Rehearse answers to expected questions	Be clear about any resources you require	Be comfortable with any technology involved	Do not teach	Keep your results secret until the presentation
Conclude by summarising your key selling points	Avoid playing organisational politics	Leave the audience wanting more	Finish on a high note	Pause regularly for feedback, expect to be challenged, and do not avoid controversial issues/topics

Persuasive presentations: key points !

☐ Presentations are a form of performance art. They serve to:
- ☐ Deliver a message
- ☐ Influence and persuade.

☐ Effective presentations combine:
- ☐ Audience analysis
- ☐ Structure
- ☐ Techniques
- ☐ Delivery
- ☐ Managing questions
- ☐ Evaluation.

☐ They should be fully rehearsed beforehand.

☐ Presentations need to be structured creatively and simply, and include:
- ☐ Pre-introduction
- ☐ Introduction
- ☐ Main body of the presentation
- ☐ Pre-ending
- ☐ Conclusion
- ☐ Question-and-answer session.

☐ The three key rules for ensuring clarity of structure are:
- ☐ Tell the audience what you are going to do
- ☐ Do it
- ☐ Remind them of what you have just done.

☐ Techniques for engaging and maintaining audience attention include:
- ☐ The use of rhetorical devices
- ☐ Imagery
- ☐ Body language
- ☐ Voice variety
- ☐ Visual aids.

☐ It is essential to reach a memorable conclusion.

but combine it with a more clinical appraisal some days after the event. Even if you conclude that the presentation was of a high standard, make a commitment to being ever more engaging, inspirational and persuasive. 'Perfection,' as Bishop Joseph Hall wrote, 'is the child of Time' (Hall, 1625: 670).

Types of presentation

Throughout the course of a manager's career, he/she may reasonably make any, or all, of the following types of presentation:

- ☐ A sales presentation
- ☐ A seminar presentation
- ☐ A presentation to superiors
- ☐ A presentation of research findings
- ☐ A presentation to inspire colleagues/teams.

While the core principles remain the same for all presentations, there are some essential differences and these are shown in Table 6.1.

☐ Persuasive report writing

Written reports, like presentations, lose power and influence if they are too long. The essential difference between the two is that the audience knows the length of time it will have to pay attention before the presentation begins.

The reader of a report, however, is literally at the mercy of the writer and often has myriad other tasks to which to attend. Consequently, the reader's level of motivation can be low and, without the benefits of being able to support the message through face-to-face interaction, the report writer has several potential obstacles to overcome. The following guidelines will help.

Activity 6.6 Write a summary of your favourite novel, film or play, providing a sense of the story, characters, style, etc., in less than 50 words. Do not include a title.

Like presenters, report writers need a detailed understanding of their audience. This will enable them to determine their purpose and the most appropriate structure, style and focus.

Audience analysis

Audience analysis centres upon answering the following questions:

- ☐ Who is my audience?
- ☐ What are its needs?
- ☐ What is its expectation?
- ☐ What language, structure and style will it most appreciate?
- ☐ What is its particular perspective/bias? How do I best reflect, accommodate or challenge that?

Activity 6.7 Select a specific audience for the summary written in Activity 6.6. Use the questions above to help you re-write/edit the summary so that it will appeal to that audience.

The report-writing process

Once the audience analysis is complete and structure, style and focus have been determined, it is time to begin the process of writing the report. This requires:

1. Time management skills.
2. Information management skills.
3. Writing and editing skills.

1. Time management skills

Schedule your various activities by working back from your deadline in the same way as you drew your timeline in the very first activity in this book (see p 11). Plan for a minimum of two drafts.

2. Information management skills

As data is collected, distinguish between key facts, secondary facts and supporting data. Simply put, key facts are those essential to your argument, without which your report would have no foundation or substance. Secondary facts provide the next layers of information. Supporting data is used to flesh out the report, but on its own would be of little consequence. For key facts to be most persuasive, they need to be supported by secondary facts and supporting data.

Activity 6.8   Read a newspaper article. Identify and distinguish between the key facts, secondary facts and supporting data.

Remember, the sequencing of information influences the conclusion drawn. The written word is certainly a powerful medium, but it can work against you, leading the reader to the wrong conclusion if you have not structured and sequenced the information to best suit your needs.

3. Writing and editing skills

It is not possible to write and edit a report at the same time. So:

☐ Aim to make the first draft as good as possible, but do not waste time trying to make it perfect
☐ When the first draft is complete, forget it for several days
☐ Remind yourself of the purpose, structure and style, and edit according to these criteria
☐ Be willing to change any of these criteria at this stage in the light of new insights or information
☐ Rewrite the report without trying to make it perfect. Now the purpose, structure and style should be fixed
☐ Forget it for several days
☐ Make the final edits
☐ Present the report.

Structure and style

The purpose of your report should be clear. A contents page, cross-referencing, clear chapter headings and the use of sub-sections should combine with bullet-pointed lists, appropriate diagrams, charts or graphs, brief linking paragraphs and, if necessary, appendices, to provide the reader with a simple, clear, easy and quick-to-read report. The structure of a strategic report, for example, could be as outlined below:

☐ Contents
☐ Executive summary: Report brief and conclusions summarised
☐ Chapter 1: External analysis

☐ Chapter 2: Internal analysis
☐ Chapter 3: SWOT and summary paragraph
☐ Conclusion: Key strategic issues identified and recommendations
☐ Appendices.

Editing one's own work is difficult. It is best to adopt a disassociated state; imagine that the report was written by someone else. An effective approach would be as follows:

☐ Ask: Do I need this sentence/paragraph/diagram? Is it essential? What is lost if I remove it?
☐ Ask: Can I write this sentence/paragraph in a better way? Refer back to your purpose, structure and style criteria
☐ Whenever possible, avoid long, complex sentences
☐ If a sentence does not work, try reversing it
☐ Aim for simplicity
☐ Edit the full report before making any changes. Use symbols to highlight the different changes needed.

Activity 6.9   Delete 10 words from your summary, without minimising its effectiveness.

Proof-reading

Print the report before proof-reading it. The written word looks different on a page from on a screen, and it is the printed version the reader will see. When proof-reading always:

☐ Read individual words first, checking for spelling mistakes
☐ Read individual sentences next, checking for structure, grammar and meaning. Ask the question: 'Can this be misinterpreted?'
☐ Read individual paragraphs next, checking for cohesion and meaning
☐ Read individual sections/chapters next, checking for purpose, structure and style
☐ Read the full report in one sitting, checking for a sense of completeness.

Activity 6.10   Give your summary a title. Then delete 10 more words. To what extent has the title made that easier to do?
Experiment by deleting the first sentence. What effect does that have?
Experiment by putting your last two sentences, or at least their message, first. What happens then?

Persuasive report writing: key points!

☐ Audience analysis is an essential prerequisite to writing persuasive reports.

☐ A clear sense of purpose must be reflected through the most simple and appropriate:

   ☐ Structure

   ☐ Style.

☐ Report writers need to possess good:

   ☐ Time management skills

   ☐ Information management skills

   ☐ Writing and editing skills.

☐ Remember:

   ☐ It is impossible to write and edit at the same time

   ☐ To aim for a minimum of two drafts

   ☐ To edit the entire report, using symbols to highlight corrections, before rewriting

   ☐ To proof-read from the printed page, not the screen.

☐ Persuasive campaigning

I hate the word 'campaign'. It limits thinking and narrows one's approach to the task in hand. It doesn't truly explain what happens when you are trying to influence and persuade, to change opinion or a course of action. And it implies a beginning and an end which, whilst it may be an accurate reflection, again hinders finding the best solution.

(Interview with Alan Barnard, 2000)

Alan Barnard is one of the UK's most able and successful campaign managers. Having worked for the Labour Party since 1989, he was made overall election co-ordinator in 1999, with responsibility for the strategic direction of election planning and for all aspects of the operational management of elections. He introduced many of the Labour Party's modern election fighting techniques and, along with Margaret McDonagh, devised the Party's general election strategy for marginal seats. He was put in charge of the last five days of campaigning during the 1997 election, during which time he was responsible for increasing the momentum of the campaign up to polling day. For Alan Barnard, the ability to manage successful campaigns is the essential element of his professional role, but how important is it for managers in other organisations? Leif Bergmann, Director of the Henley Management College, Denmark, believes it to be a core skill. He says:

Managers need to 'campaign' values, beliefs and messages to employees at all levels in the organisation. This kind of 'campaigning' is far too important to be left to others – for example, marketing departments or consultants. Communication is a distinctive management capability. Managers must, therefore, take responsibility for internal and external 'campaigns'.

(Interview with Leif Bergmann, 2001)

Alan Barnard's experience of political and business campaigning is extensive and, quite possibly, unique. It is why the Barnard Campaign model (see Figure 6.2) provides the basis for our study of the manager as a persuasive campaigner. The key elements of the CAMPAIGN model are:

- ☐ Cause
- ☐ Audience
- ☐ Message
- ☐ Publicity
- ☐ Attitudes/action
- ☐ Information
- ☐ Goals
- ☐ Non-stop.

> *Alan Barnard is an outstanding strategic campaigner. I would always want him on my side. Anyone who wants to be a persuasive campaigner should study his work and approach.*
> (Interview with Margaret McDonagh, Labour Party General Secretary (1997-2001), 2001)

Figure 6.2
The Barnard
Campaign model

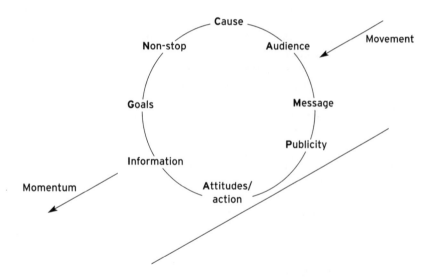

Cause

Campaigners must have a cause. Without one there is no sense of purpose, no incentive to create change, no reason to campaign. Persuasive campaigners have a commitment to a cause that fuels their energy and fires their enthusiasm. It can also force them to evaluate their moral and ethical standpoint. Questions that need to be addressed include:

- ☐ What am I prepared to do to 'win'?
- ☐ What compromises am I prepared to make?
- ☐ What lines am I willing to cross?

Barnard asserts that: 'The way campaign managers answer such questions is, essentially, an individual matter. People cannot force their values on to others.' (Interview with Barnard, 2000). While this is undeniably so, managers running campaigns within their organisation would usually want to ensure that both their cause and the nature and manner of their campaign are at least in keeping with the organisation's mission statement.

Of course, the issue of ethical management is not limited only to campaigning. Managers possess varying degrees of power and with that comes the responsibility to exercise it in a socially and environmentally appropriate manner. In *The Power of Ethical Management* (1998), Blanchard and Peale identify five key principles that underpin the application of ethical power. These are:

1. *Purpose.* This requires synergy between the individual manager's sense of purpose and that of the organisation, as reflected through its vision, values and beliefs.
2. *Pride.* A shared ethical purpose leads to a sense of pride in the behaviour and goals of the organisation, which, in turn, limits the possibility of unethical practices.
3. *Patience.* An organisation holding powerful ethical values is more likely to aim for long(er)-term success, particularly if transient, short-term successes require what is regarded as unethical behaviour.
4. *Persistence.* Shared ethical values reflect and inspire a commitment to a particular purpose and a style of achieving it. There is an ongoing determination to ensure that actions reflect values.
5. *Perspective.* Opportunities, problems and situations are evaluated from the shared ethical standpoint. There are few, if any, hurried decisions. How the organisation achieves its goals is as important as achieving them.

Activity 6.11 Think of a cause you hold dear - one that you would campaign for. What changes would be created if your campaign was successful? What would you be willing to do to ensure the success of your campaign? What would you not be willing to do? To what extent would the end justify the means?

Audience

We have already discussed the importance of knowing audience needs, experiences and expectations. To that we can add some extra insights. When discussing the importance of campaigning managers understanding their audiences, Alan Barnard says:

It's about connecting with people - communicating with them and making them feel good about the course of action you are recommending. You need to define your target audience. Not just in terms of who they are, but in terms of what they are thinking, what opinions they hold, what their aspirations and desires are, and what barriers they see to achieving those things. You also need to know how big your audience is and who, or what, influences their opinions.

(Interview with Barnard, 2000)

Barnard stresses that it is not sufficient simply to know your audience's opinions. It is also essential to understand how audience members form those opinions and the parameters of their possible actions. It is important, too, to determine what percentage of the target audience needs to be persuaded for the campaign to be successful.

Campaign managers also need to identify organisational gatekeepers – those individuals who hold the most power and influence, who have to be persuaded if the campaign is to be successful – and analyse how best to approach and convince them. This needs to be done while maintaining a continual focus on the wider audience. Information-gathering and analysis are key skills in this regard (see Chapter 5).

Activity 6.12   Refer to Activity 6.11. Define the audience your campaign would need to connect with. What are its current views on the subject? Who, or what, influences its opinions? Who are the gatekeepers? What opposition would you face from within your target audience?

Message

At the heart of the campaign is the message. It identifies the cause, its purpose and its value for the target audience. Key rules for managing the message are:

☐ Keep it simple, using simple language and concepts
☐ Repeat the core message frequently and in different ways
☐ Have an arresting approach – stand out from the crowd
☐ Stay on message – do not let anything distract you from it
☐ Ensure your message is relevant to your target audience
☐ Ensure the medium you use for delivering the message is the most appropriate
☐ Use emotion – it moves people further and faster than logic and rationale
☐ Never assume all the target audience has got the message.

It is essential to differentiate between the message and a slogan. A slogan is *not* the message. It is one way of encapsulating the message. Barnard recommends focusing on the policies and intended behaviours that highlight the message and sharing the message by stressing the benefits the target audience will experience if your campaign is successful. A memorable slogan is of most value when it reminds the audience what you are campaigning for, why you are campaigning for it, and the benefits that are unique to your proposal.

Activity 6.13   Refer to Activities 6.11 and 6.12. What will your message be? How, when and where would you deliver it?

Publicity

Publicity is achieved in part through the appropriate delivery of the message. Other publicity opportunities will occur, however, some of which will enable the campaigning manager to respond to the arguments against his/her cause, all of which must be seen as opportunities to repeat the core message. Publicity needs to be planned and sequenced throughout the campaign so that it gains momentum as the campaign reaches its climax.

Attitudes/action

These are the behaviours, skills and qualities of a persuasive campaign manager and his/her team. Barnard identifies the essential abilities of a campaign manager as:

- ☐ Leadership skills (Chapter 4)
- ☐ Team-building skills (Chapter 4)
- ☐ Creativity (Chapter 5)
- ☐ Motivation (Chapter 3)
- ☐ Delegation (Chapter 3)
- ☐ Helicopter vision (Chapter 5)
- ☐ Systemic thinking. (Chapter 5)
- ☐ Pressure management (Chapter 1)
- ☐ Image management (Chapter 1)
- ☐ Information management (Chapter 5)
- ☐ Openness to new ideas and approaches (Chapter 5)
- ☐ Energy, enthusiasm and focus.

He also makes the point that 'The campaign manager doesn't have to be the best campaigner. He or she has to be able to get the best out of everyone else' (Interview with Barnard, 2000).

Campaign managers and their teams need to:

- ☐ Have contingency plans
- ☐ Work within the agreed budget
- ☐ Research their progress among samples drawn from the target audience
- ☐ Be willing to amend their strategy and tactics in the light of that research.

Finally, campaign managers and their teams need to be willing to accept mistakes as an inevitable part of the process. According to Barnard, 'It's the team's job to minimise the impact of any mistakes that are made ... but ... a timid campaign will retreat into its shell and not have any effect' (Interview with Barnard, 2000).

Information

Information is the lifeblood of a campaign. Information about the target audience, opposition, gatekeepers, how the campaign is being received and shifts in opinion, and relevant data, needs to be updated constantly. Research is an essential, ongoing part of the campaign process. Good information management involves:

☐ Collection (information-gathering)
☐ Interpretation (understanding what it means (or could mean) to you and/or your audience)
☐ Application (using and/or sharing it to the best possible advantage).

Timing plays an important part in the overall strategy, but is of particular importance in media management. When discussing information-giving, Barnard explains:

> It's about constructing a story for your audience. The story needs to be credible, simple and easy to understand. It needs to have a start, middle and an end, and every layer of the story needs to reinforce your core message. Also every piece of information, or every part of your story has to wiggle – it has to come alive for your audience.
>
> (Interview with Barnard, 2000)

Persuasive campaigners, like great sales personnel, understand that the order in which information is presented influences the audience's eventual decision(s).

Goals

Barnard says that the starting point for a successful campaign is: 'To understand what you want to achieve. Think through why you are doing what you are doing, and what you want the outcome to be' (Interview with Barnard, 2000). During the campaign process short-term goals need to be agreed in the light of audience responses and/or new information received, although, ultimately, it is against the long-term goals that the success of the campaign will be measured. This element of Barnard's model also serves to remind the campaign manager of the need to understand, and respond positively to, the shared goals of the target audience.

Activity 6.14 Evaluate your ability as a campaign manager, by using the following grid:

Requirement	Limited ability		Very able
Leadership skills	1		5
Team-building skills	1		5
Creativity	1		5
Self-motivation	1		5
Motivating others	1		5
Delegation	1		5
Helicopter vision	1		5
Systemic thinking	1		5
Pressure management	1		5
Image management	1		5
Information management	1		5
Energy, enthusiasm and focus	1		5
Openness to new ideas and approaches	1		5

Non-stop

The most persuasive campaigners, driven by a cause, never stop campaigning, even though there is inevitably a deadline towards which they are working.

Movement and momentum

'Managing a campaign is like pushing a large boulder up a hill, so it can run down the other side' (Interview with Barnard, 2000). Barnard stresses the need not only for continual movement before and after the deadline, but for developing momentum throughout the campaign. The last four or five days, he states, are crucial. Everything that has gone before is in preparation for this last 'big push'. At this stage the campaign should have an unstoppable momentum: the 'boulder' should be at maximum speed, irresistible in its intensity.

Persuasive campaigning: key points!

☐ Managers who are leaders have to be able to campaign on a variety of levels.
☐ The eight key elements of campaigning are:
  ☐ Cause
  ☐ Audience
  ☐ Message
  ☐ Publicity
  ☐ Attitudes/action
  ☐ Information
  ☐ Goals
  ☐ Non-stop campaigning.
☐ A campaign should have continual movement and, within the initial time frame, should gather an unstoppable momentum in the final days.
☐ Persuasive campaigners:
  ☐ Are multi-skilled
  ☐ Understand their target audience
  ☐ Are adept at staying on message
  ☐ Are adept at making their message relevant and meaningful to their target audience.
☐ The success of campaigns is measured externally by matching or exceeding the expectations of observers.
☐ Success is measured internally by achieving the goals set.

Summary: selling ideas and persuasive campaigning

☐ Successful campaigning and selling of ideas is founded upon:
  ☐ Understanding and recognising the four stages of the selling process
  ☐ Understanding and motivating the target audience
  ☐ The creation of appropriate, meaningful messages

☐ Need satisfaction
☐ Having clearly defined, time-scaled goals
☐ Creating momentum
☐ Managing and learning from rejection.
☐ The core skills are those associated with:
    ☐ Managing self and self-image
    ☐ Managing one-to-one relationships
    ☐ Leadership
    ☐ Teamwork
    ☐ Creativity and creative problem-solving
    ☐ Media management
    ☐ Information-gathering, analysing and management
    ☐ Time management
    ☐ Pressure management.
☐ The aim is to influence and persuade.

A final thought

Our final thought for this chapter centres on a letter written by a first-year university student to her parents. It reinforces both Robert Louis Stevenson's observation that on occasion everyone sells something and the fact that the sequencing of information influences the way the core message is perceived. The letter is as follows:

Dear Mum and Dad,
Sorry I have not written to you sooner, but life has been rather hectic. Some months ago, I was involved in a serious car crash. The Firemen called to the scene were able to cut me out of the wreckage in a little over an hour. Fortunately, my injuries have now almost healed.
    The good thing that came out of the accident was that I fell in love with one of the firemen and we are engaged to be married. We haven't set a date yet, but it will be before it becomes obvious that I am pregnant. I know how much you will both welcome the opportunity to be grandparents! My husband to be is a fine man, as mature as you would expect from someone nearly thirty years older than me. The fact that our children will be mixed race, I see as an advantage in our multi-cultural society. I'm sure you agree! Although we haven't yet resolved the religious debate. I want our children to be Methodists, as we are, but my intended is insisting they should be Rastafarians, like him.
    Now that you have read the above, I'd like to add just one more thing. None of it is true ! There was no car crash. There is no fireman. No pregnancy. No wedding plans. No mixed race children. The truth is, I scored only 39% in my end of year exam and I'm going to have to re-sit the year. I just wanted you to get that result in perspective.
    Your loving daughter ...

References

Argyle, M. 1967. *The Psychology of Interpersonal Behaviour*. Harmondsworth: Penguin.
Blanchard, K.H. and Peale, N.V. 1988. *The Power of Ethical Management*. London: Cedar.
Guirdham, M. 1995. *International Skills at Work* (2nd edn). Hemel Hempstead: Prentice Hall.
Bishop, J.H. 1625. *Works*.
Wickham, P.A. 1999. *Management Consulting*. London: Financial Times/ Pitman Publishing.

Further reading

Wickham, P.A. 1999. *Management Consulting*. London: Financial Times/ Pitman Publishing.
Aziz, K. 2001. *Presenting To Win*. Dublin: Oak Tree Press.
Whetton, D., Cameron, K. and Woods, M. 2000. *Developing Management Skills for Europe* (2nd edn). London: Financial Times/Prentice Hall.
Blanchard, K.H. and Peale, N.V. 1988. *The Power of Ethical Management*. London: Cedar.

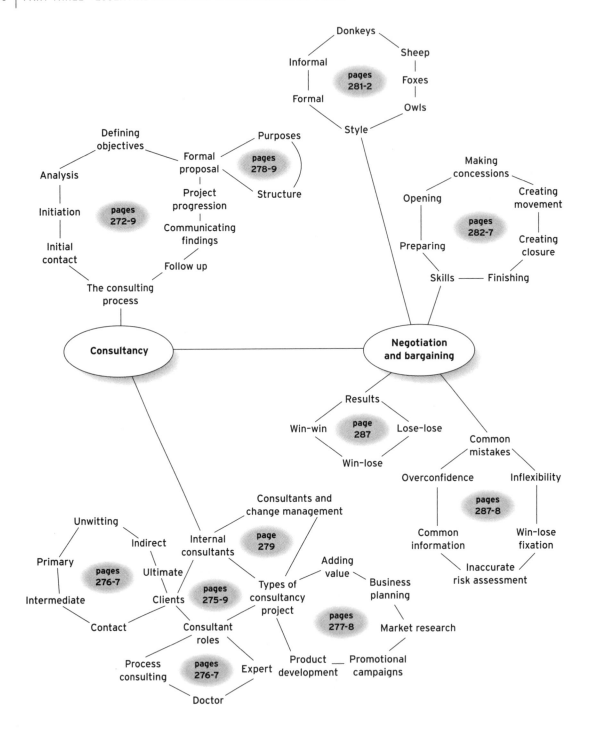

Consultancy, negotiation and bargaining

...a bargain dog never bites.

(Ogden Nash)

This chapter will develop your:

Awareness of:	Knowledge of:	Capability to:
The manager as an internal consultant.	The common activities of the consulting process: ☐ Initial contact ☐ Initiating the project ☐ Client analysis ☐ Defining objectives ☐ Formal proposal ☐ Progressing the project ☐ Communicating findings ☐ Follow-up.	Recognise and manage each stage of the consulting process.
Consultant roles and associated skills and qualities.	Types of management consulting project.	Write a project proposal.
Types of client.		
Consultancy and change management.		
The concept of negotiation and bargaining.	The six stages of the negotiation process: ☐ Preparing ☐ Opening ☐ Making concessions ☐ Creating movement ☐ Creating closure ☐ Finishing.	Negotiate successfully.
Different negotiating styles.	Associated principles and practices.	
Common negotiating mistakes.		

☐ Management consulting

Consultancy can produce meaningful and significant change. Negotiation can result in a win–win situation, with both parties recognising and sharing benefit. Bargains 'with bite' can be made. Only there is no guarantee. Operating in a consultancy role, a manager's past successes count for little if his/her current intervention fails to deliver. Every new negotiation is precisely that: *new*. It is a stand-alone interaction influenced only indirectly by previous results and associated reputations. Bargaining power shifts from situation to situation and, as with so many aspects of their role, managers need the awareness and flexibility to recognise and adapt to the newness in each situation. This, essentially, is the challenge facing managers involved in consultancy, negotiation and bargaining, whether with internal or external colleagues or clients. Like a musician, writer or actor, the manager involved in these roles is only as good as his/her most recent performance, the effects of which will usually be clear to, and felt by, a significant and vocal audience.

The consulting process

As indicated, consulting is a challenging and varied management exercise. For all its variety, however, an examination of the consulting process reveals a sequence of common activities. Philip A. Wickham identifies these as:

- ☐ Initial contact with the client
- ☐ Initiating the consulting project
- ☐ Analysis of the client's business/situation
- ☐ Defining the project objectives
- ☐ Making a formal proposal
- ☐ Progressing the project
- ☐ Communicating the findings
- ☐ Following up.

Throughout this process, the consultant needs to:

- ☐ Display good relationship-building and communication skills (Chapters 1 and 2)
- ☐ Have the ability to switch between analytical, systemic, creative and pragmatic thinking styles (Chapter 5)
- ☐ Know how to sell ideas and campaign persuasively (Chapter 6)
- ☐ Demonstrate leadership qualities, team-building and/or team management skills (Chapter 4).

And all this needs to be done with the aim of delivering an agreed result on time, to budget and within all specified parameters.

Initial contact

Consultants and clients can meet initially in formal and informal ways, with one seeking out the other or through the recommendation or involvement of a third party. The initial contact and meetings require consultants to have good image management skills, sensitivity and awareness, and the ability to create rapport. They have to convince potential clients not only of the value they can add to their business, but of their suitability to manage the people, the politics and the culture of the organisation.

Ideally, at this stage both client and consultant share a clear understanding of what is required. When this is not the case, the consultant has to help the client clarify objectives. Often clients have a sense that something is wrong or that 'things could be better', but are unclear of the causes or the most effective solutions. In this situation, the consultant needs to be adept at:

☐ Questioning (Chapter 2)
☐ Systems thinking (Chapter 5)
☐ Analysis (Chapter 5).

Project initiation

This stage can take a number of forms, from a simple verbal agreement to a written contract. For a client to make a commitment to a consultant is a significant step, and is usually regarded as such by both parties. For that reason, the first stage of project initiation is often an invitation to the consultant to make a formal bid for the work at hand. The advantage of doing so is that it ensures agreement about key elements of the project, such as:

☐ Client and consultant expectations
☐ The levels of resources the client is prepared to commit
☐ The levels and degree of communication the client and consultant will make to stakeholders.

Such factors, combined with how well the client and consultant know each other, will determine the detail and degree of formality of the project initiation.

Analysis of the current situation

At this stage, this is only a preliminary analysis, enabling the consultant to gain an initial awareness of the strengths and weaknesses of the client's business, and the opportunities and threats in the environment.

Defining objectives

This is a crucial part of the process. As Wickham writes: 'A critical element in the success of the consulting exercise is that its objectives are well defined and understood by all involved. It is the objectives of the project that the client is "buying".' (Wickham, 1999: 86). It is also important to differentiate between project objectives and project outcomes. Objectives are those things the project will achieve. Outcomes are the business's new capabilities resulting from the objectives being achieved. A consulting project should help the organisation to achieve its stated mission. To do this, the project objectives should be:

☐ Consistent (with the project's aim)
☐ Well defined (understood by all)
☐ Desirable (of benefit to the organisation)
☐ Feasible (realistic in principle)
☐ Achievable (the necessary resources are available).

The formal proposal

This is the consultant's formal statement of what he/she will do for the client (the project process) and what he/she will achieve for the client (the project objectives). In doing this, the formal proposal identifies and schedules:

☐ Information-gathering activities
☐ Information analysis
☐ Project tasks.

It is against these tasks that the progress of the actual project can be monitored and evaluated. A well-written proposal also helps direct the client's expectations, ensuring an appropriate degree of realism is maintained.

Progressing the project

This combines a variety of ongoing activities, including:

☐ Information-gathering and analysis
☐ Communication with the client
☐ Control and monitoring of the project tasks
☐ Recording and evaluating progress.

Communicating the findings

The final, formal communication of the findings acts like a full-stop at the end of a sentence, confirming to the client the value and validity of the work done, marking clearly that it is now complete and that a new 'beginning' is ready to be made.

Following up

However, despite the above, consultants and clients may both see added value in maintaining contact after the findings have been communicated. Benefits to the client include receiving additional advice on implementation and possibly securing consultant availability for future projects. Benefits to the consultant include the possibility of being offered another project, an increased likelihood of the client being willing to offer an endorsement, and the growth of his/her business network.

Internal consultants

As intimated at the start of this book, the world – including the world of work – is changing more rapidly than at any other time in our history. Managers can no longer expect simply to fulfil the requirements of a single role within a single department, as detailed in an ageing job description. Project and multi-functional teams are replacing both historical hierarchies and the formalities and security of clearly defined and often isolated and independent functions. The result is that managers need a wider variety of personal and interpersonal skills if they are to play successfully the myriad roles now required of them. One of those roles can be that of internal consultant.

Organisations and individuals are increasingly recognising the value of a permanently employed manager who adopts the role of consultant. For the manager, the challenges and opportunities are varied and exciting, requiring:

☐ Ongoing learning and skill development
☐ The ability to inspire and create change
☐ An understanding of both the external and internal resources available, what is required, and how to meet demand
☐ Strategic and planning capability.

Internal consultants follow the same processes and face many of the same issues as their external counterparts, but also have to manage additional factors created by their permanency within the organisation. For example, internal consultants need to ensure their dispassionate analysis of current situations and relationships with long-term colleagues. Internal consultants cannot afford to buy in too heavily to the accepted organisational view of its strengths and weaknesses, its unique status, or its levels of success. Rather, they have to be comfortable being *in* the organisation but not a part *of* the organisation. Of course, for the consultant-manager who can maintain this duality, there are benefits to be gained from possessing such intimate knowledge of the culture, the people and the situation. Not least, this knowledge enhances the consultant's ability to:

☐ Sell ideas
☐ Manage internal politics
☐ Inspire and create change
☐ Set the most appropriate time frames.

Activity 7.1   Imagine playing the role of internal consultant in an organisation you know well. Identify the first change you would want to sell and implement. Identify the potential barriers you would face and the likely support you would receive. Using the eight stages of the consulting process as a framework, consider how you would introduce your proposal, the objectives you would agree, and how you would progress the project.

Types of management consulting project

The varied challenges consultants face stem from differences in:

☐ The role and style of consultancy required
☐ The nature of the client
☐ The type of project to be undertaken.

Consultant roles

In his book, *Process Consultation* (1987), Edgar Schein discusses three approaches the consultant can adopt. These are determined by the issue to be addressed and, particularly, the nature of the consultant–client relationship. They are:

1. *Expert*. As the expert, the consultant analyses the problem or issue presented by the client and identifies the most appropriate solution. This approach is most suited to those situations in which the client recognises his/her lack of expertise in an area that is the consultant's acknowledged specialism.
2. *Doctor*. As the doctor, the consultant's expertise extends to diagnosing the problem prior to recommending a 'cure'. Again, this approach is most readily accepted only when the consultant is a recognised expert in his/her field.
3. *Process consulting*. Here the consultant's role is to enable those within the organisation to identify problems, then devise and implement their own solutions. In this way the consultant becomes a facilitator of change, ensuring that those who will live through and manage the change have ownership of it.

Activity 7.2   Refer back to Activity 7.1. Which of Schein's three approaches to consultancy would most suit the needs and expectations of the organisation you identified? Why? How comfortable would you be adopting that approach? Why?
  Can you think of an organisation where a different approach would be more acceptable?

The nature of the client

Schein identifies six client types, suggesting that the quality of process consulting is enhanced when the consultant interacts with a variety of individuals involved rather than a single one. Schein's client types are:

1. *Contact clients*. These make the initial contact with the consultant, introducing the possibility of the consultant's involvement with their organisation.
2. *Intermediate clients*. These become involved as the project takes shape and progresses. Intermediate clients are members of the organisation, who provide the consultant with insights, information and assistance.
3. *Primary clients*. First aware of the problem or issue because they are most obviously affected by it, the primary client pays for the solution or resolution.

4. *Unwitting clients*. These are people within the organisation who will be affected by the consultant's intervention but who are not immediately aware of that fact.
5. *Indirect clients*. Unlike unwitting clients, indirect clients recognise that they will be affected by the consultant's intervention. Despite the fact that they can exert powerful positive or negative influences, the consultant is unlikely to be immediately aware of them.
6. *Ultimate clients*. These are the people who will be affected by the consultant's intervention either directly or indirectly. They exist within and outside the organisation. Their interests need to be acknowledged and addressed by the consultant as the project develops.

Activity 7.3	Refer back to Activities 7.1 and 7.2. Identify the different client types within the organisation you have selected. How would you address the interests of your ultimate client group?

Types of project

Consultants can manage various projects. Essentially, irrespective of the project type, they are all means by which the consultants can add value to their client's business through the provision of any, or all, of the following: information; specific expertise; new perspectives; and new resources. Project types include, but are not limited to:

☐ Business planning and development
☐ Marketing research or strategy development
☐ Promotional campaigns
☐ Product development.

Business planning and development
The chance to contribute to an organisation's growth and development provides a great opportunity for consultants. Clients may have a very specific intention or direction for the consultant to pursue, or they may be far more vague. In the latter scenario, the consultant's preliminary task is to determine the organisation's current strategic position, then identify and evaluate options.

Marketing research or strategy development
The effectiveness of market research, designed to provide managers with an understanding of the level and nature of the competition they face, is based upon asking the right questions, in the right way, to the right audience, at the right time. There are four types of market research. These are:

1. *Quantitative*. Quantitative questions require quantified answers, expressed in numerical or statistical form. Quantitative research identifies and records those business factors that are most easily categorised and measured.

2. *Qualitative*. Qualitative questions are those which do not require quantified answers.
3. *Primary*. Primary research focuses on gathering and collating information that is specific to the project undertaken.
4. *Secondary*. Secondary research focuses on information that is already available and, although not originally gathered and collated for the purpose of the current project, provides additional insights.

Market research is a specialised activity that can take many forms. Consultants therefore often buy in expertise if requiring extensive and thorough market research.

Market research enables the consultant to identify the most significant business opportunities, but these cannot be taken advantage of without the application of an appropriate marketing strategy. This, in turn, is dependent on a thorough understanding of the marketing mix, which is commonly referred to as the 5Ps:

- ☐ Product
- ☐ Price
- ☐ Place
- ☐ Promotion
- ☐ Public Relations.

Promotional campaigns

The purpose of a promotional campaign is to:

- ☐ Inform (potential customers of a product or service)
- ☐ Interest (those potential customers in the product or service)
- ☐ Encourage (those customers to make a purchase).

For this to be successful, the consultant needs to understand the market sector that is being targeted, the relationship between the nature of the campaign and the likelihood, volume and duration of purchase, and all associated costs. (For a more detailed analysis of persuasive campaigning, refer to Chapter 6.)

Product development

Depending on the consultant's area of expertise, he/she can support new product development in a variety of ways, including technical advice, financial planning and market research.

Project proposal documents

The purpose of a project proposal document is three-fold:

- ☐ To make clear the aims and objectives of the project
- ☐ To make clear the value to the organisation of the project outcomes
- ☐ To make the client commit to it.

As with reports, proposals need to be brief, simple and unambiguous. They are an important tool for managing client expectations. Consulting projects at least need to meet and, ideally, surpass client expectations. The final result will invariably be compared against those targets written in the proposal.

A typical project proposal would include:

- ☐ A title
- ☐ A brief outline of the client's current situation and requirements
- ☐ Identification of the overall aim of the project
- ☐ A list of the project's objectives
- ☐ Identification of the outcomes
- ☐ A description of the consultants' intended approach
- ☐ A time schedule
- ☐ Costs to the client, including fees and expenditure.

Activity 7.4   Refer back to the previous activities. Write a project proposal, using the structure outlined above, identifying the project aim, objectives and outcomes. Ensure that it meets (and directs) the client's expectations.

Consultancy and change management

Whatever the nature of the project, the result will be change of some sort. The 'selling' and successful implementation of change is, for reasons discussed in previous chapters, a core management task. There can be any combination of logistic, emotional, cultural and training issues to be addressed. K. Lewin's (1951) 'unfreeze–change–refreeze' model (see Figure 7.1) is interesting because it implies the resistance – the rigidity – that might be encountered in the early stages, while suggesting a return to that state once the change has been consolidated.

Figure 7.1
Lewin's change
model (1951)

Unfreeze   ⟹   Change   ⟹   Refreeze

Activity 7.5   'Freeze' or 'flexible'? Consider the extent to which Lewin's model is appropriate in a rapidly changing world. Design your own, simple model to represent the ideal change process.

Management consultancy: key points!

- ☐ The consulting process is made up a sequence of common activities. These are:
  - ☐ Initial contact with the client
  - ☐ Initiating the consulting project
  - ☐ Analysis of the client's business/situation
  - ☐ Defining the project objectives
  - ☐ Making a formal proposal
  - ☐ Progressing the project
  - ☐ Communicating the findings
  - ☐ Following up.
- ☐ Management consultants need to possess:
  - ☐ Good relationship-building skills
  - ☐ Good communication skills
  - ☐ The ability to apply different thinking styles
  - ☐ The ability to sell ideas and campaign persuasively
  - ☐ Leadership qualities
  - ☐ Team-building and management skills
  - ☐ The ability to meet deadlines and work to and within agreed parameters.
- ☐ A consultant also needs to be a:
  - ☐ Committed learner
  - ☐ Change manager
  - ☐ Resource identifier and allocator
  - ☐ Strategic planner.
- ☐ There are different type of client and consultancy project. Schein identifies six client types. These are:
  - ☐ Contact clients
  - ☐ Intermediate clients
  - ☐ Primary clients
  - ☐ Unwitting clients
  - ☐ Indirect clients
  - ☐ Ultimate clients.
- ☐ Types of project include:
  - ☐ Business planning and development
  - ☐ Marketing research or strategy development
  - ☐ Promotional campaigns
  - ☐ Product development.

☐ Negotiation and bargaining

Unlike the creative process which contains myriad paradoxes, negotiation and bargaining is founded on only one. Such is its significance, however, that it alone is the primary cause of all the difficulties negotiators face. The paradox is this: *People only negotiate and bargain when there is something of value they wish to attain. This desire, or need, is both the negotiator's starting point and the weakness that can be exploited by those with whom they are negotiating.* Thankfully, all sides in a negotiation bring with them their own needs and associated vulnerabilities. While these may not always balance out – one side may be perceived to be in the weaker starting position – there are always opportunities for the skilled negotiator to strengthen his/her bargaining power as the interaction progresses. This usually begins with negotiators:

☐ Agreeing the boundaries within which the negotiations will focus
☐ Denying their need for a particular outcome
☐ Stressing the gulf that exists between the parties and the improbability of a successful result.

This is often followed by the development of informal talks, alongside the more formal meetings, exploring without commitment the most likely areas of agreement. This, in turn, leads to a move by one party that is designed to force the other side into making a decision. A key element in this three-phase approach to negotiating is timing, with both parties moving through the process at the same pace. Ann Douglas explains it thus: 'So far as the actions of the parties are concerned, the main imperative is that the movements of the two sides be synchronised to take on the phases of the bargaining sequence concurrently' (Douglas, 1957: 69–81).

Negotiating style

This can be either informal or formal. The degree of formality is often determined by the nature of the negotiations and, particularly, the relationship between the two parties. Informal negotiations emphasise the relationship between the two parties, and encourage a focus on the *spirit* of any agreement reached. Formal negotiations, through their focus on the written word, often favour the party with the strongest power base, limit the likelihood of informal talks and understandings, and emphasise the *letter* of any agreement reached.

For many managers, negotiations are part of an ongoing relationship with internal or external colleagues, clients or potential clients. An informal approach would, whenever possible, be the most appropriate in these situations, bearing in mind that the more formal the process, the more the advantage lies with the party with the strongest power base.

Understanding negotiating style is a key aspect of Gavin Kennedy's practical and engaging book, the title of which sums up his thoughts on the subject: *Everything is Negotiable* (2000). Kennedy identifies four sets of negotiating characteristics, which he labels:

1. *Donkey.* 'Donkeys' are those negotiators who are unaware of what can be achieved, demonstrate stubborn, emotional defiance in the face of unacceptable offers, and are often limited by what Kennedy describes as 'deep, though pragmatically flawed "principles"' (Kennedy, 2000:6).
2. *Sheep.* 'Sheep' are negotiators who are unable to fight for their interests, are often too concerned with not annoying the other party and, ultimately, are too easily influenced by others.
3. *Fox.* 'Foxes' are pragmatic, results-focused negotiators, who are capable of exploiting the weaknesses of others but who run the risk of being unnecessarily devious.
4. *Owl.* 'Owls' are negotiators who are respected not only for what they do, but also how they do it. 'Owls' understand the benefits of developing appropriate relationships within the negotiating process, are able to defend against any threats they face, and take advantage of any opportunities that appear.

Activity 7.6   Which of Kennedy's four negotiating characteristics closely describes your current negotiating style? Identify friends or colleagues who belong in the other categories.

Negotiating skills

The three-phase approach, outlined above, can be broken down into six stages, each requiring specific skills. These are:

☐ Preparing
☐ Opening
☐ Making concessions
☐ Creating movement
☐ Creating closure
☐ Finishing.

Kennedy writes: 'In my experience, there is no such thing as *advanced* negotiating skills. There is only the constant application of your core skills to ever more complex situations' (Kennedy, 2000: 8, original emphasis).

Activity 7.7   Think of a current situation about which you might enter into negotiation. List the things you need to know and do in preparation.

Preparing

As with meetings and presentations, preparation is the essential first component of the negotiating process. Sun Tzu's martial dictum is as appropriate to the negotiating room as it is to the battlefield:

Know the other and know yourself:
One hundred challenges without danger;
Know not the other and yet know yourself:
One triumph for one defeat;
Know not the other and know not yourself:
Every challenge is certain peril.

(Wing, 1989: 51)

Understanding self includes an awareness of:

☐ The strengths and weaknesses of your personal negotiating style and experience
☐ Your and/or your company's needs and 'bottom line'
☐ The ways you and/or your company are perceived by the other party
☐ The strengths and weaknesses of what you have to offer
☐ What you and/or your company would regard as a 'win'.

Understanding the other party includes an awareness of:

☐ Their negotiating style and experience
☐ Their needs and 'bottom line'
☐ The benefits (to you) of what they have to offer
☐ What they would regard as a 'win'.

Understanding the environment includes an awareness of:

☐ The time frame within which you have to negotiate
☐ Any external factors or forces that could influence the process.

Pre-negotiation preparation enables managers to identify their objectives and targets (those results they would willingly accept) and their resistant point (the worst possible result they could accept). It also enables them to bring the most appropriate style and substance to the negotiating table, to time the development of the interaction accurately and, ultimately, to achieve a deal through their understanding of the other party's objectives and resistant point, and by making it clear that they can provide what the other party wants. Preparation should be based on the belief that the negotiation will lead to an agreement, and that the process itself serves merely to determine the all-important terms.

Activity 7.8   Refer to Activity 7.7. What will be the most successful possible result for you? What will be your 'bottom line'?

Opening

A sound negotiation principle is: *There is no such thing as a first offer that is too good to refuse!* In other words, no matter how good the other party's opening offer appears to be, resist the natural temptation to grab at an apparent bargain.

Instead, turn it down. Unless the other party is totally devoid of negotiating skill, its opening will almost certainly be a 'bargain dog that never bites'.

Openings in a negotiation are like those in a chess match. They are both of great importance and are employed to disguise the forthcoming strategy and objectives. In negotiation, openings can have a significant impact on the eventual result and therefore need to be managed skilfully. The purpose of the negotiator's opening move is two-fold:

☐ Setting his/her own offer at the most appropriate level. This is usually a long way removed from any predetermined targets
☐ Responding to the other party's opening offer in a way that is deemed most appropriate, based on an understanding gained during the planning stage. This is usually a form of rejection.

As experienced negotiators are aware of both these purposes, there is usually no time advantage to be gained by making the opening offer a serious commitment. This is simply because the other party will automatically view it as a level that is significantly below what you are prepared to offer. Another point to bear in mind is that even if the first offer is the best one available, negotiators cannot be sure of that, and so cannot feel they have accomplished their best possible result until they have applied all available techniques and exhausted all available options. Simply put, to be fulfilled, negotiators have to negotiate their way to success in much the same way as chess masters have to move pieces across the board. Also, there is no personal or professional satisfaction in accepting a 'win' that appears to be too easily offered!

Activity 7.9   Refer to Activity 7.8. What would be your opening offer? What opening offer would you expect the other party to make? How, and why, would you reject it?

Making concessions and creating movement

Concessions feature in all negotiations but, as with most things, there is a right and a wrong way (and a right and a wrong time) to apply them. Essentially, the principle is: *In a negotiation, give nothing away for free – make the other party pay for every (apparent) concession you make.* In other words, preface any concession you may offer with the phrase: 'If I do this, I expect you to do this ...'

Concessions can be viewed as stepping stones in the negotiation journey, which is why they should rarely be presented as an ultimatum. Negotiators who pretend that certain concessions represent their last offer can find themselves struggling to convince the other party when they really do mean to halt. Also, it is hard to keep the momentum of the negotiation going if one party frequently suggests it has made its last offer. This approach has to be balanced, of course, by giving the impression that you cannot be easily moved, by possessing and demonstrating a strong resolve and, if facing an equally tough negotiator, by an acceptance that deadlocks happen. The belief that every negotiation can lead to a successful deal should not blind one to the fact that occasionally they do not. If there is a choice to be made between giving in to tough demands from the other party or being tough back and accepting the likelihood of a deadlock, choose the deadlock. After all, there isn't a lock that can't be picked eventually – assuming both parties have something the other side needs.

Concessions freely given, that do not reflect a trade-off between a small shift in your position for, ideally, a more significant one in the other party's, simply undermine your credibility and increase the other party's confidence in its ability to achieve its ideal exit point. Possibly the worst thing a negotiator can do is to make a concession as a 'sign of goodwill'. Goodwill concessions do not soften up the other side and encourage it to reply in kind. Rather, the opposite is more likely to occur. Once the other party gets something for nothing, it will expect to get more for exactly the same price! Imagine what would happen if a dog trainer decided to reward his German Shepherd with a titbit before it had responded to his command to sit. The answer is obvious: the dog suddenly has no incentive to change its position in response to the trainer's voice. It has learnt that it can get something for nothing and will doggedly (pardon the pun) pursue that approach. No matter how clever a German Shepherd may be, negotiators are smarter and learn more quickly.

According to the *Oxford Thesaurus*, the literal meaning of the word concession is 'submission (or) surrender'. Managers acting as negotiators have to know how to use concessions without surrendering something they intended to retain. Negotiators are not in the business of yielding anything, but of making gains. This is achieved not only by ensuring that they always receive more than they give, but by refusing to be influenced or intimidated by the behaviour of the other party. Aggressive negotiators who use bullying tactics to make others submit are successful because they make their opposition forget one key point: *Behaviour should have no direct effect on the outcome!* No matter how aggressive the other party is, experienced negotiators do not allow themselves to be distracted from their task; they never allow behaviour to become the issue. Also, they never forget that the only reason people negotiate is because neither side has the power nor the will to force a settlement on their terms. Given this, the concept of a bullying negotiator is almost a contradiction in terms.

Be aware also that while threats are a common feature in many negotiations, and do sometimes produce compliance, they always create resentment, which, more often than not, results in a counter-threat and the creation of a vicious circle. The other point to be aware of when managing intimidating opponents is that their image – personal, organisational or environmental – should be ignored in exactly the same way as their behaviour. Whatever the tactics employed, they need to be mentally sidelined. Remember:

☐ The only thing that matters is the issue
☐ The other party cannot intimidate you without your permission. So don't give it.

The SWISH technique described in Chapter 1 can be used to create a positive mental state, resistant to any intimidating tactics.

Activity 7.10   Refer to Activities 7.8 and 7.9. What concessions, if any, would you be prepared to make as 'stepping stones' towards achieving a successful conclusion? How, and when, would you introduce and justify each concession? In each instance, what would be the least you would expect in return?

Creating closure

As the negotiation progresses the pressure to reach closure increases, sometimes creating a sense of anxiety in less experienced negotiators. This can be taken advantage of by a skilled opponent, who will attempt to provoke the other party into a move towards closure on less than favourable terms. Impatience, anxiety or simply a powerful need to reach completion, are common weaknesses that can undermine useful work done early in the negotiating process.

The emotional pressures are often driven by the so-called 'flight, freeze or fight' syndrome explained in Chapter 1. The need to reach completion is a learned response and must be understood as such. In terms of a negotiation, the concept of completion needs to be interpreted as a final result that satisfies your targets or, alternatively, as a deadlock when agreement cannot be reached. Any other form of completion is a failure. If the other party begins to show signs of anxiety, impatience, etc., a move towards closure can be made by:

☐ Offering an inducement (e.g. 'If you agree with this now, in the future I'll help you by ...')
☐ Pretending you think an agreement has been reached (e.g. 'I'm really pleased we've been able to agree terms ...')
☐ Pretending a breakdown is imminent (e.g. 'If we don't resolve this aspect now, everything else we've agreed is null and void ...').

If your move does not work, be prepared to renew the negotiation and bear in mind the previous warning about the danger of using threats, implied or otherwise.

Activity 7.11   Refer to the previous Activities. In your negotiation, what signs would indicate that a move towards closure was appropriate? What type of move would be most effective in that instance? Why?

Finishing

Negotiations that do not end in a deadlock end in a compromise, few of which reflect equal measures of success for both parties. Usually, the side that has prepared better and/or applied better tactics will be closer to achieving its predetermined target. The final offer needs to be made in a way that clearly differentiates it from everything that has gone before. This can be achieved in a variety of ways, including:

☐ Changing personal style and demeanour
☐ Presenting the offer in a different format, e.g. a written format
☐ In a team situation, having the most senior member make the offer.

Above all else, it has to be clear that there is now no more room for manoeuvre.

Activity 7.12	Refer to the previous Activities. Explain and justify how you would 'flag up' your final offer.

The perfect result?

The results of the negotiation can be evaluated against the following types:

☐ *Lose–lose.* This does not automatically apply to a deadlock or a breakdown, either of which may be a reflection of the fact that there are irreconcilable differences between the parties. A lose–lose situation is one in which neither party regards the conclusion as satisfactory.
☐ *Win–lose.* This describes an outcome in which one party clearly achieves its targets and the other blatantly does not.
☐ *Win–win.* This describes an outcome in which both parties feel they have benefited. The prevailing belief that a successful deal could be reached has been proved true.

The manner of the 'perfect result' is greatly influenced by the nature and purpose of the negotiation. If it is part of a long-term business relationship, for example, both parties would most probably be aiming for a win–win situation. On the other hand, if the negotiation is a one-off meeting, the aim would be to out-negotiate the other and create a win–lose outcome.

However the perfect result is defined, managers operating as negotiators need to draw upon many of their skills in communication, understanding people and image management, in combination with specific negotiation skills and tactics, if they are to have any chance of achieving success. They must also avoid the most common mistakes.

Activity 7.13	Refer to the previous Activities. What would be the perfect result of your negotiation?

Common negotiating mistakes

In *Negotiating Rationally* (1992), Bazerman and Neale identify five mistakes that are a common cause of negotiation failure or breakdown. These are:

☐ Inflexibility – irrationally refusing to move from a position
☐ Regarding all negotiations as win–lose affairs
☐ Inaccurate risk assessment – failing to evaluate the true costs of concessions, etc

☐ Over-reliance on easily available information
☐ Over-confidence.

Cross-cultural negotiations

The successful management of negotiations with colleagues and clients from different countries requires a high level of the communication skills contained in Chapter 1, the negotiating skills covered in this chapter and the cross-cultural knowledge and skills described in Chapter 8. Without overstating the point, the challenges facing international negotiators far outweigh those facing managers operating only within their own country. As increasing numbers of organisations are operating within the global market, these are skills that few managers can afford to be without.

Negotiation and bargaining: key points!

☐ People only negotiate when another party holds something of value they wish to acquire.
☐ Negotiations can be both formal and informal.
☐ Formal negotiations:
  ☐ Favour the party with the strongest power base
  ☐ Limit the likelihood of informal talks and understandings
  ☐ Emphasise the *letter* of any agreement reached.
☐ Informal negotiations:
  ☐ Emphasise the relationship between the two parties
  ☐ Encourage a focus on the *spirit* of any agreement reached
☐ The six steps in the negotiating process are:
  ☐ Preparing
  ☐ Opening
  ☐ Making concessions
  ☐ Creating movement
  ☐ Creating closure
  ☐ Finishing.
☐ Skilled negotiators:
  ☐ Are fully prepared and have clear targets for which to aim
  ☐ Know that everything is negotiable
  ☐ Give no free concessions
  ☐ Are never intimidated or distracted by behaviour or environments.

Summary: consultancy, negotiation and bargaining

☐ Successful consultancy, negotiation and bargaining are founded upon:
  ☐ An understanding of client/other party needs and expectations
  ☐ The belief that everything is negotiable
  ☐ Comprehensive preparation
  ☐ Having clearly defined, time-scaled goals
  ☐ Courage.
☐ The core skills are those associated with:
  ☐ Management of self and self-image
  ☐ Managing one-to-one relationships
  ☐ Developing others
  ☐ Leadership
  ☐ Teamwork
  ☐ Creative problem-solving
  ☐ Selling ideas and persuasive campaigning
  ☐ Strategic planning
  ☐ Change management
  ☐ Time management.
☐ The aim is to achieve or exceed targets within the predetermined time frame without paying an unacceptable price.

A final thought

The will to win is not nearly as important as the will to prepare to win.

Anonymous

References

Bazerman, M.H. and Neale, M.A. 1992. *Negotiating Rationality*. New York: Free Press.

Douglas, A. 1957. 'The peaceful settlement of industrial and inter-group disputes', *Journal of Conflict Resolution*, Vol. 1: 69–81.

Kennedy, G. 2000. *Everything is Negotiable*. London: Random House.

Lewin, K. 1951. *Field Theory in Social Science*. New York: Harper.

Schein, E.H. 1987. *Process Consultation* (Vol. I). Reading, MA: Addison-Wesley.

Wickham, P. A. 1999. *Management Consulting*. London: Financial Times/Pitman Publishing.

Wing, R.L. 1989. *The Art of Strategy*. A translation of Sun Tzu's *The Art of War*. Wellingborough, Northamptonshire: The Aquarian Press.

Further reading

Wickham, P.A. 1999. *Management Consulting*. London: Financial Times/Pitman Publishing.

Kennedy, G. 2000. *Everything is Negotiable*. London: Random House.

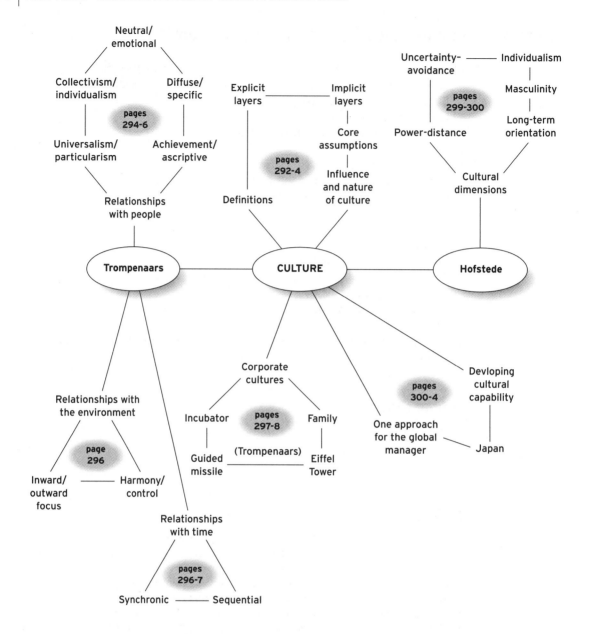

Cross-cultural management

A fish only discovers its need for water when it is no longer in it. Our culture is like water to a fish. It sustains us. We live and breathe through it.

(Fons Trompenaars)

This chapter will develop your:

Awareness of:	Knowledge of:	Capability to:
The concept of culture.	The explicit and implicit cultural layers.	Recognise the different ways culture is reflected and demonstrated.
The concept of 'cultural capability'.	Key cultural elements. Relationships with: ☐ People ☐ Time ☐ The environment.	Present the most appropriate self-image and create rapport with people from different cultures.
The relationship between this topic and previous skills covered in this book.	Common cross-cultural management mistakes and problems.	
The relationship between national and organisational culture.	Organisational cultural types: ☐ The Family ☐ The Eiffel Tower ☐ The Guided Missile ☐ The Incubator.	Identify organisational cultural types and related management styles.

☐ Fons Trompenaars

In many respects, the contents of this chapter – the knowledge and skills needed by the global manager – brings together core elements of the other chapters in this book. Understanding the role and power of beliefs, the different styles and expressions of intrapersonal and interpersonal communication, the need for creativity, and cross-cultural attitudes towards teamwork, leadership and change, are all essential components of this one topic.

Culture has been defined in a variety of ways. Edgar Schein defines it as: 'The deeper level of basic assumptions and beliefs that are shared by members of an organisation, that operate unconsciously and define a basic "taken for granted" [that] fashions an organisation's view of itself and its environment' (Schein, 1992), while Fons Trompenaars writes: 'Culture is the way in which people solve problems' (Trompenaars, 1993: 6). All organisations develop an internal culture. Indeed, individual functions within an organisation develop their own 'ways of doing things'. It must be remembered, however, that these 'ways' reflect the assumptions and beliefs referred to by Schein. Knowing *how* people in other cultures behave is not as important as understanding *why* they behave in the ways they do.

Managers moving from one organisation, or one function, to another need to be sensitive to and, perhaps in the first instance, adapt their style and image to meet the expectations of their new colleagues. As national culture influences corporate culture this issue is magnified many times over when trying to create appropriate relationships with foreign colleagues. The flexibility required to lead, manage, present, sell, inspire, support or train effectively in the global arena can therefore be seen as one key measurement of a manager's personal and interpersonal skills.

Activity 8.1   Brainstorm the differences between your own nationality and any one other. Give yourself only three minutes. How many differences did you write down? How easy was it?

Take a moment to consider any difficulties that may arise because of these differences if working with people from this culture.

The concept of culture

In his seminal work, *Riding the Waves of Culture* (1993), Fons Trompenaars argues that any form of social interaction or meaningful communication presupposes common ways of processing information among the people involved. This sense of mutual dependence is due to the fact that the people involved share a 'connected system of meanings' – a shared definition of what a situation means. How do these shared beliefs and interpretations come about? They come about because of the existence of mutual expectations. These occur on many different levels, incorporating the explicit, the implicit and the subconscious.

Activity 8.2 Write your own personal definition of culture. Now list what you consider to be the key elements of culture - those aspects of life most influenced by culture. Finally, see if you can name anything that is *not* encompassed by, or affected by, the concept of culture.

The explicit cultural layer

This incorporates those elements of a culture you observe easily and quickly. In other words, this refers to what we might call the 'tourists' view' of a culture. Examples of this explicit layer include language, food, fashion, buildings, monuments and religious shrines. The key point for the global manager to remember is that these explicit differences are actually reflections of important implicit and/or subconscious differences. Our interpretation of someone else's 'explicit cultural layer' says more about us, and where we come from, than it does about them. To a great extent, our existing world view (our mindsets, beliefs, values, etc.) is culturally driven.

The implicit cultural layer

On this level are the values, and norms of the group, organisation or country. Trompenaars defines the norms as the 'mutual sense a group has of what is "right" and "wrong"', whereas values 'determine the definition of "good and bad", and are therefore closely related to the ideals shared by the group.' (Trompenaars, 1993: 22, 23). A culture is generally stable when the norms reflect the values of the group. Tension occurs when this is not the case and, if the imbalance is not corrected, this tension can develop into action designed to create change.

Norms operate on a conscious or subconscious level to create a feeling within people of how they *should* behave. Values create a feeling of how people *desire* to behave. Even when different cultures share the same values, it does not automatically follow that they will express those values through the same behaviour. For example, two cultures may share the value that 'hard work is essential for a successful society'; however, their behavioural norms may lead to two different sets of behaviour, with one culture praising and rewarding individual effort and drive, while the other emphasises teamwork. Why do different groups of people choose different norms and values? Primarily because of the core assumptions they hold about the nature and purpose of existence.

Core assumptions about existence - the subconscious level

The most basic value people share is for survival, with communities often struggling against nature, or challenges posed by other groups. Such problems are eventually solved automatically. Groups of people therefore organise themselves in such a way as to increase the effectiveness of their problem-solving processes. Because different groups developed in different geographical regions, they faced different natural problems/issues, and formed different sets of logical assumptions about them.

Changes in culture tend to occur when people discover new and better ways of solving problems and challenges; in other words, when the old ways no longer provide the best opportunities for survival. As a basic principle, it is most easy to create support for cultural change when people realise that the survival of their community is at stake.

The influence and nature of culture

Culture directs actions. Clifford Geertz defines culture as the means by which people 'communicate, perpetuate, and develop their knowledge about attitudes towards life. Culture is the fabric of meaning in terms of which human beings interpret their experience and guide their action' (Geertz, 1973). Culture, then, is:

☐ Man-made
☐ Agreed by others
☐ Passed on to future generations.

It gives people a meaningful context in which to communicate, think about themselves and understand the world and their role in it. Differences in culture stem from the different shared meanings people attribute to their environment. Essentially, without people interacting with each other and their environment, there would be no such thing as culture. It exists only because we do.

Activity 8.3 Consider your own national culture. What are your shared norms and values? Can you identify any ways in which the geography of your country has influenced your cultural attitudes?

Key cultural elements

The research of Fons Trompenaars and Geert Hofstede has identified a number of broad cultural elements or criteria through which a preliminary understanding of a specific culture can be attained. Trompenaars states that these criteria relate to three kinds of relationship. These are:

1. Relationships with other people.
2. Relationships with the environment.
3. Relationships with time.

1. Relationships with people

These are sub-divided into the following five categories:

- ☐ Universalism versus particularism
- ☐ Collectivism versus individualism
- ☐ Neutral versus emotional
- ☐ Diffuse versus specific
- ☐ Achievement versus ascriptive.

Universalism versus particularism

In a universalist culture, most people share the value that rules are meant to be followed and following the rules is more important than judging each situation on its own merits. People will probably follow the rules even if it is not in their best interests to do so. An example of a country that tends towards universalism is Switzerland. In a particularist culture, people will adhere to rules, but place a greater value on being able to make decisions based on the particular nature of each situation. An example of a country that tends towards particularism is Venezuela.

Collectivism versus individualism

In a collectivist culture, people tend to value teamwork. An example of a country that tends towards collectivism is Nepal. In an individualist culture, people tend to value, encourage and reward individual performance. An example of a country that tends towards individualism is the USA.

Neutral versus emotional

This refers to the range of feelings and emotions expressed. In a primarily neutral society, people will not show their emotions. This does not mean they are emotionless, but rather that they hide their feelings – possibly only openly expressing them in certain, socially acceptable, situations. An example of a country that tends towards neutrality is the UK. In a primarily emotional society, the opposite tends to be true. People are expressive, openly passionate and emotive. An example of a country that tends towards the emotional end of the scale is Italy.

Diffuse versus specific

This refers to the nature of the relationship that is expected. In a society that tends to value diffuse relationships, people expect to develop a deep, long-term relationship in which they get to know each other on far more than a superficial level. Thus a work relationship can also impact on one's social life. An example of a country that tends to favour diffuse relationships is China. In a society that tends to value specific relationships, people will differentiate more clearly between business colleagues, friends, family, etc. In other words, in this type of society there is no need for a business relationship to become anything more personal. An example of a country that tends to favour specific relationships is Switzerland.

Achievement versus ascriptive

In an achievement-orientated society, people value the status a person acquires through his/her own effort and initiative. Individuals who have achieved great things, perhaps starting from lowly beginnings, would be seen as role models to others in a similar position. An example of a country that tends to favour individual achievements is the USA. In an ascription-orientated society, people can hold valued status because of their family connections, or the university they attended, or the important social contacts they have. An example of a country that tends to favour ascription is Nepal.

Activity 8.4	Imagine you are meeting with important potential business partners from the USA and Nepal. How would you adapt your language, style and focus to create rapport with each?

2. Relationships with the environment

In essence, Trompenaars identifies two differences in cultural attitudes towards nature. These are harmony or control, and inward or outward focus.

Harmony or control

Cultures that value working towards harmony with nature see man as part of nature and believe that, for man to survive, the human race must go along with nature's laws, directions and forces. An example of a country that favours harmony is Egypt. Cultures that value control of nature believe it is important for the human race to find ways of imposing its will on natural forces. An example of a country favouring this approach is Brazil.

Inward or outward focus

Cultures that value an inner focus tend to encourage the view that power comes from within, that external elements can be controlled, and that it is important to do so. Such cultures generally believe that it is worth trying to control nature and, in a business context, would regard organisations as mechanistic – that is, controlled by the will of its operators. An example of a country in which an inner focus would find support is Portugal. Cultures that value an outward focus generally seek harmony with nature and, in a business context, regard organisations as products of their environment. An example of a country favouring an outward focus is Japan.

3. Relationships with time

Anthropologists have argued for many years that attitudes to time reflect people's perception of the meaning and values of life. Essentially, cultural attitudes towards time vary according to the degree to which they regard the passing of time as either *sequential* or *synchronic*. For those with a sequential view, time is regarded as a series of passing events. To the synchronic view, the past, present and future are all interrelated. People in sequential cultures tend to place great emphasis on punctuality; they see time as a precious commodity that cannot be wasted. From the synchronic viewpoint, however, punctuality is not necessarily so significant. Essentially, cultures promote different ways of perceiving the relationship between the past, present and future. An example of a country that places great emphasis on the future and its relationship with the present, and far less emphasis on the past, is the USA. An example of a country that values the present and the future, but also places great value on the relationship between the past and the present is the UK. Understanding how another individual, organisation or national culture tends to view time, provides valuable insights for the manager working in the global market.

Activity 8.5   Consider the possible beliefs, attitudes and behaviours of a person who is committed to the concept that 'time is money'. How might these be different from a person who is committed to the concept of reincarnation?

Imagine that you have a series of meetings arranged with each of these people. How would your approach and attitude change to reflect these differences?

Corporate cultures

Trompenaars identifies four types of corporate culture, which in turn can be allied to specific national cultures. He calls these:

☐ The Family
☐ The Eiffel Tower
☐ The Guided Missile
☐ The Incubator.

The Family

This is a culture that combines an established hierarchy with close, personal relationships. The ideal result is a power-orientated, supportive and caring environment. Relationships within the Family culture tend to be diffuse – there is a focus on the development of people, and problems or disagreements are rarely aired beyond the confines of the organisation. The Family culture is popular in countries such as France and India.

The Eiffel Tower

This is a culture based around a formal bureaucracy, narrow at the top, with clearly established roles throughout and a broad and stable base. The focus is on structure rather than function. The Eiffel Tower culture is popular in countries such as Germany and Austria.

The Guided Missile

This is a culture that is impersonal and task-orientated, an approach reflected through the use of cross-disciplinary teams or project groups. Such groups are usually temporary in nature, disbanding once the project is finished, creating relationships that are fleeting. The Guided Missile culture is popular in Britain and the USA.

The Incubator

This is a culture that prioritises the development of individuals. The organisation is viewed as an 'incubator' for personal fulfilment and has minimal structure or hierarchy, preferring instead an environment of intense emotional commitment. This mixture of informality and spontaneous creativity usually means that organisations built around the Incubator culture are limited in size. The Incubator culture is popular in Sweden.

Activity 8.6   Which of Trompenaars's four types of corporate culture have you experienced? Which did you (or would you) feel most comfortable within? Why? Which culture would you find it most difficult to adapt to? Why?

Fons Trompenaars: key points!

☐ Trompenaars's cultural elements are based on three different relationships:
  ☐ With people
  ☐ With the environment
  ☐ With time.

☐ The four key corporate cultures are:
  ☐ The Family
  ☐ The Eiffel Tower
  ☐ The Guided Missile
  ☐ The Incubator.

☐ By understanding the drivers of behaviour, the global manager is more capable of:
  ☐ Matching and mirroring foreign colleagues
  ☐ Creating the most appropriate relationship.

☐ It should be remembered, however, that not everyone in any culture exhibits all the behaviours and attitudes that comprise the cultural norm.

☐ This point should be borne in mind also when considering the work of Geert Hofstede.

☐ Geert Hofstede

A social psychologist at the University of Limberg, the Netherlands, Hofstede carried out an extensive survey into cultural characteristics in the early 1970s. Consequently, he identified four cultural dimensions and placed individual national cultures on a scale from high to low within each dimension. Hofstede's four cultural dimensions are:

1. Power-distance.
2. Uncertainty-avoidance.
3. Individualism.
4. Masculinity.

More recently, he added a fifth dimension, 'long-term orientation', determining that the willingness to delay satisfaction and reward was linked to economic dynamism.

1. Power-distance

This reflects how far a culture encourages superiors to exert power. In a high power-distance culture:

☐ Inequality is accepted.
☐ Everyone knows his/her place.
☐ Managers make decisions and tell their subordinates what to do.
☐ There are few disagreements between managers and those they manage.

An example of a country that favours high power–distance is India.
    In a low power–distance culture, the opposite is true. Here:

☐ People are regarded as colleagues.
☐ Inequalities are minimised.
☐ People are consulted before decisions are made.

An example of a country that tends towards low power–distance is Austria.

2. Uncertainty-avoidance

This reflects the ease with which a culture copes with uncertainty, change and newness. In a high uncertainty-avoidance culture, people feel the need for order and clarity, and feel threatened by uncertainty. An example of a country that tends towards high uncertainty-avoidance is Greece.
    In a low uncertainty-avoidance culture, people more easily accept the uncertainties of life and each day is taken as it comes. Australia, for example, would be placed low–medium on the uncertainty-avoidance scale.

3. Individualism

This reflects the degree to which a culture encourages individual as opposed to collectivist or group-centred concerns. An example of a country that demonstrates individualist characteristics is the USA.

4. Masculinity

This reflects the extent to which a culture values performance, money, material standards and ambition. In a 'masculine' culture, these values are clearly evident. An example of a country with pronounced 'masculine' values is the USA.

At the other end of the scale, 'feminine' cultures are those which value quality of life, the environment and good service. An example of a country with 'feminine' values is the Netherlands.

Activity 8.7   Consider the following countries and decide where you will place them on the scale for each of Hofstede's first four dimensions: France; the UK; India; Spain; and Israel.

(The answers can be found at the end of this chapter.)

Geert Hofstede: key points!

☐ Hofstede's five cultural dimensions are:
  ☐ Power-distance
  ☐ Uncertainty-avoidance
  ☐ Individualism
  ☐ Masculinity
  ☐ Long-term orientation.

☐ Countries can be placed at any point on each scale, from low to high.

☐ As with Trompenaars's work, Hofstede's findings provide a valuable starting point for developing international management and communication skills.

☐ Developing cultural capability

This section provides the opportunity to consider any cultural bias you may hold, and to apply the theory you have learned, through a consideration of a specific national culture. The country selected is: *Japan*. The reasons for selecting Japan are as follows:

☐ People from western countries tend to acknowledge many apparent differences between Japanese culture and their own

☐ Such obvious differences make Japan an apparently easy – and useful – 'first case' for people wishing to develop their cultural capability

☐ There is increasing interaction between Japanese and western businesses.

Activity 8.8   Read the following statements quickly. Record your first reaction to each, and then move on.

What is the truth?

1. The Japanese have a suicidal tendency.
2. The Japanese culture is completely different from any other culture on earth.
3. As a general rule, the Japanese fear very little.
4. The Japanese are the toughest people to negotiate with.
5. Japan is essentially a sexist, male-dominated society.
6. The Japanese are less emotional than westerners.
7. Japanese businesses are dominated by their Chairmen - they hold the power.
8. Many Japanese are prejudiced against westerners.
9. The Japanese thrive on conflict and competition.
10. Modern-day Japan is still heavily influenced by its past.
11. The Emperor is regarded as a god.
12. It is impossible for a foreigner to be accepted by the Japanese.
13. The Japanese believe themselves superior to any other race.

It is likely that you instinctively agreed or disagreed with each statement in Activity 8.8 – even if you have never worked with the Japanese, or lived in their country. The point of the activity is to highlight the ease with which people can stereotype, or make sweeping generalisations, based on little or no research or experience. If we find it easy to generalise about other people, then they find it just as easy to generalise about us!

Activity 8.9   Write down both Trompenaars's and Hofstede's cultural criteria and dimensions. Read the following information about Japan. Your aim is to determine where Japanese culture fits in Trompenaars's relationship-driven criteria and on the scales of Hofstede's original four dimensions.

Understanding Japan

The islands of Japan

The geography of the islands is unaccommodating. Only 15 per cent of the total land is arable, only 4 per cent pasture and grassland. Approximately four-fifths of Japan is mountainous. The people inhabit the edges of the country. The islands are volcanic in nature and approximately 40 volcanoes remain active. About every ten years a new island appears. The islands also lie close to two major fault lines, resulting in a 10 per cent share of world earthquake energy.

Japan is *in* Asia but, in many respects, is not *of* Asia. Its unique position, influenced by contrasting cultures, created the need for the Japanese to develop a culture unique in its own right.

Doing business in Japan

In Japan it is of paramount importance to establish whether or not you are a person with whom it is desirable to do business. In other words, the relationship is all important. A 'new' relationship must reinforce the security and stability of the existing network of relationships and not detract from it. The success of Japanese business is founded to a great extent on smooth personal relations within the company and equally harmonious relations within the business community at large. In Japan the important element is *how* business is done rather than *how much* business is done. The latter is derived from the former.

Business relationships are on a personal level, based on mutual trust, and are binding. They bring obligations on both sides. They cannot therefore be casually entered into. In the preliminary stage, an introduction is vital. When someone acts as a go-between for you, you are immediately under an obligation to him/her. *Giri*, 'the weight hardest to bear', is a crucial aspect of the Japanese psyche. If you wish to have respect, you must recognise and honour your obligations.

The first meeting

The first meeting marks the start of what may become a long-term relationship. Hence there is no need to rush.

All Japanese business people carry *meishi*, calling cards. The *meishi* is a standard-bearer, identifying business and status. As such it is treated with respect – it is never creased or damaged.

Communication at this first meeting can be awkward. Personal questions will not be asked unless personal information has been volunteered. Physical contact will not be made.

Maintaining the business relationship

The concept of *giri* implies that the relationship will become more and more binding with the passage of time. The notion of life-employment, until recently never questioned in Japan, illustrates the Japanese attitude to business relationships.

Relationships between companies and their customers are equally binding. Obligations must be met. Once a relationship is entered into, contact is maintained even if there is nothing specific to discuss. Confrontation is avoided whenever possible.

Consensus-building and the *ringi* system

Japanese companies operate a group decision-making system known as *ringi*. It is a multi-step procedure for building consensus and involves a complex set of negotiations through which different viewpoints are considered and accommodated. Proposals are circulated at sectional, divisional and corporate levels. This is followed by a discussion of the proposal in an attempt to develop a consensus. It is a slow process, but has the advantage of precluding a disagreement once a consensus has been reached.

In Japanese organisations, informal and formal mechanisms for communication exist, allowing information to be passed from the low ranks to upper management via middle management. Thus a lower-ranking person in an important division may at any given time have more active influence than a person in a higher-ranking position.

Contracts

In the past, contracts were not common in Japan. Westerners and Japanese still often differ in the way they regard contracts. To the Japanese, a contract is a binding signal of intent, but there is always scope for some details and practices to change. After all, in a relationship built on trust, what's the problem?

Understanding Japan – results

- ☐ Overall, Japanese culture values a collectivist approach
- ☐ People tend to have an outward focus and aim to achieve harmony with their environment
- ☐ Relationships tend to be diffuse
- ☐ People tend to be 'neutral', not openly showing their emotions
- ☐ Japanese culture emphasises ascribed status, placing emphasis on titles, seniority, etc. rather than purely on achievement
- ☐ The Japanese tend to demonstrate a synchronic attitude towards time (this is revealed in their attitudes to the ongoing nature of negotiations and/or relationships).

Japanese culture also demonstrates:

- ☐ Medium power-distance traits
- ☐ High uncertainty-avoidance
- ☐ High masculinity.

Activity 8.10 What are the implications of this understanding for the global manager about to work with the Japanese and/or in Japan? Write down a list of the mistakes that could be made that would hinder the development of the most appropriate relationship. Now make notes describing how the perfect global manager would behave, think, respond, etc. Note also how many of the topics, behaviours, skills and issues outlined above relate to those discussed in previous chapters.

Understanding cultures: an approach for the global manager

One approach to understanding a different culture is as follows:

1. List everything you know about culture 'A'.
2. Place the contents of your list within the three cultural layers – explicit, implicit and subconscious.
3. Note the layer with which you are most familiar.
4. Highlight those elements of your list which are assumptions rather than facts.
5. Discover where culture 'A' fits within Trompenaars's cultural criteria and Hofstede's dimensions.
6. Summarise your learning by completing the following sentences. For culture 'A':
   ☐ The norms are ...
   ☐ The core values are ...
   ☐ The core beliefs are ...
7. With this as your foundation, deepen your understanding of the culture by:
   ☐ Reading appropriate texts
   ☐ Questioning people with relevant experience (be aware of their assumptions and any bias they may hold).

Your aim is to move beyond the 'tourists' view' to associate valued behaviours with the beliefs and core assumptions that underpin them, and to understand why people within the culture behave as they do.

Developing cultural capability: key points!

☐ For the global manager, there is no single best way to manage.

☐ Effective global managers understand that:
  ☐ Having the best product at the best price does not always guarantee success
  ☐ Of equal importance is the ability to meet the relationship and management needs and expectations of foreign colleagues and/or partners.

☐ Effective global managers achieve their goals by combining their:
  ☐ Technical expertise
  ☐ Understanding of the drivers of cultural behaviour
  ☐ Communication skills
  ☐ Creative skills.

Summary: cross-cultural management

- Successful cross-cultural management is founded upon:
  - An understanding that there is no one best way to manage
  - An understanding that business practices and management styles are influenced greatly by national culture
  - An awareness of the different levels of cultural influence.
- The core skills are those associated with:
  - Management of self and self-image
  - Developing one-to-one relationships
  - Leadership
  - Teamwork
  - Creative problem-solving
  - Selling, influencing and persuading
  - Consultancy, negotiation and bargaining.
- The aim is to achieve your goal(s) through the ability to adapt your management, leadership, selling, campaigning or negotiating style to best suit the needs and expectations of clients and colleagues from different cultures.

A final thought

Cultural capability is essential for anyone working in the international arena. Imagine the difficulties a European politician would face if he/she lacked cultural capability. Actually, you do not have to imagine. The following is an abridged version of a real event.

An English minister and his team met their Italian counterparts for the first time, with the aim of reaching agreement over a specific issue. The meeting quickly took a turn for the worse, with first the Italian delegation and then the English one walking out of the negotiating room. What was the reason for the difficulty? It was expressed thus by the English minister: 'How can you possibly have a reasoned discussion with people who lose their temper and shout so easily? It really isn't cricket.' And it was expressed by the Italian minister thus: 'How can you possibly work with people who care so little about this important topic that they show no emotion?'

It seems that even passion and reason are the results of cultural shaping!

Answers to the Hofstede Activity

France

High power-distance.
High uncertainty-avoidance.
Medium to high individualism.
Medium masculinity.

The UK

Low to medium power-distance.
Low to medium uncertainty-avoidance.
High individualism.
High masculinity.

India

High power-distance.
Low to medium uncertainty-avoidance.
Low individualism.
Medium masculinity.

Spain

High power-distance.
High uncertainty-avoidance.
Medium to high individualism.
Medium masculinity.

Israel

Low power-distance.
Medium to high uncertainty-avoidance.
Medium individualism.
Medium to high masculinity.

References

Geertz, C. 1973. *The Interpretation of Culture*. New York: Basic Books.
Schein, E. 1992. *Organisation, Culture and Leadership*. San Francisco, CA: Jossey-Bass.
Trompenaars, F. 1993. *Riding the Waves of Culture*. London: Nicholas Brealey Publishing.
Hofstede, G. 1980. *Culture's Consequences*. Calif.: Sage Publications.

Further reading

Schein, E. 1992. *Organisation, Culture and Leadership*. San Francisco, CA: Jossey Bass.
Trompenaars F. 1993. *Riding the Waves of Culture*. London: Nicholas Brealey Publishing.
Geertz, C. 1973. *The Interpretation of Culture*. New York: Basic Books.

Part Four

Leading and learning

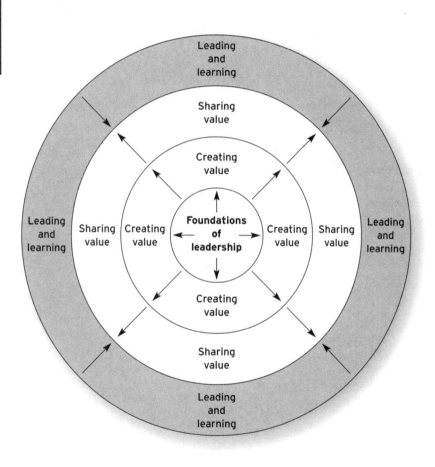

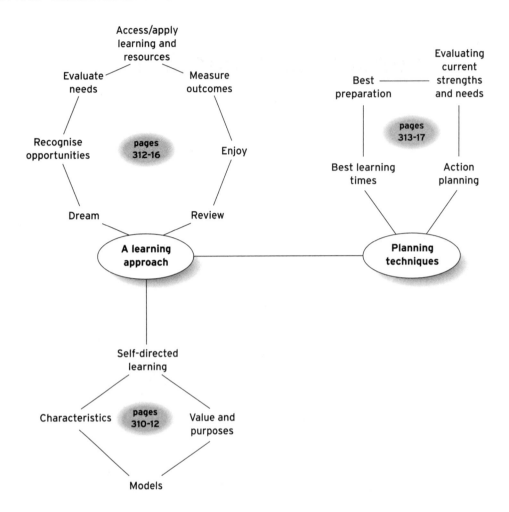

09

Planning and managing personal development

They know enough who know how to learn.

(Henry Brooks Adams)

This chapter will develop your:

Awareness of:	Knowledge of:	Capability to:
The concept of self-directed learning (SDL).	Self-directed learning (SDL) models and characteristics.	Evaluate your personal and professional developmental needs.
The concept of balanced learning.	The DREAM(ER) approach to personal and professional development.	Create a virtuous learning circle within a balanced lifestyle.

☐ Self-directed learning

As stated at the start of this book, the ultimate measure of learning can be seen as *an increased ability to take appropriate action*. For lifelong generative learners, personal and professional development is an essential part of a balanced lifestyle that provides appropriate time for the management of work demands, family and social life, study, leisure and new and/or unexpected events. As such, the planning and managing of personal development must aim to increase knowledge and enhance capability without damaging or negating any of the other elements within the balanced framework.

Managers and organisations as a whole certainly have a responsibility to encourage and enable learning, but learning is ultimately an individual activity. No one else but the individual can learn. According to Manz and Manz:

> *Members of organizations need to be not only lifelong learners but also learners in control of what they know and how they go about obtaining and assimilating information. This philosophy is directly related to the components of a self-directed learning process. Given the rapid rate of change and growth of knowledge in today's world, people must continuously learn and update their skills, and they must acquire much of this learning on their own.*
>
> (Manz and Manz, 1991: 5)

The value and appropriateness of workplace self-directed learning (SDL) have been espoused by many writers, who argue that:

☐ It is in keeping with the western concept of self-reliance and individualism (Ravid, 1987)
☐ It is a way of creating and maintaining the flexibility and adaptability that workers and, by extension, organisations need to ensure their future well-being (Pedler *et al.*, 1990)
☐ It is in keeping with post-modern society, in which rapid change and unknown futures create a necessity for learning organisations (Senge, 1993).

Different definitions of self-directed learning in the workplace exist and these, in turn, have influenced models of SDL. These include:

1. Learning without a teacher.
2. Learner characteristic models.
3. Learning skill models.
4. Constructionist perspectives.

1. Learning without a teacher

The focus here is on systematic self-teaching. The individual learner is responsible for managing, directing and driving forward the learning process. The characteristic of teacher-less learning has been adapted over time with educational substitutes in the form of videos, computers, etc. filling the original void. The content is usually predetermined, which leaves the learner with decisions to make only regarding the time and place of study. Summarising this model, Piskurich wrote: 'SDL is a training aid in which trainees master packages of predetermined material, at their own pace, without the aid of an instructor' (Piskurich, 1983: 4).

2. Learner characteristic models

The focus again is on the individual, but this time on the psychological and social predispositions that the best learners have. These include:

☐ A concept of themselves as independent learners
☐ Tolerance of risk
☐ Creativity
☐ A long-term learning perspective
☐ Self-awareness and self-management
☐ Self-motivation
☐ Acceptance of the responsibility for their own learning.

Ravid makes reference to these qualities when defining workplace SDL as:

An approach to learning, training and upgrading based on the individual's ability to sense what is relevant and important, and to solve problems; to be aware of sources of information and use them; to be flexible in viewing things, independent in thinking, curious, initiating and persistent.

(Ravid, 1987: 102)

Ravid also goes on to make the points that SDL 'aims at collaborative, professional work, replacing the dependency on an authority figure with the support of peers' (104), and that 'Self-directed learning does not take place in a vacuum. The character of an organization's internal work environment has long been recognized as influential' (102).

3. Learning skills models

The focus here is on 'learning to learn' – giving learners the skills to enable them to control and direct their own learning. Naisbitt and Aburdene wrote:

In a world that is constantly changing, there is no one subject or set of subjects that will serve you for the foreseeable future, let alone the rest of your life. The most important skill to acquire now is learning how to learn.

(Naisbitt and Aburdene, 1985)

The gist is that organisations committed to enabling SDL must identify the core learning skills, and develop their workers' competencies in them. This is why, according to Cheren: 'In a very short time enhancing learning competence has come to be accepted as an important training function' (Cheren, 1990: 268).

4. Constructionist perspectives

The focus here is on how employees and organisations learn from experience, using review techniques and developing collective meanings that can be used to enhance effectiveness. The notion of self-directed learning is implicit within this approach. As Watkins and Marsick state: 'In a learning organisation, the individual is a catalyst of his/her own learning' (Watkins and Marsick, 1990: 298). Although this learning is strongly influenced by the organisational context, the perception is of a shift towards organisations 'powered by self-developing people, continually changing shape and direction' (Pedler *et al.*, 1990: 15).

The characteristics and appropriateness of SDL in the workplace

The essential characteristics of SDL that relate to the work context are:

☐ Freedom, choice or control
☐ External challenges and pressures
☐ Excitement and stimulation
☐ Awareness of self and others
☐ Learning with, and from, others.

The appropriateness of SDL in the workplace is dependent upon both employer and employee agreeing what is acceptable. This, in turn, depends upon there being congruency between the individual's beliefs, values and goals and those of the organisation. The greater the overlap, the better the conditions to support SDL. Organisations committed to SDL therefore need to ensure they employ individuals who share their corporate beliefs, values and goals.

Personal development, however, is not purely a work-related activity. Indeed, some would question the morality of some approaches to SDL in the workplace. At what point does encouragement of, or insistence upon, professional self-development become exploitation? The focus on a balanced approach to personal and professional development put forward in this book is one method of ensuring the appropriateness of one's learning.

☐ Dreaming and learning

Human beings do not have to be taught how to dream. Rather, we have to be reminded of the need to dream deliberately. Great generative learners are also great dreamers, in the sense that they are aware of possibilities and/or imagine valuable new realities which inspire their need to learn. If learning is not

---

Activity 9.1

Review your response to that first Activity (Activity A). How accurately does it reflect the dreams you hold about how successful you could be?

If you stopped reading now and dreamt of the perfect life, would it be at all different from the timeline you drew? If so, repeat that first Activity so that your response is totally consistent with your dream. Use that to help you identify your learning needs.

inspired by a dream, it is more burden than growth. Dreams that do not inspire learning are best reserved for the confusion of sleep. As a basic principle: *If you are committed to lifelong learning, practise the art of dreaming.*

The very first activity in this book (Activity A on p. 5) was an exercise in dreaming – an invitation to imagine your perfect future. Now look at Activity 9.1.

Learning times and methods of preparation

In Chapter 1, you identified your perfect learning environment. The questionnaire in Activity 9.2 will enable you to evaluate your management of two other key components of the learning process. These are:

☐ The times you learn best
☐ The ways you prepare best.

Activity 9.2   Answer all the following questions:

Time
1. What time(s) of the day do I study best? ....
2. I study at these times:
   Sometimes   Always   Never
   Because ....
3. The duration of the study period is determined by the task:
   Sometimes   Always   Never
   Because ....
4. The ideal frequency of my study periods is:
   .... times per day
   .... times per week.
5. I achieve this frequency:
   Sometimes   Always   Never
   Because ....

Preparation
1. I identify an achievable study goal for each study period:
   Sometimes   Always   Never
   Because ....
2. I gather sufficient information/resources in preparation for my study periods:
   Sometimes   Always   Never
   Because ....
3. I use a period of preparation time to create the emotional and physical state that optimises my learning performance:
   Sometimes   Always   Never
   Because...
4. The emotional and physical state that optimises my learning performance is:
   ....
   (Examples include: excited, relaxed, determined, pressured, etc.)
5. I can create this emotional and physical state by employing the following thoughts/behaviours/routines:
   ....

Evaluation of current skills levels

Life-long learners need to acknowledge:

☐ The dream(s) they need to turn into a reality
☐ The value and relevance of their current experiences and skills
☐ Sources of support and learning
☐ Measures of progress.

Activity 9.3 enables an evaluation of your level of ability at the key skills contained within this book. The results of this evaluation can be rewritten under the heading shown in Activity 9.4.

Activity 9.3   For each skill, score your ability on a rating of 1 (no ability) to 5 (highly skilled), and its current and future relevance on a rating of 1 (no relevance) to 5 (vitally important).

Skill	Ability	Current relevance	Future relevance
Face-to-face communication			
Managing pressure			
Managing self-image			
Motivating self			
Motivating others			
Delegation			
Time management			
Questioning			
Whole-body listening			
Interviewing			
Networking			
Conflict management			
Learning			
Assessment and appraisal			
Mentoring			
Counselling			
Team-building			
Team player			
Leadership			
Helicopter vision			
Systemic thinking			
Divergent thinking (creating ideas)			
Convergent thinking (evaluating ideas)			
Persuading and 'selling'			
Implementing			
Presenting			
Report writing			
Negotiating			
Managing consultancy projects			
Cross-cultural management			

Activity 9.4 Under the following headings, identify your:

Current strengths	Required strengths	Current weaknesses

Action planning and measuring success

The DREAM approach to learning can be summarised thus:

☐ Dream
☐ Recognise opportunities to dream the dream into a reality
☐ Evaluate learning needs
☐ Access and apply learning and necessary resources
☐ Measure outcomes.

Two additional elements, which essentially underpin the others, connect the DREAM to a DREAMER. These are:

☐ Enjoy
☐ Review.

Enjoy

Simply put, if you are not having fun, you are more likely to stop and less likely to achieve your full potential. People learn best, have the most physical and emotional energy, and gain the most valuable insights, when they are playing and in good humour. If the thought of your personal and professional development does not make you smile, if you do not regard it for the most part as a joy and a treat, how successful are you likely to be? And why do you do it?

Making learning fun
The following list is not exclusive and its contents can be used in combination:

☐ Regard learning as a reward rather than work
☐ Use music, art or a particular poem or thought to stimulate you within your learning environment
☐ Take time to energise yourself, physically and mentally, before beginning a study period. You might sing a song and/or dance for a few minutes, or use the SWISH technique (see Chapter 1)
☐ Create a mental association between learning and an image, memory or story that always makes you smile

☐ Designate certain pieces of clothing as 'learning clothes'. Make them bright and cheerful. Always – and only – wear them when you study
☐ Place images (or reminders) of your dream, your desired future, in your learning environment. Use them to inspire you
☐ Never refer to your learning as 'work'.

Activity 9.5   Add your own ideas and methods to the above list.

Review

This is at the heart of the learning process. While mentoring, appraisal and assessment play an important part in providing feedback and ensuring review, an individual commitment to this practice is essential for the serious (sorry, cheerful) learner. Without review, learning is limited and action plans are difficult to create. In one sense, the entire learning process hinges on the ability to review accurately, perceptively and frequently.

Learning logs are one useful way of ensuring review. A learning log is a simple, written record of:

☐ Experiences
☐ Behaviours
☐ Outcomes
☐ Conclusions drawn.

As Plato reminded us at the start of this book, 'The beginning is the most important part of the work', and so it is with learning logs. Making the commitment and finding the time to start a learning log is often more difficult than keeping it going. However, people who write diaries do not think of them as work and invariably keep them up to date. A learning log can be thought of as a learning diary that helps to increase awareness and understanding, and to direct future action. People who favour mind maps to traditional note-taking can use this format to record and review their experiences.

Activity 9.6   Keep a learning log for one week. Take a few minutes at the end of each day to record your experiences, your perception of the outcomes and your performance. Identify any learning points. You might use the following headings: event; desired outcome/actual outcome; my performance; learning points. Or you might use a mind map.
    At the end of the week, determine how you can simplify the log. Use this as your permanent 'personal development diary'.

Having identified learning needs, an action plan can be drawn up to guide and direct future learning.

Activity 9.7   Select one learning need you identified in Activity 9.6. Plan how you will address it using the following headings:

Aim: ....

Intermediate goals: ....

Timescale :

    Start ....

    Finish ....

Procedure:

    Step 1 ....

    Step 2 ....

    Step 3 ....

    Step 4 ....
    (Identify all necessary stages in the procedure.)

Resources and support needed: ....
(Include professional, academic, technological, emotional, etc.)

Measure(s) of success: ....

Rewards: ....
(Identify how and when you or others will reward your efforts.)

Planning and managing personal development: key points!

☐ Planning and managing personal development is an essential part of a balanced lifestyle.

☐ Managers and organisations have a responsibility to encourage and enable learning, but learning is ultimately an individual activity.

☐ Many writers argue that self-directed learning is valuable because it is:

    ☐ In keeping with the western concept of self-reliance and individualism

    ☐ A way of creating and maintaining the flexibility and adaptability that workers and organisations need to ensure their future well-being

    ☐ In keeping with our rapidly-changing society, which creates a need for learning organisations.

☐ Models of SDL include:

    ☐ Learning without a teacher

    ☐ Learner characteristic models

    ☐ Learning skill models

    ☐ Constructionist perspectives.

☐ The essential characteristics of SDL that relate to the work context are:

    ☐ Freedom, choice or control

    ☐ External challenges and pressures

☐ Excitement and stimulation
☐ Awareness of self and others
☐ Learning with and from others.
☐ Effective lifelong learners:
  ☐ Dream
  ☐ Recognise opportunities
  ☐ Evaluate learning needs
  ☐ Access and apply learning and necessary resources
  ☐ Measure outcomes
  ☐ Enjoy the learning process
  ☐ Review their progress and change their perceptions and behaviours in the light of lessons learned.
☐ They also create:
  ☐ Inspiring learning environments
  ☐ The most effective physical and emotional learning states within themselves
  ☐ Opportunities to study at the times when they learn best.

Summary: planning and managing personal development

☐ Successful personal development is founded upon:
  ☐ A balanced approach to personal and professional demands, desires and needs
  ☐ A commitment to lifelong learning
  ☐ A willingness to dream
  ☐ An analysis of personal needs, strengths, weaknesses and learning style.
☐ The core skills are those associated with:
  ☐ Management of self and self-image
  ☐ Generative learning
  ☐ Creative problem-solving
  ☐ Time management.
☐ The aim is to turn dreams into a reality by achieving high-level, sustainable, balanced performance through learning processes that are personally and professionally appropriate and acceptable.

A final thought

Sticks and stones may break my bones, but words will never hurt me.

The adage argues against the power of language and, while it is true that no known combination of vowels and consonants can be bone-breaking, words can have a powerful effect. So, we will end with one final activity, and one final thought, because managers who are committed to their own learning, leadership and the empowerment of others within the context of a balanced lifestyle need to:

☐ Maintain a positive approach
☐ Understand the holistic, interactive nature of learning and skill development.

Activity 9.8   Make a commitment to stop using limiting or negative words. Replace them with those that encourage learning and growth. We offer some suggestions below. Add some of your own.

Banish:	Replace with:	
'But'	'And'	
'Change'	'Learn'	
'Problem'	'Opportunity'	
'Failure'	'Feedback'	
'Work	'Play'	
'They'	'We'	(With regard to work colleagues.)

And, finally, one of the great benefits of constantly developing personal and interpersonal skills is that each time we do it, we learn something new about ourselves. And this, of course, takes us right back to Chapter 1 …

References

Cheren, M. 1990. 'Promoting active learning in the workplace', in R.M. Smith and Associates (eds), *Learning to Learn across the Lifespan*. San Francisco, CA: Jossey-Bass.

Manz, C.C. and Manz, K.P. 1991. 'Strategies for facilitating self-directed learning: a process for enhancing human resource development', *Human Resource Development Quarterly*, Vol. 2 (1): 3–12.

Naisbitt, J. and Aburdene, P. 1985. *Re-inventing the Corporation*. New York: Warner Books.

Pedlar, M., Burgoyne, J., Boydell, J. and Welshman, G. 1990. *Self-Development in Organizations*. London: McGraw-Hill.

Piskurich, G.M. 1983. *Self-directed Learning: A Practical Guide to Design, Development and Implementation*. San Francisco, CA: Jossey-Bass.

Ravid, G. 1987. 'Self-directed Learning in Industry', in V.J. Marsick (ed.), *Learning in the Workplace*. London: Croom Helm.

Senge, P. 1993. *The Fifth Discipline*. London: Century Business.

Watkins, K.E. and Marsick, V.J. 1990. *Sculpting the Learning Organization*. San Francisco, CA: Jossey-Bass.

Further reading

Pedler, M., Burgoyne, J., Boydell, J. and Welshman, G. 1990. *Self-development in Organizations*. London: McGraw-Hill.

Watkins, K.E. and Marsick, V.J. 1990. *Sculpting the Learning Organization*. San Francisco, CA: Jossey-Bass.

Senge, P. 1993. *The Fifth Discipline*. London: Century Business.

INDEX

5I Creativity model *see* creative intelligence
Aburdene, P. 311
achievement-orientated society 296
ACTH 50
Adair, J. 167–70
adrenalin 50, 51
advertising
   AIDA acronym 243–5
   see also selling
Alderfer, C., ERG theory 45, 46
amygdala 51–2
anticipatory stressors 55
appraisal 150–5
   behavioural criteria 152
   development plans 155
   interview 153–5
   job purpose and accountabilities 151
   monitoring and reviewing performance 153
   objectives 152
Argyle, M. 239–40
Argyris, C. 178
ascription-oriented society 296
assertiveness 37–42
   avoiding interrruptions 40
   body language 39–41
   compliments 41
   description 37
   eliciting response 40–1
   how to say no 39–40
   verbal 39
association 125
audience, campaigns 262–3
audience analysis 248, 257

Bandler, R. 10
bargaining *see* negotiation and bargaining

Barnard, A. 260–6
barriers to learning 129–31
Bazerman, M.H. 287
behaviour 19–20
behaviour interpretation 85–9
   assumptions 86–7
   cues 85–6
   judging 87–8
   sensory acuity 88
behaviourist learning 125
Belbin, M. 187
beliefs 12–17
   how they work 14–15
   negative 13, 14, 15–17
   personal belief audit 15
   reframing 16–17
Bennis, W. 161, 162, 175, 191
Bergman, L. 260
bisociation 226
Blake, R.R. 164
Block, P. 134
blue sky thinking 222
body language 39–41, 253
Body Shop, The 81
Bond, D. 90
brain 131–2
brainstorming 222–3
Brown, A. 169–70, 174
Brown, M. 224
brown paper processing 222
Buzan, T. 224

campaign manager, essential qualities 264
campaigning 260–6
   attitudes/actions of management team 264
   audience 262–3

campaigning *Continued*
  Barnard Campaign model 261–6
  cause 261–2
  ethical management 262
  goals 265
  importance 260
  information 264–5
  message 263
  publicity 264
Canon 65–6
capabilities 18–19
change management, and consultancy 279
Chappell, J. 149
Cheren, M. 311
coercive power 3
cognitive learning 124–5
collectivist culture 295
communication loop 70–1, 78
communication synapse 72, 73
compliments 41
conflict management 107–15
  accommodation 112
  avoiding or minimising conflict 110–11
  causes of conflict 108–10
  collaboration 112–13
  compromise 112
  confrontation 112
  constructive conflict 107, 108
  cross-cultural conflicts 115
  definitions of conflict 107
  destructive conflict 107, 108
  divide and rule 113
  employing mediator 113–14
  networking 111
  suppressing or working through differences
    113
convergent thinking 227
conversations, unwanted 80
Cooper, Colonel J. 50
corporate culture 297–8
corticotrophin 50
cortisol 50, 51
creative intelligence 220, 231, 232
creative intelligence – 5I creativity model 210–31
  identity 212–19
    appropriate attitudes 218–19
    forcefield analysis 216–17
    heuristics 213–14
    information – depicting 216
    information analysis 214–15

information gathering 213–14
    information reliability and relevance 218
  imagine 219–26
    appropriate attitudes 226
    bisociation 226
    blue sky thinking 222
    brainstorming 222–3
    distortion and negation 223–4
    divergent thinking 219–20
    mind mapping 224–5
    provoking newness 221
    word association 224
  implement 229–31
  interpret 226–9
    appropriate attitudes 228
    convergent thinking 227
    forcefield analysis 216
    Walt Disney Strategy 227–8
  invent 229
cultural capability, developing 300–4
culture
  concept of 292–4
    changes 294
    explicit cultural layer 293
    implicit cultural layer 293
    subconscious level 293–4
  corporate 297–8
  definition 292
  Hofstede's dimensions 299–300
  relationships with environment 296
  relationships with people 294–6
  relationships with time 296–7
customer relationships 89–93
  completing the circle 92–3
  customer loyalty 93
  matching messages 91–2
  perimeter planning 90–1

De Pree, M. 166
delegation 140–4, 169
  factors to consider 141–2
  role underload 143
  upward 143
  work overload 143
depression 51
dialogue, compared with discussion 188
Digman's Five Factor Model 30
discussion, compared with dialogue 188
divergent thinking 219–20

double-loop learning 125
Douglas, A. 281
dreaming 5
  and learning 312–17
Dulewicz, V. 174

Einstein 132
emotional intelligence 174
emotions 21–4
  pacing 80
empowerment 133–40
  barriers – overcoming 134–9
    creation of goals 138
    culture 134–5
    modelling 137
    personal and interpersonal skills 135–9
    relationships built on trust 138
    training 136–7
  definitions 134
encounter stressors 52
environments 20–1, 173–4
ERG theory 46
ethical management 262
expectancy theory of motivation 43
expert power 3, 171
Eysenck, 25

fear 130, 131
fight, flight or freeze syndrome 49–52, 286
fight or flight syndrome 49
flexibility 238
flow, and learning 132–3
forcefield analysis 216–17
formal negotiations 281
Freud, S. 22
Friedman, M. 27–8

Gardner, H. 21–2, 22, 70
generative learning 125–6
generative powers 3
Glass, N. 133, 150
goals, creation and empowerment 138
Goffman, E. 31, 34, 35, 36
Goleman, D. 21, 23, 81–2, 111, 133, 174
Golembiewski, R.T. 138
goodwill concessions 285
Greenberg, J. 28
Grinder, J. 10

group, definition 176
groups and teams 176–91
  Belbin's team roles 187
  classification 178
  cultures 189
  effectiveness 180–2
  Hawthorne experiments 179–80
  interaction 184
  leader as team builder 186–9
  nature 177–8
  open communications 188
  potential conflicts 188
  problems 185–6
    hidden agendas 186
    team anxiety 185
    team-think 185–6
  purposes 180
  social processes 184
  team development 182–4
  team learning concept 188–9
  trust 188
  VROOM approach 189
Guilford, R.R. 27
Guirdham, M. 85, 86, 94, 238–9

habitual thoughts and behaviour 77
Hackman, J.R. 46
Handy, C. 143, 171
Hatch, T. 70
hawk vision 199
Hawthorne experiments 179–80
helicopter vision 199
Herzberg, F., motivators and hygiene factors 47
heuristics 213–14
Higgs, M. 174
Hofstede, G. 294, 299–300
Holmes, T.H. 53
Honey, P. 127–9
Hunt, J. 107

image management 30–7
  first impressions 32
  introductions 33–4
  Johari window 31
  maintaining personal image 34–6
  personal versus public perception 31
  self-presentation 31–2
imagery 252
individualist culture 295

influence 172–4
  see also persuasion; power
informal negotiations 281
information
  analysis 214–15, 263
  breakdown as cause of conflict 109
  compared with knowledge 3
  gathering 213–14, 263
  reliability and relevance 218
integrity 175
intelligences 21–2
internal consultants 275
  see also management consultants
interpersonal intelligence 70, 78
interpersonal skills 60, 135–9
interviews 97–106
  appraisal 153–5
    preparation 154–5
    purpose 153–4
    timing 154
  cue cards 103
  information gathering 101, 102
  interviewee 102–5
    answering questions 104–5
    first impressions 104
    preparation 103–4
    use of cue cards 103
  mind maps 100, 103
  process 100–2
    closure 101, 105
    evaluation 101, 105
    feedback 102, 105
    introduction 101
  selection interview 97–102
    interviewer's responsibilities 97
    interviewer's skills 98
    purpose 98
    questioning 98–9
    silence 100
    whole-body active listening 98, 99–100
  value of 106
intrapsychic intelligence 22

Janis, I. 185–6
Janusian thinking 207–8
Japan 300–4
  contracts 303
  first meeting 302
  geography 301–2

giri 302
  maintaining business relationship 302
  meshi 302
  ringi system 302–3
Jones, E.E. 36
Jordan, M. 191

Kennedy, G. 281–2
Knight, S. 137
knowledge, compared with information 3
Kobasa, S.C. 28
Koch, R. 58–9
Kolb, D.A., learning cycle 122–4
Kotter, J. 55, 166
Kunce, J.T., Personal Styles Inventory 29

language 74–6
  Meta Model 76
  Milton Model 75–6
  structures 200
Lawler, E.E. 46
leaders
  compared with managers 162
  responsibilities 166
  as team builders 186–9
leadership 161–76
  action-centred 167–70
  best fit approach 169–70
  contingency theories 165–7
  defining 161–2
  influence 172–4
  power 170–2
  qualities 174–5
  style 163–5
    autocratic 163, 164
    democratic 163, 164
    and lifecycle 166–7
  traits 162–3
learning 19, 122–33
  action planning and measuring success 315–16
  barriers 129–31
  behaviourist 125
  cognitive 124–5
  double-loop 125
  and dreaming 312–17
  evaluation of current skills levels 314
  and flow 132–3
  generative 125–6

human potential 131–2
Kolb's learning cycle 122–4
lifelong 126–7, 135, 145, 310, 314
methods of preparation 313
mistakes 131
reactive 122
review 316
self-directed 310–12
stages 122
styles 127–9
times 313
see also training
learning logs 316
LeDoux, J. 52
Levi Strauss 162–3
Lewin, K. 279
lifelong learning 126–7, 135, 145, 310, 314
listening skills 34

McConkie, M. 138
McCoy, G. 90
McDonagh, M. 260, 261
McGregor, D.M., Theory X and Theory Y
    Assumptions 44–5, 135
McKinsey's 7S model 215
management consultants 272–80
    business planning and development 277
    and change management 279
    client types 276–7
    consulting process 272–5
    internal 275
    marketing research and strategy development
        277–8
    product development 278
    project proposal documents 278–9
    project types 277–8
    promotional campaigns 278
    roles 276
managers
    compared with leaders 162
    responsibilities, training 145, 146–8, 149–50
    as role models 19–20
managing one-to-one relationships
    communication loop 70–1, 78
    customers 89–93
        completing the circle 92–3
        loyalty 93
        matching messages 91–2
        perimeter planning 90–1

interpreting behaviour 85–9
    assumptions 86–7
    cues 85–6
    judging 87–8
    sensory acuity 88
perception filters 72–8
    beliefs and values 74
    habitual thoughts and behaviour 77
    language 74–6
    memories 74
    perception of time 76–7
power 93–5
    formal 93–4
    imagined 94–5
    informal 94
rapport *see separate entry*
representation systems 82–4
    auditory system 83
    kinesthetic system 83
    lead system 83
    preferred system 82
    visual system 83
with superiors 95–6
Manz, C.C. & K.P. 310
market research 277–8
marketing mix 278
Marsick, V.J. 312
Mary Kay Cosmetics Company 81
Maslow, A.H., hierarchy of needs 45–6
matching and mirroring 79–80
Matsushita, K. 134
Mayer, J.D. 22, 23
Mayo, E. 179
meaning and motivation 124–5
mediators 113–14
memories 74
mentors 149–50
message
    campaigns 263
    interpretation 72
metaphor 11
Miller, M.A. 53
mind mapping 62, 100, 103, 224–5
mistakes 131
Mitarai, Dr T. 65–6
modelling others 137
Molden, D. 75
motivation 42–8, 169
    self-motivation 47–8

motivation *Continued*
  theories and models 43–7
    Alderfer's ERG Theory 46
    expectancy theory 43
    Herzberg's motivators and hygiene factors 47
    McGregor's Theory X and Theory Y Assumptions 44–5, 135
    Maslow's hierarchy of needs 45–6
    Vroom's Two-factor Theory 44
Mouton, J.S. 164
Mumford, A. 127–9
Myers-Briggs Type Indicator 28

Naisbitt, J. 311
Nanus, B. 162
Neale, M.A. 287
needs, Maslow's hierarchy of needs 45–6
negotiation and bargaining 173, 272, 281–8
  bargaining style 281–2
  common mistakes 287–8
  cross-cultural negotiations 288
  goodwill concessions 285
  negotiating skills 282–7
    finishing 286–7
    making concessions and creating movement 284–5
    move towards closure 286
    opening 283–4
    preparation 282–3
  threats 285
Neuro-Linguistic Programming (NLP) 10
noradrenalin 50

O'Connor, J. 79
Oliver, M. 116
Ornstein, R. 131–2

pacing and leading 80
particularist culture 295
Pavlov, I. 125
Pedler, M. *et al* 310, 312
perception filters 72–8
  beliefs and values 74
  habitual thoughts and behaviour 77
  language 74–6
    Meta Model 76
    Milton Model 75–6
  memories 74
  perception of time 76–7

performance, monitoring and reviewing 153
personal development, planning and managing 309–19
personal identity 10–12
personal image *see* image management
personal magnetism 173
personal power 172
personal and professional development 310
personality 25–30
  extrovert 25
  introvert 25
  traits 27–30
    definition 27
    Digman's Five Factor Model 30
    Kunce's Personal Styles Inventory 29
    Myers-Briggs Type Indicator 28
    Type A and Type B individuals 27–8
persuasion 173, 238–40, 242
  key points 247
  persuasive styles 238–40
  see also assertiveness; campaigning; presentation; report writing; selling
Peters, T. 107–8, 110, 111
politicians, use of language 75–6
position power 171
power 3–4
  coercive 3
  definitions 3
  expert 3
  formal 93–4
  generative 3
  imagined 94–5
  informal 94
  leadership 170–2
    expert power 171
    personal power 172
    position power 171
    resource power 171
    use of power 172
  and relationships 93–5
  see also influence
presentations 247–56
  anecdotes and examples 249
  audience analysis 248
  evaluation 254–5
  maintaining audience interest 249
  managing questions 254
  notes 249
  purpose 247

rehearsal 254
structure 248–57
    conclusion 251
    introduction 250–1
    main body 251
    pre-ending 251
    pre-introduction 249–50
    questions 251, 254
techniques 251–3
    body language 253
    hand-outs 253
    imagery 252
    rhetorical devices 252
    visual aids 253
    voice variety 253
types 255
venue 254
pressure *see* stress and pressure management
problem management 196–210
    causes and symptoms 197–8
    definition of problem 206–8
    evaluation of problem 208–9
    helicopter vision 199
    systems thinking 199–205
        balancing feedback systems 202–3
        delays 203–4
        feedback loops 199, 201, 205
        and language 200–4
        reinforcing systems 202
        slump in sales 204–5
proof-reading 259
PsychoNeuroImmunology (PNI) 49–52
publicity 264

questioning 98–9

Rahe, R.H. 53
rapport 78–82, 84
    and manipulation 81–2
    matching and mirroring 79–80
    pacing emotions 80
    pacing and leading 80
pacing values 81
Ravid, G. 310, 311
reactive learning 122
Reddin, W.J. 165
reframing 16–17
rejection, managing 246
repetition 39, 125

report writing 256–60
    audience analysis 257
    information management skills 257–8
    proof-reading 259
    structure and style 258–9
    time management skills 257
    writing and editing skills 258, 259
representation systems *see under* managing
        one-to-one relationships
resource power 171
resources, as cause of conflict 110
response, eliciting 40–1
rhetorical devices 252
Robbins, A. 15, 47–8
Roddick, A. 81
Rokeach, M. 17
role models 19–20, 137
Rosenman, R.H. 27–8
Roseto, Pennsylvania 60
Rotter, J.B. 138
Russell, P. 224

Salovey, P. 22
Schein, E. 176, 276, 292
Schmidt, W.H. 165–6
selection interview *see under* interviews
self management and understanding 10–25
    behaviour 19–20
    beliefs 12–17
        how they work 14–15
        negative – adverse effects of 13, 14
        negative – techniques to remove 15–17
        personal belief audit 15
        reframing 16–17
    capabilities 18–19
    emotions 21–4
    environments 20–1, 22–3
    personal identity 10–12
    self-motivation 23–4
    values 17–18
self-awareness 22–3
self-directed learning 310–12
self-motivation 23–4, 47–8
self-presentation 31–2
selling 240–7
    characteristics of best sales people 240
    CHIPS analysis 245–6
    decision 242
    managing rejection 246

selling *Continued*
  process 240–3
  visual aids 244–5
  see also advertising; persuasion
Senge, P. 19, 70, 86, 144, 170, 178, 188, 199, 310
sensitivity 27
sensory acuity 88
sequential cultures 297
Seymour, J. 79
situational stressors 53–5
social proof 12–13
Social Readjustment Rating Scale 53
Sondhi, R. 162
  DOPE model of time management 55–60,
    140
Sperry, R. 131–2
stress and pressure management 48–65
  biology of stress 49–52
    amygdala 51–2
  colour coding 50–1, 53, 64
  coping strategies 60–4
    anticipatory stressors 61–3
    Balanced Learning Performance System
      63–4
    encounter stressors 60–1
    general strategies 63–4
    Personal Safety Pyramid 62
  hormonal responses 50
  most stressful events 53
  stressors 52–5
    anticipatory 55
    Emotional Gateways to Change 53–5
    encounter stressors 52
    situational stressors 53–5
    time 55
  time management 55–60
    80/20 principle 58–9
    DOPE model 55–8, 140
    symptoms of poor management 59–60
    value 59
superiors, relationships with 95–6
SWISH 56, 315
SWOT analysis 103, 104, 209
synchronic cultures 297
synectics 206–7
systems thinking 62, 199–205
  feedback loops 199, 201, 205

and language 200–4
reinforcing systems 202

Tannenbaum, R. 165–6
teams *see* groups and teams
terminal values 17–18
threats 285
time, perception of 76–7
time management *see under* stress and pressure
    management
training 136–7, 144–50
  behaviour and language 148
  environment 148
  gap 145
  goals 147–8
  needs analysis 146
  off-the-job 146
  on-the-job 146
  responsibilities 144–5
    managers 145, 146–8, 149–50
  structure of sessions 148
  timing 148
  see also learning
Trompenaars, F. 292–8
trust, relationships built on 138
TSH 50
Tuckamn, B. 182
Type A and Type B individuals 27–8
Tzu, S. 107

uncertainty, as cause of conflict 109
univeralist culture 295
upward delegation 143

values 17–18, 74, 81
visual aids 216, 244–5, 253
voice 253
Vroom, V.H., Two-factor Theory 44

Walt Disney Strategy 227–8
Watkins, K.E. 312
Watson, C. 149
whole-body active listening 98, 99–100
Wickham, P.A. 238, 272, 273
word association 224

Zaidel, E. 132